The Information Revolution and National

Significant Issues Series

SIGNIFICANT ISSUES SERIES papers are written for and published by the Center for Strategic and International Studies.

Director of Studies: Erik R. Peterson

Director of Publications: James R. Dunton

Managing Editor: Roberta L. Howard

Editorial Assistant: Kathleen M. McTigue

The Center for Strategic and International Studies (CSIS), established in 1962, is a private, tax-exempt institution focusing on international public policy issues. Its research is nonpartisan and nonproprietary.

CSIS is dedicated to policy analysis and impact. It seeks to inform and shape selected policy decisions in government and the private sector to meet the increasingly complex and difficult global challenges that leaders will confront in the next century. It achieves this mission in three ways: by generating strategic analysis that is anticipatory and interdisciplinary; by convening policymakers and other influential parties to assess key issues; and by building structures for policy action.

CSIS does not take specific public policy positions. Accordingly, all views, positions, and conclusions expressed in this publication should be understood to be solely those of the authors.

❖   ❖   ❖

The Center for Strategic and International Studies
1800 K Street, N.W.
Washington, D.C.   20006
Telephone: (202) 887-0200
Fax: (202) 775-3199
E-mail: info@csis.org
Web site: http://www.csis.org/

The Information Revolution and National Security
Dimensions and Directions

Edited by *Stuart J. D. Schwartzstein*
Foreword by *Adm. William A. Owens*

THE CENTER FOR STRATEGIC & INTERNATIONAL STUDIES
Washington, D.C.

Significant Issues Series, Volume XVIII, Number 3
© 1996 by The Center for Strategic and International Studies
Washington, D.C. 20006
Printed on recycled paper in the United States of America

99 98 97 96   5 4 3 2 1

ISSN 0736-7136
ISBN 0-89206-288-6

Library of Congress Cataloging-in-Publication Data

The information revolution and national security : dimensions and
    directions / edited by Stuart J. D. Schwartzstein.
        p. cm. -- (Significant issues series, ISSN 0736-7136 ;
    v. 18, no. 3)
    Includes bibliographical references.
    ISBN 0-89206-288-6
      1. Military doctrine—United States.   2. Information warfare—
    United States.   3. National Security—United States.
    4. Information technology—United States.   I. Schwartzstein,
    Stuart J. D.   II. Center for Strategic and International
    Studies (Washington, D.C.)   III. Series.
UA23.I39   1996
355.3'43—dc20   96-42159
                                                        CIP

Contents

Foreword *Adm. William A. Owens*   ix

Introduction *Stuart J. D. Schwartzstein*   xv

About the Contributors   xxiii

Acknowledgments   xxxi

**Part I: Thinking about the Information Revolution—
Issues and Implications**

1
Analogue to the Industrial Revolution   3
George E. Pickett Jr.

2
Thinking about Information Infrastructure   9
Brian Kahin

3
Information Security: Planning for the Deluge   15
Alfred A. Jones

4
Financial Systems: Instabilities and Conflict   24
Martin Shubik

5
**Information Warfare and National Security: Some First
Amendment Issues**   37
James R. Ferguson

6
Law, Civil Society, and National Security: International Dimensions   46

Henrikas Yushkiavitshus

7
The Information Warrior   54

John W. Rendon Jr.

8
**The View from the White House:
A Public Policy Perspective   63**

Michael R. Nelson

9
The Ten-Foot-Tall Electron: Finding Security in the Web   68

Larry Seaquist

Part II: Conflict in the Information Age

10
Resilience and Vulnerability in the Information Age   79

R. James Woolsey

11
The War After Byte City   86

Michael Vlahos

12
**Another View of Information Warfare:
Conflict in the Information Age   109**

Jeffrey R. Cooper

13
Information, Power, and Grand Strategy: In Athena's Camp   132

John Arquilla and David Ronfeldt

14
Global Swarming, Virtual Security, and Bosnia **181**
James Der Derian

15
Regional Powers and Information Warfare **194**
Ahmed S. Hashim

16
The Impact of the Information Revolution on Strategy and Doctrine **218**
Daniel Gouré

17
Information Warfare: The Burden of History and Hubris **233**
C. Kenneth Allard

Selected Bibliography *C. Edward Peartree* 251

Foreword

Adm. William A. Owens

"Revolution" is a powerful word. It connotes action and significant, rapid change; it can mean events around which we build our sense of history and heroism. The term stirs favorable emotions in the United States because our historical roots lie in revolution. Perhaps that is why it pops up so often in advertising, often attached to things that have little real chance of historical note or of inspiring heroic effort, however good they may be in getting our clothes cleaner, our teeth brighter, or our cars sleeker. The unfortunate result of this inuring overuse and dilution is, of course, that we may be slow to recognize real revolutions. Real revolutions are truly important; they affect lives and the course of history. They demand considerable discussion, debate, and dialogue . . . if we are to master them.

The information revolution and the revolution in military affairs (RMA) that stems from it are real revolutions. As the essays that follow suggest, they are stirring the debates, insights, and passions that always accompany periods of rapid and significant innovation—particularly in the United States. The world will increasingly refer to what is occurring as the "American" revolution in military affairs; although military thought outside the United States reflects some aspects of what is under way, it is here that the discussion is deepest and the technologies that drive the revolution the most robust and here that the integration of those technologies with each other and with military organization and doctrine has already begun.

Like all true revolutions, the American revolution in military affairs involves big changes—changes that occur (or that we recognize) suddenly and that spread across institutions, doctrine, behavior, and the way we think about using military force. Again, as is the case with real revolutions, this one is surrounded by confusion because revolutionary change means giving up old ways of doing things. (Indeed, the anxiety of deep, fast, and widespread innovation lies not in accepting the new so much as in surrendering the old.) Therefore, it is important to understand the genesis and foundation of this revolution if we are to control it and bring it to fruition.

The following essays give an intellectual depth and better understanding of what drives these changes in the Pentagon. Together, they point out that the American revolution in military affairs stems from the way several particular information technologies will interact. Most of the senior military and civilian leaders inside the Pentagon agree on the specific technologies involved. They are the technologies that allow us to gather, process, and fuse information on a very large geographical area in real time, all the time; technologies that allow us to transfer that information to our forces with accuracy and speed; and technologies that give us the capacity to use military force with speed, accuracy, precision, and great effect over long distances. There is agreement on their interaction. We have decided, collectively, to build what some of us call the "system of systems"; namely, interactions that will give us dominant battlespace knowledge and the capacity to take full military advantage of that knowledge.

Evidence of the agreement is in the defense budget, in the recommendations of the Chairman's Program Assessment, and in the white papers, staff studies, and battle laboratories of the military services. Budgets for the programs that will give us the system of systems are growing much faster now, at rates considerably above the overall defense budget. The Chairman's Program Assessment recommended this growth, a recommendation generated largely by intense, in-depth discussion among the senior military leadership and the work over the last two years of the Joint Requirements Oversight Council (JROC). Whether it is the army's discussion of Force XXI, the navy's Forward . . . from the Sea, the air force's Global Reach, Global Power and subsequent assessments, or the marines' Sea Dragon, the basic argument is similar, reflecting commitment to radically improved situational awareness, agile communications, and precision weaponry. The decision-makers inside the Pentagon agree on the path to the future.

Deciding to take this revolutionary path was not easy. In an era when the defense budget is not going to rise appreciably, reallocating resources in favor of the system of systems means cannibalizing long-favored programmatic children to nurture the new arrivals. Yet, we have decided to do so.

We have less agreement on how fast we should go down this path—how much we should accelerate the emergence of the system of systems—and what we should give up to do so. Nonetheless, the commitment on direction is clear and, I believe, irrevocable. As a result, the United States will be the first nation to emerge in the postrevolutionary era, equipped with unmatched capabilities, perhaps with capabilities that will change the character of military conflict as we have known it for centuries.

Although we are now on the revolutionary path and have accepted the prospect of large-scale innovation that occurs relatively quickly and spreads across institutions, doctrine, and thought, not everything is settled. We lack a firm consensus on two important dimensions of this American revolution. The first is what it means, more specifically, for military organization and doctrine. The second is what it means for U.S. foreign policy and America's role in world affairs.

Most of us inside the Pentagon believe U.S. military organizations will change, perhaps dramatically. So far, however, we have come to this deductively, not from the empirical, detailed assessments and experiments we must yet undertake. Still, the kind of information-empowered, dominantly knowledgeable forces in our common vision seem to call for flattened, less hierarchical organizations, and the very concept of being able to "see" a large battlefield with great fidelity raises intriguing possibilities. If, for example, we will know where enemy forces are and what they are doing—in detail and in real time—and can engage them with highly accurate, precise, reliable, and effective longer-range weapons, why would we need our present numbers and kind of close air support forces? Indeed, does not that capability suggest that the need to hold units in reserve at the tactical and operational levels will become an anachronism? There is surely a subtle relationship between the kind and size of logistics structures we need and the precise, real-time logistics data we will have on both tactical requirements and matériel flows. In short, the American revolution in military affairs carries a whole range of force structure questions we have not yet answered. We sense, collectively, that they loom just over the horizon, but this dimension of the revolution remains unclear, with little firm agreement on what is to be done.

Part of this ambiguity reflects the profound challenge the American revolution in military affairs posits to the Clausewitz view of warfare, the notion of the "fog and friction" of armed conflict. Carl von Clausewitz probably articulated as well and as systematically as anyone what experienced warriors sense to be true—that the clash of armed forces is so complicated as to seem chaotic, so ambiguous that even the simplest plans and actions become difficult to execute, so uncertain as to constitute an impenetrable "fog" that rules out predictability. First expressed by Clausewitz in the first decade of the nineteenth century, these views have lain beneath military thought in the United States and elsewhere throughout the twentieth century. Today, we see them reflected in doctrine (for example, in the assumption that fog and friction are an inherent part of military operations), in structure (for example, in the idea that units held in reserve act as a hedge against the "inevitable" fog and friction of war), and in the design of our command and control systems (for example, in the consciously built redundancy we seek to ensure the transmission of information and orders in the face of unexpected breakdowns and delays).

To be fair, architects of the American revolution in military affairs have never claimed to be able to dissipate completely the fog of war or eliminate fully the friction encountered in conflicts. They *have* argued that the revolution can introduce such a great disparity in the extent to which fog and friction apply to one of the sides in a conflict as to give that side a dominance in war seldom, if ever, before equaled.

This important nuance aside, the American revolution in military affairs challenges one of the central assumptions of how we currently think about the use of military force—and behaviors and institutions built upon that assumption. This challenge is, ultimately, what makes it a true revolution.

It is no wonder, then, that we have not yet reached a consensus on the full doctrinal and structural implications of the revolution. Yet, as in the decision to embark upon the revolution, we have committed ourselves to working out these implications. This effort, too, is probably irrevocable, and our willingness to think seriously about such things will increase our revolutionary lead.

As we deal with these basic questions, we will have to address the equally interesting issue of what the revolution will mean to U.S. foreign policy. If the revolution lives up to its military promise of unequaled potency, this potency will not necessarily make achieving the goals of U.S. foreign policy any easier, particularly the goal of building a stable, just, and free world over the long term. The disparity in military power the revolution offers the United States poses a challenging dilemma: how can we use this power to deter and compel—by convincing others that they cannot prevail against us—without frightening the rest of the world into trying to counter or balance our power? We have not yet agreed on the answer. We have hardly posed the question.

Where does this American revolution stand as we approach the next millennium? We find it in full swing. We have embarked on the revolutionary path, the system of systems is already emerging, and—most important—we have accepted the promise and risk of innovation. We have not, however, reached a full agreement on how fast we will traverse this course or on what the journey will entail. The American revolution in military affairs is under way. It is not yet consummated.

The time is therefore ripe for further discussion, debate, and insights. Because the essays that follow advance our understanding of this very real revolution, they will add to our national capacity to seize and use it.

Introduction

Stuart J. D. Schwartzstein

> Par ma foi! il y a plus de quarante ans que je dis de
> la prose sans que j'en susse rien
> —Moliere, *Le Bourgeois Gentilhomme*

Rather like Molière's Monsieur Jourdain, who discovers that he has been speaking prose for more than 40 years, many of us recently have become aware of information and its ubiquity— although, for good reasons, we have greater difficulty in defining it than we have in defining prose. Like prose, information is, of course, not new. What is of recent vintage, however, are computers and computer networks: electronic means of storing and communicating information, means that have changed the ways in which we use information, widened significantly the availability of information of all kinds, increased the speed with which information is obtained, and contributed to the exponential increases in volume of information. Computers have also helped in revealing much of the complexity of the world around us and understanding information at a variety of levels and in ways heretofore not possible. Thus, what has been at times called the computer revolution has, in turn—and particularly with the development of computer networks—led to what is often referred to as the "information revolution."

This information revolution includes the significant changes being brought about by the development and widespread (and growing) use of powerful computers, software, computer networks, and advanced, high-speed communications, all of which are themselves bringing about change and in their totality are having a transforming effect in a number of areas. If there is a current debate over whether the changes that we are seeing, both the technological developments and their impacts, constitute enough of a discontinuity with the past to warrant the term "revolution," what is clear to most observers is that the changes that have taken place are, at the very least, significant and far-reaching. (The word "revolution," as Michael Vlahos points out in his essay, has become a commonplace, used with great frequency but with little understanding of what it really means.)

Use of the term "information revolution" also forces us to think about what we mean by information. As John Arquilla and David Ronfeldt point out, "Most people think they know information when they see it"—but of course there are a variety of definitions, and, indeed, how we think about information has been evolving even as various technologies give us greater availability of information, change the ways in which we can use it, and provide us with much that has heretofore not been possible.

Within developed countries, the impacts on business and industry, organizations, institutions, governments, media, education, and entertainment—virtually every aspect of life—have not only been significant but are continuing to be felt directly and in second- and third-order effects. In less-developed countries the impacts are also beginning to be felt, if usually only to a relatively small degree. Nonetheless, the changes are not only internal to societies and nation-states but global and are having real impacts on relations between countries around the world. More broadly, how individuals see themselves, organize themselves, and, on a global basis, interact is also changing, although clearly the pace, directions, and effects of change vary enormously around the world.

The development, growth, exploration, and, now, exploitation and in some important respects settlement of cyberspace are perhaps what is truly revolutionary and what may well alter significantly the ways in which we live. The electronic frontier is emerging in a number of dimensions: as geography, memory, society, school, forum, and market; as reality, "hyperreality," and wonderland as fantastic as Lewis Carroll imagined. Time, space, distance, and identity are challenged. Perhaps what is most extraordinary is that in the span of just a few years—the last decade of the twentieth century—the kinds of visions that very recently were considered only science fiction and the imaginative excesses of a few writers are indeed becoming part of everyday life.

The changes, however, that we are seeing are not complete but ongoing, and many of us suspect that the information revolution is still in its early stage—a stage marked, indeed, by continued rapid technological change (in some areas at exponential rates) and little agreement as to what larger meanings we might assign to it or what analytical frameworks are appropriate. For many, including Jeff Cooper and Chip Pickett, the appropriate analogue is the industrial revolution; others, like Dan Gouré, see many of the changes as part of larger transformations that have spanned the twentieth century. There is, of course, a wide range of views, from those who see computers as ushering in the millennium (with a capital *M*) to those who believe that it is more a matter of hyperbole than substance and that relatively little is changing.

Necessarily embedded in any discussion of information and extremely important to any analysis of changes within our society (and, indeed, globally) are questions related to the news media: what media provide, to whom, with what speed, and with what accuracy and what effects. Some of the questions are old ones (or at least not new ones) related to the question of what information can or should be openly available in wartime or a conflict situation, particularly thorny questions for a democratic society in which the freedom of the press is an important value and one of the legal foundations of government. What are in the United States First Amendment rights have implications for a wide range of other issues in an information age characterized by high-speed communications and the ability to transmit news, including war-fighting and scenes of carnage and destruction, into the homes of citizens throughout the country. New technologies have also brought new issues, such as the availability of encryption, to the fore in a way not seen before.

Even as we struggle with questions as to how we might view the changes that are encapsulated in the phrase "information revolution," there is the very important practical issue of how to deal with them. Technological change continues to outpace the ability of most individuals and governments—and, indeed, of many businesses—to adapt to the change. It might well be said that an increasing number of technology cycles can fit into any one policy cycle. At the risk of stating the obvious, such a lag can create real vulnerabilities where national security is concerned.

It is the implications of the changes being wrought by the information revolution on national security that are, perhaps, most compelling. The history of war-fighting in this century has been one in which technological changes have played a major role in the outcome; and the ability of nations to defend themselves effectively has, in large measure, depended on access to technology at least equal to that of the adversary. The recognition that information technologies not only are transforming daily life in modern industrial societies but are among those critical to military capabilities has given rise to a good deal of interest—indeed, almost a cottage industry—in what is often termed "information warfare." The use of information technologies is the basis for the "revolution in military affairs" and the "military-technical revolution," as well as a large number of predictions and statements as to how profound change is altering the ways in which we can and should conduct warfare and defend ourselves. The transformation is seen by a number of analysts as similar to that which, with the industrial revolution, brought about industrial-based militaries and industrial warfare.

The recognition that information technologies are changing war-fighting capabilities as well as creating new vulnerabilities has also led to considerable debate over weaponry and weapons systems, for which planning and budgeting usually must be done many years in advance of actual deployment. The degree to which various "smart" weapons confer advantage remains debatable; at the same time, there is awareness that with new weapons there are frequently new vulnerabilities. There is, too, as pointed out in several essays in this volume, the fact that most of the technologies responsible for the information revolution have been created by the civil sector, not the military, and that increasingly the flow of technology is from civilian research and development to military, not the reverse, as had been the case for the first four decades following World War II. Difficult questions related to weapons and war-fighting capabilities have become considerably more difficult and complex with the information revolution, particularly with an erosion between civilian and defense sectors.

This volume is not, however, about information warfare, however that may be defined. As the title indicates, it concerns the information revolution and national security, which means that what we are considering is much broader: the changes being wrought by new and emerging information and communications technologies—including but not limited to computer hardware, software, networks, and satellites—to national security (which, at least for the purposes of this volume, may be defined as the ability of a nation to defend its civilian society and protect its vital interests, primarily through military capabilities). This, in turn, demands that we consider how the ways in which we live and the ways in which we do business and govern our societies are changing and what vulnerabilities we must address. As the information technology revolution progresses, globalizing and transforming commerce, politics, law, culture, and perhaps society itself, the types of conflicts and crises with which we must contend are also changing. In this context, we need to think about how the information revolution directly affects national security in a number of areas and how we may even be seeing changing concepts of "nation" and "security." We need also to think about the indirect effects, such as the effects on our society's resilience—which James Woolsey considers in his essay—as well as new means of providing and ensuring security, the subject of several essays in this volume.

It is also important to recognize that the velocity of change continues to increase. The shelf life of many high-tech products is short, and the speed of development of new products continues to increase. This itself poses many problems and challenges for a society and government that, accustomed as they may be to change—more than most in the world—find themselves struggling to deal with that rapid change. It is interesting to contrast that with the relatively—and often not even relatively—slow pace at which government continues to move in many areas.

The role of government in this era also deserves a good deal of thought. Given that national security is—and, for the foreseeable future, must be—the responsibility of government, can our government cope with the rapid changes that are taking place? We know that all bureaucracies (including our national security bureaucracies) fight hardest when fighting to perpetuate themselves. We also know that bureaucracies tend to see issues as those for which their own strengths and structures make them indispensable. One of the great difficulties for our government is changing and adapting to change despite bureaucratic infighting. We know that many of our present governmental policies and structures—many unchanged for decades or longer—are out of date and well behind the rapid changes in information and communications technologies.

The range of issues and subjects that can quite properly be subsumed under our title is, certainly, immense. This volume is not intended to cover all aspects, nor does it aspire to constituting a definitive text. This volume is intended as an introduction to the subject, one in which a number of perspectives and

schools of thought are reflected. Our sense is that it does provide
well what is stated in the subtitle: dimensions and directions.

The essays here—the work of scholars, senior policymakers,
and experts in a variety of fields—are divided into two sections,
each covering a significant aspect of the larger subject.

The first part deals primarily with many of the developments and broad implications for society of the information revolution—beginning with Chip Pickett's observations on how we
should think about the information revolution and Brian Kahin's
comments on understanding the information infrastructure.
Fred Jones looks at the security of information systems, while
Martin Shubik analyzes how we might assess risk to financial
systems in the digital age. First Amendment issues relating to
national security are Jim Ferguson's topic, while UNESCO Assistant Director General for Communications, Information, and
Informatics Henrikas Yushkiavitshus reminds us that information issues are also global in scope and impact. John Rendon
looks at the role of the media, and Mike Nelson gives us the view
from the White House on public policy considerations in the
information age. Finally, Larry Seaquist warns us against exag-
gerating many of the changes taking place and becoming mes-
merized by a "ten-foot-tall electron."

The second section takes us, in large measure, to different
perspectives and much of the current thinking on information
warfare, defense, and the changes in the conduct of conflict that
are resulting from new information technologies. Much of the
work here deals with the impact that current and coming
changes will have on militaries and, more broadly, national security policy. Jim Woolsey and Mike Vlahos take a broad look at
conflict in the information age, giving their perspectives on the
resilience our society needs and the creativity our military needs
to survive such conflict. Jeffrey Cooper analyzes how to look at
conflict in a postindustrial age and offers a taxonomy on which
we may base much of our thinking. John Arquilla and David
Ronfeldt place information within the context of national power
and examine its growing role in the formulation of grand strategy. Arguing that information is no longer a mere adjunct of
material power but is now a distinct "fourth dimension," they
offer a compelling case for the proposition that the strategic use
of information is (and will be increasingly) a critical factor in
national success or failure. Next, James Der Derian provides a
different perspective on the use of information, discussing "virtual reality" and wargames in the context of Bosnia. Ahmed

Hashim also has a regional focus, looking at developments in information and their impacts on strategy as they are viewed in China and elsewhere in what we often refer to as the Third World. Moving again to the broader outlook, Dan Gouré, in a somewhat dissenting view, sees many of the changes often hailed as information warfare as less than revolutionary but, instead, as successors to changes brought about much earlier this century. Finally, Kenneth Allard examines the challenges facing the U.S. national security establishment as it attempts to reorganize itself around the information revolution and maintain its leading edge as the world's preeminent military power— pointing out the dangers of resting on our information warfare laurels.

It is our hope that this volume makes at least a modest contribution, perhaps in better delineating the issues and fostering understanding of the changes that are taking place, long-term and short-term.

About the Contributors

C. Kenneth Allard, an active duty colonel in the U.S. Army, is Senior Military Fellow at the Institute for National Strategic Studies, National Defense University. In addition to operational intelligence assignments in the United States and overseas, he has served on the faculty of the United States Military Academy, as special assistant to the army chief of staff, and as dean of students of the National War College. He is the author of *Somalia Operations: Lessons Learned* (1995) and is a contributor to *Turning Point: The Gulf War and U.S. Military Strategy* (1994). His book *Command, Control and the Common Defense* won the 1991 National Security Book Award. Colonel Allard holds a Ph.D. from the Fletcher School of Law and Diplomacy and an M.P.A. from Harvard University.

John Arquilla is associate professor of national security affairs at the Naval Postgraduate School. Prior to his current position, he taught strategic analysis at the RAND Graduate School of Policy Studies and worked as an analyst for U.S. Central Command, the Joint Staff, and various intelligence agencies. Among his publications are "Cyberwar is Coming!" (*Comparative Strategy*, Fall 1993), "The Strategic Implications of Information Dominance," (*Strategic Review*, Summer 1994), "Welcome to the Revolution in Military Affairs," (*Comparative Strategy*, Fall 1995) all coauthored with David Ronfeldt, and the book *From Troy to Entebbe: Literary and Historical Perspectives on Special Operations* (1996). Mr. Arquilla received his B.A. from Rosary College and his M.A. and Ph.D from Stanford University.

Jeffrey R. Cooper is director of the Center for Information Strategy and Policy at Science Applications International Corporation (SAIC). His 30-year career in defense analysis has included positions at the Hudson Institute, SRS Technologies, the Johns Hopkins University School of Advanced International Studies, the U.S. Arms Control and Disarmament Agency, and the Department of Energy as assistant to Secretary of Energy James Schlesinger. Mr. Cooper's recent work has focused on information warfare and the revolution in military affairs. His writings include *Another View of the Revolution in Military Affairs* (1994) for the U.S. Army War College. He received his undergraduate and graduate education at the Johns Hopkins University.

James Der Derian is a professor of political science at the University of Massachusetts at Amherst. A former visiting fellow at St. Antony's College, Oxford, he has taught at Columbia University, the University of Southern California, and Gardner and Lancaster State Prisons. He is the author of *On Diplomacy: A Genealogy of Western Estrangement, Antidiplomacy: Spies, Terror, Speed and War, International/Intertextual Relations: Postmodern Readings of World Politics* (coeditor), and *International Theory: Critical Investigations* (editor). A frequent contributor to *Wired*, his most recent book is *Virtual Security*. Mr. Der Derian is a graduate of McGill University and was a Rhodes scholar at the University of Oxford.

James R. Ferguson is a partner with Sonnenschein Nath & Rosenthal in Chicago. He teaches courses on foreign policy and national security at the Northwestern University School of Law, and has written widely on issues involving national security and the First Amendment. His articles have appeared in *Science, Technology and Human Values, Legal Times, The Cornell Law Review* and *The Harvard Civil Liberties Law Review*.

Daniel Gouré is deputy director of Political-Military Studies at the Center for Strategic and International Studies. Before joining CSIS, he served in the Office of the Secretary of Defense as director of the Office of Strategic Competitiveness. Prior to his work there, he served in the U.S. Arms Control and Disarmament Agency and in the private sector as a defense analyst with Systems Planning Corporation, Science Applications International Corporation, and the Center for Naval Analyses. He has published widely in such journals as *Orbis, Comparative Strategy, Signal, Military Technology*, and *NATO's 16 Nations*. He has a B.A. from Pomona College and an M.A. and Ph.D from the Johns Hopkins University.

Ahmed S. Hashim is a senior associate in Political-Military Studies at the Center for Strategic and International Studies, where he has worked on Persian Gulf security, global technology diffusion, and the revolution in military affairs among Third World nations. Prior to CSIS, he held positions at the International Institute for Strategic Studies and the Los Alamos National Laboratory. Among his publications are "Iraq Five Years After Desert Storm," (*Current History*, January 1996), "Military Science and Technology Policies of the Islamic Republic of Iran," in *Military Technology and Offensive Capacity in South Asia* (1996), and *The Crisis of the Iranian State: Domestic, Foreign and Security Policies in Post-Khomeini Iran* (Adelphi Paper, 1995). He received a B.A. from the University of Warwick and his M.Sc. and Ph.D from the Massachusetts Institute of Technology.

Alfred A. Jones is director of information security services at Electronic Data Systems where his work includes developing information security services and products that will integrate functions across platforms, networks, and software products. Prior to his current post, he served as division manager for corporate information security where he was responsible for information security policy development, deployment, and operations across EDS's worldwide networks. A former U.S. Navy submarine officer, Mr. Jones holds a degree in electrical engineering from Pennsylvania State University.

Brian Kahin is director of the Information Infrastructure Project in the Science, Technology, and Public Policy Program at Harvard University's John F. Kennedy School of Government. Mr. Kahin is also general counsel for the Interactive Multimedia Association. He has acted as a consultant for EDUCOM and the U.S. Congress Office of Technology Assessment, and serves as an adviser on the U.S. State Department Advisory Committee on International Communications and Information Policy. His publications include *Public Access to the Internet* (coedited with James Keller, 1995) and *Standards Development and Information Infrastructure* (coedited with Jane Abbate, 1995). He received his B.A. and J.D. from Harvard University.

Michael R. Nelson is special assistant for information technology in the Office of Science and Technology Policy at the White House. Mr. Nelson has worked extensively on a range of information policy, information technology, and telecommunications policy issues related to the National Information Infrastructure (NII) and Global Information Infrastructure (GII) initiatives. A former staff member on the Senate Commerce Committee and

Science Subcommittee, he was lead Senate staffer on Senator Al Gore's High-Performance Computing legislation. He holds a B.S. from the California Institute of Technology and a Ph.D. from the Massachusetts Institute of Technology.

Adm. William A. Owens (Ret.) is executive vice president of Science Applications International Corporation and the former vice chairman of the Joint Chiefs of Staff in the Clinton administration. Prior to his confirmation as vice chairman, Admiral Owens served as first deputy chief of naval operations for Resources, Warfare Requirements, and Assessments, as commander of the Sixth Fleet and of NATO's Naval Striking and Support Forces Southern Europe, and as senior military assistant to the secretary of defense. Earlier in his career Admiral Owens served as a member of the U.S. Navy's first Strategic Studies Group and as a nuclear submarine officer. Among Admiral Owen's recent publications is "America's Information Edge" (*Foreign Affairs*, March/April 1996) coauthored with Joseph Nye. He holds a B.S. from the U.S. Naval Academy and M.A. degrees from Oxford University and the George Washington University.

C. Edward Peartree is a research assistant in Political-Military Studies at the Center for Strategic and International Studies where he has worked on information warfare, defense science and technology, and various issues pertaining to the impact of the information revolution on international security. Prior to joining CSIS, he worked as an editor and writer in television and documentary films. An editorial board member of George Washington University's *International Affairs Review*, he received a B.A. from the Johns Hopkins University and an M.A. from George Washington University's Elliott School of International Affairs.

George E. Pickett Jr. is the director of the Northrop Grumman Corporation Analysis Center. A former U.S. Army officer, he served in a variety of command and intelligence positions. Mr. Pickett has also served on the National Security Council and the Office of the Secretary of Defense on net assessment and intelligence management projects, and he was a senior staff member on the Senate Intelligence Committee responsible for the budgets of tactical and certain national intelligence programs. Prior to his work at Northrop Grumman in threat analysis, defense planning, and industry strategy, Mr. Pickett worked as a systems engineer and systems planner in private industry. He holds a B.A. from Yale University and an M.B.A. from the Harvard Business School.

John W. Rendon Jr. is cofounder and president of the Rendon Group. Mr. Rendon has served as senior strategic consultant to the Governments of Panama, Kuwait, Haiti, and Aruba, as well as a number of international corporations. He also directs strategic planning sessions on public relations and conducts seminars and classes on the American political system. He has lectured at the Kennedy Institute, the University of Massachusetts, the American Political Science Convention, Georgetown University and other institutions. A former executive director and national political director of the Democratic National Committee, he served as a member of President Jimmy Carter's senior campaign staff.

David Ronfeldt is a senior social scientist in the International Studies group at RAND. Originally a specialist in U.S.-Latin American security issues, his work is now focused primarily on the global information revolution and information-age modes of conflict. Among his publications are "Cyberwar is Coming!" (*Comparative Strategy*, Fall 1993), "The Strategic Implications of Information Dominance" (*Strategic Review*, Summer 1994), "Welcome to the Revolution in Military Affairs" (*Comparative Strategy*, Fall 1995), all coauthored with John Arquilla, and *Tribes, Institutions, Markets, Networks: A Framework About Societal Evolution* (RAND, 1996). He holds a Ph.D from Stanford University.

Stuart J.D. Schwartzstein is currently a fellow at the Centre for International Studies of the London School of Economics and associate director of the Office of Naval Research Europe in London. Until recently he was a visiting fellow at the Center for Strategic and International Studies on assignment from the Office of the Under Secretary for Policy, Office of the Secretary of Defense. He has worked on international science and technology cooperation, defense industrial cooperation, export control, and nonproliferation issues and has served as an adviser to the National Science Foundation. A former Foreign Service officer in the U.S. Department of State, he has also worked on population, environmental security, and humanitarian relief projects. His most recent article is "The Impact of the Information

Revolution on International Relations" (IPTS Report, July 1996). Mr. Schwartzstein received his B.A. from the University of Pittsburgh and studied at the Institut d'Etudes Politiques of the University of Paris and the Wharton School.

Larry Seaquist is founding chairman and CEO of the Strategy Group, an independent nonprofit organization working on international public policy issues. An international security strategist, Mr. Seaquist is a senior adviser to the director general of UNESCO and a frequent lecturer at universities and executive seminars. A former U.S. Navy officer and combatant ship commander, he also served tours on the Joint Staff and the Office of the Under Secretary of Defense for Policy, where he was acting assistant deputy under secretary of defense (policy planning) and director of the policy research program. An affiliate of and adviser to numerous organizations, including the International Institute for Strategic Studies, the Brookings Institution, and the Center for Strategic and International Studies, he is currently working on the forthcoming book, *Waging Peace: Civilization in a Disorderly World.*

Martin Shubik is Seymour H. Knox Professor of Economics at Yale University. Prior to his affiliation with Yale, Mr. Shubik taught at the University of Melbourne, the University of Chile, Santiago, and Pennsylvania State University. He has also worked in the private sector at IBM and General Electric and has served as a consultant to a wide variety of private and governmental organizations, including RAND, the Ford Foundation, ARPA, and NASA. Mr. Shubik has been a fellow at Princeton University and the American Academy of Arts and Sciences and an external faculty member at the Santa Fe Institute. Among his publications are "Strategic Purpose and the International Economy" (*Orbis,* 1983) with Paul Bracken, "Open Questions in Defense Economics and Economic Warfare" (*Journal of Conflict Resolution,* 1989) with R. Verkerke, and "Terrorism, Technology and the Socio-economics of Death" (*SOM Research Paper,* 1995). Mr. Shubik has a B.A. and M.A. from the University of Toronto and a Ph.D from Princeton University.

Michael Vlahos is a senior fellow at the Progress & Freedom Foundation and Olin Fellow at the Paul H. Nitze School of Advanced International Studies of Johns Hopkins University. Prior to his current positions, Mr. Vlahos was a project director at the Center for Naval Analyses, director of the Center for the Study of Foreign Affairs at the Foreign Service Institute, U.S. Department of State, and a strategic analyst with the Central Intelligence Agency. He has also served as a consultant to the Johns Hopkins Applied Physics Laboratory and RAND and has been a visiting lecturer at the Army Command and General Staff College. He received his B.A. from Yale University and his M.A. and Ph.D from the Fletcher School of Law and Diplomacy.

R. James Woolsey is a former director of Central Intelligence and currently a partner at Shea and Gardner. Prior to his tenure at the Central Intelligence Agency he served as ambassador and U.S. representative to the Negotiation on Conventional Armed Forces in Europe (CFE), as under secretary of the U.S. Navy, and as general counsel of the Senate Committee on Armed Services. Mr. Woolsey is a trustee of a variety organizations, including the Smithsonian Institution and the Center for Strategic and International Studies, and has published widely on defense and foreign policy issues. A Rhodes scholar, he received a B.A. from Stanford University and an LL.B from Yale University.

Henrikas Yushkiavitshus is assistant director-general for Communication, Information and Informatics, UNESCO. Before joining UNESCO in 1990, he was the vice chairman of the USSR State Committee for Television and Radio Broadcasting and Chairman of the Interministerial Committee for Radio and Television Development. A member of many international communications and broadcast media organizations, including the Radio, Television and Media Coordination Committee of the International Olympic Committee, he is the recipient of a number of international awards, including an Emmy from the U.S. Academy of Television Arts and Sciences. Mr. Yushkiavitshus received a degree in radio communications and broadcast engineering from the Leningrad Electrotechnical Communication Institute.

Acknowledgments

We extend our sincere thanks and appreciation to the Robert R. McCormick Tribune Foundation of Chicago, its president and CEO, Neal Creighton, and its executive vice president, Richard A. Behrenhausen, for their generous support, without which neither this publication nor the conference for which many of the materials here were originally prepared would have been possible. We are particularly grateful for the opportunity McCormick Tribune provided in enabling us to pursue a general topic without restraints or conditions, one that gave us a good deal of intellectual freedom and resulted, we think, in an imaginative approach to a difficult subject. Our thanks, too, to Messrs. Creighton and Behrenhausen for their excellent advice and guidance.

Our thanks also to the United Nations Educational, Scientific and Cultural Organization for additional encouragement and support for this publication and in particular to its assistant director general for communication, information and informatics.

The National Strategy Forum of Chicago, under the able leadership of its president, Richard E. Friedman, and with the assistance of John M. Flanagin and Colleen Grady, has been an invaluable collaborator, particularly in the organization of the conference, but also in constituting an excellent source of advice and encouragement.

Here at CSIS the work of a number of individuals made this publication possible. Dan Gouré, Bill Taylor, and Ahmed Hashim have provided both assistance and excellent sources of information and advice. Most notably, C. Edward Peartree is deserving of both thanks and gratitude for his hard and careful work in putting together this volume, as well as his yeoman efforts on the conference and a host of related activities.

Part I

Thinking about the Information Revolution—Issues and Implications

1

Analogue to the Industrial Revolution

George E. Pickett Jr.

Many are making forecasts about the content and timing of the information revolution. These forecasts often address one or more of four subjects: (1) projecting the nature and effect of the explosion in information and information-related technologies; (2) describing the matching impact on the flow and use of information; (3) estimating the impact of such information on the institutions, structures, and operations of the business environment, nations, the public sector, and individual lives; and, finally, (4) projecting the potential impact on conflict between nations and subnational groups in the next century. This short essay raises some issues for consideration in the practice of making and following these forecasts.

The analogue for this "revolution" is the industrial revolution, not a political revolution, because the former communicates the scale in time as well as in content. As much as the information revolution may collapse the time of action to seconds on an operational level, it will be much like the industrial revolution in the time it takes to be fully adopted throughout society. The world is more technologically advanced than it was in the industrial revolution, and that advancement should accelerate the time required to have an impact. Nevertheless, those who forecast a change measured in only a few decades should be required to offer some evidence. Perhaps a half-century or more is a better estimate, and that is a half-century in addition to the four decades that have already passed since the invention of the transistor.

Forecasts are going to be wrong. Although we need to probe the complexity of this change, the pattern of forecasting in the past is that even brilliant people have marginal hit rates. Some examples are merely interesting, such as projections in the early twentieth century that families would have airplanes in their garages the same way they had cars (an example of basing an estimate on recent social and industrial experience and overlooking the inherent asymmetries of the technologies and their applications). Estimates that had more serious implications (for corporations in this case) were forecasts in the 1950s that the number of computers in the United States in the year 2000 would be on the order of 1,000 systems.

There are several problems in forecasting the decades ahead: the risk of imagining that information itself will make the projections more accurate (i.e., we have more data and thus are probably more accurate); the danger of becoming captured by the power of forecasters' words and not recognizing the absence of content; and the fact that all prognosticators carry into their estimates subtle assumptions about how the world operates. One implication of these problems is that we need approaches to planning that incorporate (rather than overlook) our assumptions, hopes, and errors. New ways to plan may be even more important than in the past because global integration can mean that mistakes can be propagated through many economies or their consequences can be more costly. The corporate environment may provide some useful hints in this regard; in the past several decades, new techniques have emerged such as policy-oriented scenario planning, core competencies, and adaptive organizational approaches.

For governments, there should be time to interpret and react to this revolution. Nations cannot be overly relaxed about the changes occurring, but there is ample time for sensible policies to evolve. Moreover, the search for a single, fixed solution in public policy (a "point solution") should be approached with some skepticism. If people are likely to be wrong about detailed forecasts, the policies built on those forecasts are also likely to be wrong. From a public policy viewpoint, the selection of point solutions by business is generally satisfactory because there are a number of firms involved. Mistakes that lead to disappearances of individual firms are acceptable and make little difference to the public. Such, however, is not the case in the public sector. Nations that make the wrong bets on the future can pay a high price. That leads to the paradox that the appropriate approach to this revolution from a national point of view may be evolutionary.

A key characteristic of the evolutionary approach is an acceptance of multiple approaches to solving problems or challenges. Moreover, the emphasis is not just on getting right answers to the challenges, but also on developing ways to learn as much as possible from the failures. A challenge for public institutions is quickly recognizing mistakes, trimming the bad ideas to invest in the good ones, and capturing and disseminating the lessons learned (which should be easier in an information-focused organization).

Some nations and organizations will move faster than others in this revolution.   The information revolution will change the calculus of natural advantage among nations and other organizations. Much as the changes in the middle of this century have shown that one state's possession of certain raw resources (with notable exceptions) provides only a limited guarantee of worldwide prominence, this revolution may continue to redefine comparative advantage. As forecasters have projected, information competence does not respect geopolitical boundaries, and a technology that is largely based on sand is hard to restrict to a few nations that have all the raw materials. (Indeed, the raw materials of this revolution are far from concrete, based as they are on understanding science, technology, organizations, people, and so on.)

Where should forecasters look for ideas about how to assess the early winners in this competition? Studying nations is potentially a step, as they struggle with the policy implications of information and the issues of sovereignty, law, and public policy. Industry may also present interesting insights because firms move more quickly than nations and suffer the results more rapidly. For example, companies like Wal-Mart have shown how communication technology can change the competitive landscape of even general merchandising. Intel and Microsoft have shown that the pace of technological change can redefine the competitive structure of an entire industry in less than a decade. Arguably, information is even at the heart of a range of competitive strategies that exploit time to get ahead as opposed to cost, price, distribution, market presence, location, and so forth. Such time-based strategies include just-in-time inventory, accelerating product development, and integrating development and manufacturing.

In thinking about the implications of this revolution, one has to be cautious about the more subtle aspects of conceptual frameworks.   As companies have found to their dismay, when the environment shifts in a dramatic fashion, their ability to respond is constrained more by the assumptions held by their people and embedded in their organization than by limitations in resources and technology. Thus, IBM arguably held the resources and technology to dominate the emerging microcomputer market. Not only was its resource base huge, but its laboratories invented some of the key technologies and its manufacturing some of the key processes. Its roller coaster ride in the 1980s resulted from subtle assumptions (e.g., believing that hardware would be more critical than software, as had been the case in mainframes) and more obvious ones (e.g., believing people would be loyal to the IBM name brand).

Today's world is composed of large institutions, both of government and of private enterprise, and their conceptual frameworks are important. It is comparatively easy to be cautious about making errors in forecasting technologies although the questions are complex (e.g., will microelectronics encounter limits of nature and cost?). Some aspects of growth forecasts are also complex but self-evident (e.g., there are always limits to exponential growth, and the computer industry has already had a long sustained run). The deeper and more subtle issues are nontechnical or quasi-technical. If the information revolution occurs, it will increase the volume and speed of knowledge flows, and the impact will not be just on technology and systems, but on people and organizations. For example, how far will work be redefined? How much further will our view of organizational structures and processes change beyond the departures already occurring from the views of the early twentieth century? Will our notions of how human beings think and act continue to change as we understand the brain and evolution more completely and as we observe how people operate in an environment ruled by greater volumes, flow, and velocities of information? Is there a point at which the technical discipline of architecture must be melded with the role of human decision-making and organizational design in order for information technology to progress?

The difficult challenge in forecasting this revolution may be ferreting out the implicit assumptions we make about how people and organizations operate, and how those may change. For example, some people are concerned about the proliferation of security systems to protect communications and databases; they believe a key weakness is the absence of a standard. One underlying assumption in this judgment is that standards can be set and updated by a central organization (i.e., government) quickly enough to keep pace with the growth in information technologies (and attempts to attack the products of those technologies). An even deeper assumption is that centralized approaches are the solutions to problems of protection. A counterview might be that information technology continues to develop at rates that defy comprehensive understanding. The process of trying to set standards may be valuable because it disseminates information about security, but setting actual standards may be beyond organizational capability as long as rates of change are high. Indeed, perhaps we should encourage the decentralized generation of protective systems, if only because it complicates the job of those who wish to penetrate systems. This example is admittedly mundane, but it demonstrates the importance of understanding our deeper beliefs about the keys to successfully dealing with the future.

Perhaps the most important aspect of the information revolution is the development not of the technology but of adaptive institutions and the processes by which they operate. Excessive focus on technology has probably been a typical characteristic of estimating future change in the United States. The previously cited example of an airplane in every garage reflected the influence of the automobile and its manufacturing technology (which provided the popular mental model for forecasters to use). Since the middle of the century, businesses have come to appreciate more fully the strategic competitiveness aspect of success, understanding that building a better mousetrap is no guarantee of future success without attendant moves in the areas of distribution, design, manufacturing, presence, promotion, and so on (the failure of the Beta video standard being an example). More broadly, Japanese successes in numerous fields have certainly alerted us to the importance of organizing how people work. Finally, major new ideas in business strategy (e.g., competition based on time or portfolio management) have alerted us to much more complex models of change and leadership than simply inventing technology.

In this information technology future, technology may ironically become a less significant determinant of the rate and content of the realized future than it has been in the past. It will still be important, and a necessary precondition to the possibility of change. At least as important, however, are other variables that determine the rate and content of the technology that eventually is applied in ways central to how humans think, work, and interact. An important element of that success will be the institutional activities that translate and exploit the technologies of information, because it will be through them that the technological advances are converted into uses. As is already being seen, the ability of organizations to adapt quickly and reshape themselves to these technologies is an essential element of that success. The question is whether we will see new forms of organization emerge to increase the rate at which change is adapted to and exploited. For example, the penetration of information systems is a threat against which even in peacetime we are gaining concrete experience in preventing and in ameliorating its effects. What we may be overlooking is that government organizations and the private sector are developing institutional and process competencies for confronting this threat (which is very real for them), and those competencies may be much more important than any particular remedy that appears.

As we consider the information revolution and its implications, we need to consider its analogues, the complexity and velocity of change, and how we manage that change. Perhaps most important, we need to examine the underlying assumptions we hold—without which examination we are unlikely to be able to do the analytical work necessary for forecasts of any value.

2

Thinking about Information Infrastructure

Brian Kahin

There are some basic questions about the way that information technology is transforming the world that receive less attention than is appropriate. Even the people who think there are important issues often struggle with the inadequacies of concepts like the "superhighway" (a concept that I find fundamentally misleading, even dangerous). The difficulty comes in part from trying to generate excitement about a national initiative (even if the government is not directing it). Although some people do get excited about four-lane highways, it is not as much as people get excited about or used to get excited about the space race. In some ways I think that the National Information Infrastructure (NII) initiative, as the administration has been pursuing it, has been conceptually much closer to the space race than to a superhighway in that it is a technology initiative.

Nevertheless, the NII initiative is different in at least two respects from the space race: it is unclear what the roles of the government and the private sector should be in this initiative, and it lacks the concreteness of putting a man on the moon, which was something the government was uniquely situated to do. We did not expect private enterprise to put a man on the moon, so the government did it by creating a new agency—the National Aeronautics and Space Administration. Clearly, it is mostly the private sector's role to create an information infrastructure, but it is a much more difficult initiative to visualize and talk about because it is a collection of abstract issues. This initiative is not about projecting ourselves in space or about building anything gigantic. It is really more of a disappearing act. It is about shrinking components, shrinking computers, shrinking distances, shrinking costs, and disappearing barriers. It is about the ultimate dematerialization of information and about globalization at the same time.

We can see this paradox very clearly in the transformation of publishing. Publishing is no longer the manufacture of books that are distributed physically to thousands of different locations and archived in huge collections. Publishing now is about globally accessible information. Instead of having thousands or millions of copies, you only need to have one copy, and that copy is accessible worldwide. Under the economic model of the Internet it is accessible worldwide at the same cost wherever you are in the world. I think this model will hold up.

This transformation, this image of globally accessible information, is not as simple as it appears to be. You may have heard that information wants to be free; but this means that we have to devise new ways of mediating and configuring access to information over networks if we are going to maintain a marketplace for information.

The real transforming metaphor here is the network. It is not the simple shift from wire-based telephony and coaxial cable and optical fiber, although I would not deny the very powerful image in that optical fiber. What is really important is the breakdown of two classical models of networking: the switched point-to-point model of traditional telephony and the broadcast-like model of cable television and direct satellite broadcast. The real difference lies in the notion of addressability. We are moving away from the networks of simple homogeneous users—everybody connected at the same three-kilohertz analog channel, everybody with more or less the same analog device in their right hand—to a much more complex network that is very difficult for people to visualize. It is very hard for people to understand the Internet intellectually unless they have had some kind of experience with the tools available for use over the Internet. Instead of homogeneous nodes of users, we now have users that have names and domain names that can be mapped to network addresses. We have computers that are addressable on the network, other networks addressable on the network, and information or media elements—information of any kind—fully addressable on the network.

We have a network of networks. This part of the Internet is very hard for people to understand. If you hear somebody say "networks like the Internet," you know that person does not understand the Internet. The Internet is not a network like Compuserve. The Internet is similar to what you might call the global telephone system—not a singular system, but a system of systems.

Furthermore, you have the concept of overlay networks. Again the Internet demonstrates this concept because it is an overlay on underlying physical telecommunications facilities. The Internet can overlay anything from satellite to cable to wireless to dial-the-regular-public-switch network-based lines, anything. It is a hostile overlay network in that it is indifferent to whatever the networks below it are.

These networks are different from traditional networks in that there are degrees of interoperability. Interoperability is a big issue. Some networks may be interoperable with other networks for some functions but not for others. You may have access to the Internet for certain kinds of functionality but not for others.

Finally, we have the reality of networks that are no longer based in physical structure but are just based in information. This characteristic is to some degree true of the Internet in that much of the Internet is defined by databases that are essentially routing tables, address servers, or domain-name servers that translate numeric addresses into the domain names that we all recognize. You can set up a network with a database. You can tear it down instantly. The sunk investment is almost nothing in an information-defined network. A mailing list is a network. A mail exploder is a network. A group of interlinked websites is a network. You can see in the interlinking of networks different degrees of functionality in different configurations, a breakdown between the concept of the network and the concept of processing.

Networks are no longer limited to generic models. The networks can be defined and designed for particular tasks or particular enterprises. It is no longer a question of being on or off the network, a fact that leads us into very difficult issues of network design and mediating access to information about network design. The breakdown or blurring of boundaries that everybody talks about actually leads into a variety of new structures or new boundaries. The nature of the boundary is no longer the simple wall it used to be. At one extreme there are very, very strong walls, the kind of walls that are available through encryption and that are much stronger than anything that exists in an analog environment. At the other are the globalization of information and the instant accessibility of information all over the world, making things seem without boundaries in a way.

Another key concept is disintermediation. Functions that are linked to physical process disappear, and people, institutions, or industries performing those roles are threatened by disintermediation. Authors can now have the opportunity of dealing directly with readers. At the same time, however, there are new ways of adding value, of intermediating, of linking and packaging, of filtering, and of analyzing. All these become, in the long run, much more important.

Reduction of cost is another aspect. There are some very large reductions of direct cost, for example, in the fact that you can pass an enormous amount of information through optical fiber, which is much cheaper than the copper it replaces. What happens, however, when these direct costs are decreased because information becomes more efficiently carried? The transaction costs become significant.

There are also different kinds of transaction costs. One is sometimes referred to as information costs, which is the cost of locating information. You can have information more cheaply available, but you still have the problem of finding the information you want. There are ways of addressing those information costs, but these information costs become much more significant in comparison to direct costs.

Finally there are the transaction costs associated with institutions, laws, regulations, and industry practices—costs that do not go away as easily as direct costs, and so they become more important. There is a theory that we can use information technology as it has been used in financial markets to reduce those transaction costs. What once was an exchange located in a particular building in London suddenly becomes a worldwide market. It may not be easy, however, to reduce those costs when you are dealing with national laws or regulations that control the use of those services.

Finally, I would like to show a map (figure 1) of how converging industries look as businesses rather than as technologies. There is a convergence of the different businesses of content and telecommunications facilities, a convergence driven to a large extent by technological convergence. To a large extent the market lags behind the technology, and the policy development lags behind the market.

We no longer have distinct content industries, such as we had in print publishing or the movie industry, or distinct telecommunications industries and distinct computer industries, such as we had 15 years ago. We have, in fact, the creation of new industries that are part of this three-cornered continuum. In this environment businesses face not so much a problem as an opportunity or a set of unprecedented opportunities. There are all sorts of ways to add value within this space, and this is only one dimension of that space. It does not reflect applications in

Figure 1

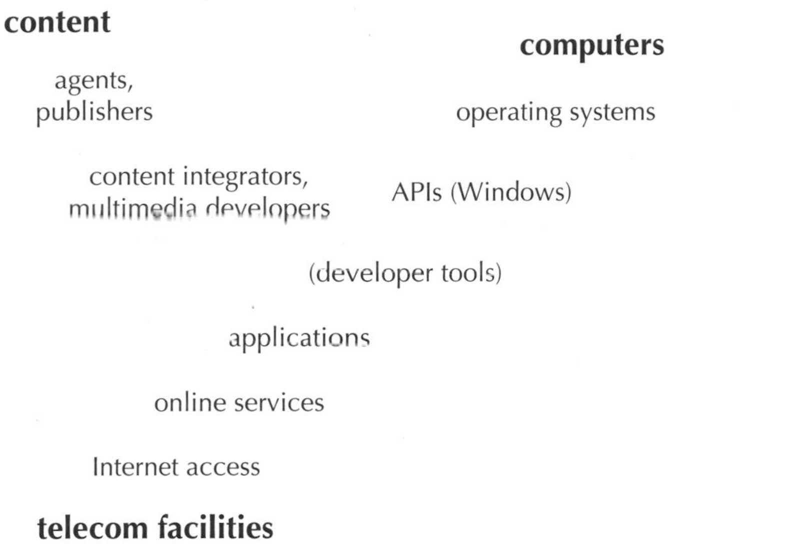

---

content

                                          computers

agents,
publishers   operating systems

content integrators,
multimedia developers   APIs (Windows)

(developer tools)

applications

online services

Internet access

telecom facilities

---

specific industries or specific sectors, such as health or banking, but just general purpose infrastructure. There are so many ways for adding value and for strategic positioning that it is overwhelming.

For policymakers the situation is overwhelming, but there is no opportunity to be seized other than that of helping the development of the market. There are, conceivably, things to protect against and some specific opportunities in areas where the public sector has played a major role, such as education. In general, however, it is very hard to design a coherent policy vision around this, although the administration is trying to do so with the NII initiative. And that is what the vision of a global infrastructure in some respects aspires to.

Finally, I want to point out that along with this convergence of businesses and industries a policy convergence is occurring. Certain policy values are associated with content: First Amendment rights, copyright, and public libraries; very different policy values are associated with telecommunications, universal service, and interconnection. There are fewer policy values associated with computing. Historically computing has been an unregulated market in which intellectual property and antitrust provide the operating ground rules. As the industries converge, however, the policy domains converge. The problem policymakers face is: how do you reconcile the principle of interconnection with the competition that we associate with the computer industry and with software?

Within this map I want to point out that there are three classical models for infrastructure emerging. One is that of telecommunications facilities and the transformation of traditional network facilities, cable, satellite delivery, and telepathy. Its own particular problem is that it requires an enormous amount of capital, but that is where the superhighway metaphor directs you. The other model is the Internet, which does not necessarily involve owned facilities and therefore operates at a higher level. The investments required for Internet activity are really quite small, largely because it is premised on interconnecting private networks that have already been justified for other reasons. In the end, what has made the Internet so successful is a very collaborative and interactive standards process, as well as precedents for interconnection that have allowed these different networks to operate as if they were a coordinated whole. Finally, there is the published software model, which figures prominently in the issues surrounding the evolution of Microsoft, the epitome of the published software model, which has shown how it is possible to leverage a strong position in operating systems down into other parts of the infrastructure.

In conclusion, what we see here is new, unfamiliar terrain in which positioning is absolutely critical because it determines strategic options in a very fluid environment. We see companies go to great lengths to acquire market share, forgoing short-term profits if necessary. At the same time, the market demands open standards, so that it is difficult to assert and maintain proprietary advantage.

We have never seen anything quite like this before: high levels of private investment and extreme competition in a standards-based, multidimensional, infrastructure-like environment. The scale of the investment and the unusually powerful economic factors are driving technological and market change at an unprecedented pace. This development challenges not just the immediate stakeholders but every sector of the economy. It challenges every form of human enterprise because it can integrate enterprise, good or evil, around the globe.

3

Information Security: Planning for the Deluge

Alfred A. Jones

Information security is directly linked to the issue of control of information assets. Without controls, information security is difficult, if not impossible, to apply in any environment. I suggest that the effectiveness of controls over information assets has been declining for the past 30 years, and the rate of this loss of control is increasing. Automated controls were quite stringent when an organization's computer facility was located in an isolated room or building and all computer-based work, including programming, keypunching of programs, running programs, and printing computational results, occurred in that facility—controls were inherent in the physically localized process. This confinement of process provided an inherent level of information security because access to these facilities was easily limited.

The effectiveness of this innate security began its downward trend when electronic linkages among these computer facilities integrated these facilities into a computer-net utility. With the arrival of data networks, the information security problem became much larger. In the same vein, the advent of client-server architecture (a network and application configuration that divides processing between clients, such as desktop or laptop computers, and servers, such as larger computers at the hub of the networked client computers) continues to increase the size and complexity of this problem. When business processes migrated to the desktop, the controls were left at the mainframe. With the connective realities of local area networks (LANs), wide area networks, the Internet, workgroup computing, messaging, and electronic commerce, the information assets contained in the Global Information Infrastructure (GII) are dispersed well beyond the physical walls of the originally isolated data centers. Security for these dispersed assets lags behind the spread of this ubiquitous computer-net utility.

Exacerbating this problem of loss of control is the increasing amount of data being generated and transmitted throughout computer-net utilities. The rate of growth is nonlinear, compounding arithmetically, possibly even exponentially. With information growth continuing at this explosive rate, control, as we now know it, becomes the first fatality. Security of this information then becomes difficult at best and impractical for most.

Does this mean that there is no hope, that free access to all information is the new paradigm? The answer is, of course, no. The realities of capitalism and profit continue to operate robustly throughout most of the world. The experience of Electronic Data Systems, Inc. with customers and prospective customers from all over the world and from all industries and governing organizations reveals that decision-makers are becoming aware of this security-versus-little-or-no-security issue and its implication for the future. They read stories in business magazines and daily newspapers of computer virus contamination, financial losses due to computer fraud, and damage to systems by disgruntled employees in retribution for real or perceived slights. Businesspeople understand the larger issue of poor enterprise-wide security because of the potential damage it can do to their businesses, even if they do not understand the causes that are amplifying it.

Another observation we can make from experience is that nationally established security standards and directions do not readily translate into the solutions needed for truly global operations. The security objectives, needs, and solutions of nation-states are not those of global commercial organizations. The impediments restricting the global use of robust encryption mechanisms, the disparities relating to product certifications, the varied legal requirements surrounding privacy of personal information, and the inconsistencies in copyright and intellectual property rights provide a very confusing basis upon which to build a GII.

When it becomes too difficult to do business in a certain locale because of burdensome legislation, restrictions on global operations, and intrusive oversight requirements, enterprises may find it more profitable to relocate their business. With the computer-net utility in place, it will become increasingly easier to move business because electronic relocations will not impose the severe financial penalty of physical relocations. Two hundred years ago, Benjamin Franklin said, "Merchants have no country. The mere spot where they stand does not constitute so strong an attachment as that from which they draw their gain." This sage observation contains a strong message for us today doing business using the GII.

Controlling Information Assets

From what we have seen of organizations' attempts to gain or maintain control of their information assets, these efforts, for the most part, are creating more chaos than control. Formal ownership of information assets with its attendant accountability and authority is confused. Who in an organization, by their assigned role, owns the information assets presented on a screen that is composed of data from multiple sources originating from databases possibly located across the globe? When asked, some managers will acknowledge their ownership of a specific file. In other cases, managers will acknowledge ownership of files because they are contained within a computer-based application under their control. In still other cases, managers will compete for ownership of very corporately visible files. Without ownership definition, assignment of value and authority for access have a weak foundation.

Assignment of value to information assets seems more art than science, a qualitative rather than quantitative equation. If one asks six people to estimate the value of something physical such as an automobile, their estimates are closely clustered. If, however, one asks six people to estimate the value of a database containing the marketing plans and targeted customer populace for an organization, their estimates will range widely. Valuation practices for information assets do not follow any generally accepted process.

Key culprits in this confusion over defining and implementing enterprise-wide security are the information protection practitioners themselves. Over time, they have done a very questionable job of defining and specifying their requirements, on an enterprise-wide scale, to the vendor community. The vendor community has attempted to give the information protection experts what they have myopically requested, and the vendors have attempted to integrate these pleas for functionality with the selected security functionality they believed would be marketable. The result is a disparate set of security functionality that heavily overlaps from product to product, has gaping holes in the functionality spectrum, and requires specially trained technicians to deal with each product. As one security executive from a global financial firm recently put it, "Vendors, please stop listening to us until we really understand what we need."

What is needed is an information security function that works across a heterogeneous configuration of platforms to provide secure linkage across enterprises that have a crazy-quilt mixture of equipment, operating systems, networking systems, and database management systems. This is the real world for large companies doing business across the globe in this era of mergers, acquisitions, and industry convergence.

From a technological perspective, information security is a unique animal. Some people consider it an adjunct function to the operating system. Some consider it a systems management function. Others know it as an application. In fact, information security is all of these. Its functionality is unique in that it is integral to the operating system, inherent to any network, and interacts with the user just like an application. Information security must perform its functions in all areas of the information infrastructure. Even with such a complex and wide-ranging purpose, the using community expects, and should get, easy installation, configuration, and maintenance of the information security product.

User-friendly interfacing with security products is not a dream. It can be provided. As I perform my business functions, I should not have to adapt to the security processes. The security processes should adapt to the way I do business. For example, I should be able to give access permission to an employee by notifying the security system of this new permission without having to be trained in the special computer language of the security system. I should be able to "point and click" the access permission using a mouse on a graphical display that is designed with business symbols and deducible steps. Conducting security transactions should be as easy as adding a new employee to the compensation system.

Why do we persist in thinking that information security administration falls only within the domain of a systems administrator who has been trained in the cryptic language of an information security product? Should the administrative assistant, with surrogate authority granted by the information owner, be capable of modifying the access permissions of people within a security domain? The answer is yes. Applying the same look and feel of other Windows-based applications, and not having to know the special language of the underlying security product, the assistant should be able to administer the security within a domain. Moving the administration closer to the using community, or even within the using community, provides better control, greater responsiveness, and customer convenience. We must reengineer our thinking about security functionality with the same sensitivities we use in reengineering our business applications.

Under this assumption, then, we must plan our security infrastructure with the same discipline with which we construct our plans for business and technological advances. There must be a direct correlation between the security charter of an organization and the mission statement of the business. There must be compliance by the security architecture with the governing technical direction of the organization. The security plan must be based on a total risk assessment that identifies the threats, the probability of threat occurrence, the targets, the vulnerability of the targets, and the value of the targets. Without this basic work on the security structure, an organization's technological infrastructure is seriously faulty.

Planning a sound security structure requires an organization to integrate its security across all computer platforms and linked networks to enable coherent enterprise-wide security policies. If an organization's security policies are properly constructed, they will not have to be changed each time the underlying technology changes. Yes, security procedures may change when this occurs, but it is the procedure that changes, not the policy. If policies are truly based on principles, they will apply to both mainframe domains and LAN domains. They will apply to centralized administration and decentralized administration. It is the local interpretation of the centralized policies that provides the maximum strength to the security structure.

In many instances, our security work with customers reveals that mainframe-based legacy and distributed security system structures remain separate. Typically, the management information systems (MIS) organization is heavily involved in mainframe security, and in many cases, the distributed infrastructure grew up outside of the MIS organization's sphere of control. The nature of the distributed infrastructure is such that security becomes even more complex than that of the mainframe world. With security in this arena being almost an afterthought by many organizations, the continuity between the two domains is generally weak or nonexistent. This lack of continuity can be a pitfall in an organization's planning. Security policies and standards of operation should universally apply to the entire enterprise.

A security architecture that is singularly focused on technology yields only a partial, and possibly doomed, solution. Properly constructed policies in combination with a properly trained user organization provides the fullest human-computer security solution. We all are aware of recent spying cases, disgruntled employee activities within our own organizations, and breaches of security defended by people who just wanted to get the job done. Technology, by itself, is no more than half of the security solution available to protect an organization from situations like these. People who understand responsibility and accountability, in combination with an ethical set of values, are the primary barrier in a total security program. Relying on technology to control and protect information completely is ill advised. Security awareness on the part of individuals is as important as technological wizardry in forming a secure infrastructure for an organization.

As most security practitioners will acknowledge, security solutions for emerging technology lag behind that technology's deployment. Until the technology developers become sensitized to the security issues of these advances, we will react to new technology after its deployment by constructing add-on or patchwork security solutions, as opposed to integrating the security features into the technology before release.

A recent example of this is object-oriented technology. Object-oriented technology centers on creating units of programming, views of information, or associations of certain data to other data for the purposes of creating reusable "things." Compositing objects can make system development proceed faster because many of the processes contained within any system occur multiple times. The same is true for views of data extracted from many sources. Security, then, becomes a contextual problem based on usage of these reusable things. I submit that the security solution for object-oriented technology is currently nonexistent.

Without proper planning that includes people and policies in addition to technology, the foundation for an organization's infrastructure will be weak and will create chaos. Distributed security, with its inherent complexity, adds another dimensional challenge to this chaos. We all know that gaining control of a chaotic situation is expensive. Our resources are better spent on planning the total solution, not patching the holes in a security domain installed as an afterthought.

So what is the future? What are the trends, technologies, and issues that we must consider in our efforts to keep control of our information assets?

The Role of Government?

While the inevitability of technological advancement is clear, it is equally clear that too much government regulation can inhibit the advancement of the information age, resulting in higher prices and reduced availability of services on a worldwide information infrastructure. The free market, not regulation, will provide optimal security solutions on this infrastructure.

We know that barriers can be built around such issues as privacy, intellectual property rights, transborder data flow, and protectionist policies. The government's role, however, is to legitimately facilitate and advocate greater competition in a free-market society. It must move to eliminate trade, investment, and technical barriers in order to stimulate open movement of products and services across borders. Government and the private sector must work together in a spirit of cooperation to remove barriers that block the promise of the Global Information Infrastructure. The GII will contribute to the increasing permeability of nation-state borders. This, in turn, will contribute to the increased exchange of information, ideas, and intellectual thought, not to mention increased markets, trade and business expansion, much of it through secure electronic means.

Conclusion

This Global Information Infrastructure will not be based on one underlying network or framework. It will consist of many networks offered by many service agents offering many services. The one-size-fits-all vision does not acknowledge the impact of free-market influences. The Internet is growing and will continue to grow in importance as a part of this infrastructure, but it will not be the most secure communication framework. It will suffice for the business envisioned to be contained on it. It will not suffice for business transactions that require security levels well above this baseline. Large global organizations will rely on more than one communication framework to conduct their business. Just as there are tollways, interstate highways, two-lane roads, and country lanes, there will be multiple paths, each with a certain level of security, by which one will traverse the Global Information Infrastructure.

Another control issue that will require attention in this network-linked world is resource addressability. To have controls over anything, one must be able to identify uniquely each "resource" (things such as personal computers on a network and printers linked to a network). This is done with unique addresses for each and every resource that is connected to the network. One can imagine the confusion if a command is issued to a resource at an address that is duplicated on the network . . . confusion reigns. Therefore, just as each of us has a unique mailing address to ensure that we get only the mail directed to us, each resource must have unique addressability for control purposes. As security practitioners know, unique addressability to each resource in the security domain is required in order to impose the proper controls for its usage. As the boundaries of security domains expand beyond data centers, campuses, and enterprises, the issue of duplicate addresses will temporarily hinder the growth of the information infrastructure. The emergence of standardized directories capable of handling the huge inventory of resource addresses will enable improved security.

A current security issue that will take on greater importance in the future is robotic safety. Networked computing power must incorporate sound security for robotic control systems. Safety considerations will require responsibility in design and implementation of systems that will affect people's well-being. For example, downloading software changes to vehicle-based systems that affect the vehicle's operation must have ingrained security. Remote operation of mechanical devices must contain security functionality to prevent harm or injury. Laser-based surgical procedures assisted by software programs must have the proper controls incorporated to ensure maximum safety for the patient. As more and more tasks are relegated to computer control, the security dimension of this human-task-to-computer-task transfer looms larger in importance.

Object-oriented technologies will require a practical redefinition of data labeling and asset ownership. These already difficult tasks may have become practically impossible with the advent of this technology. Who owns an information view of data composed of files and databases located across an enterprise? What sophisticated artificial intelligence determines the sensitivity of a composite of nonvalued data element? We will be required to take a higher or macro-level view for labeling and ownership assignment of information assets because it is pragmatically impossible to have each and every owner of the pieces of information that go into the construction of a screen full of information give their formal permissions for access. Many of these composited views of informational elements are created dynamically such that one cannot even predict where or how that element is going to be used or viewed next.

Security, now and in the future, begins with the critical processes of identification and authentication (I&A). Smart cards containing more than just I&A functionality (business, financial, and social information for interactive uses) and passive biometric identification will have key places in tomorrow's communications technology and software applications. Emphasis on I&A will increase dramatically, even in those information environments such as public forums where security is not a major concern because, even in the networked world, people will want to know with whom they are communicating.

The hypothesis I put forward at the beginning of this paper is predicated on the belief that the loss of control over information assets is under way, aided by the ubiquity of computer literacy and an explosion of information. A futurist recently produced this sound byte: "Information will double every 73 days by the year 2020—plan accordingly." This prediction has merit but generates cause for concern for the information security professional. What are we to do to secure this information deluge?

The answer I put forth is one that, in the light of key factors influencing the direction of technology and business, gives us a chance to provide the appropriate level of security without being washed away in this flood of information: We must plan for securing selected information only for the period of time that it has value, protects privacy, or affords safety. We cannot and should not attempt to secure all information. That is futile and a waste of resources. By continually applying this criterion to filter the information being generated, we will be able to perform the task we have been assigned—securing that which is worth securing.

4

Financial Systems: Instabilities and Conflict

Martin Shubik

Although this essay contains a certain amount of history and some specific facts for context, my emphasis is on posing questions and puzzling over the issues we need to confront. I wish to stress that my observations are preliminary and that considerably more work on this topic is justified by the defense needs of our society. Nonetheless, it must be set in the context of other priorities. As we know, economists worry about the optimal assignment of resources. A criterion used is that a marginal expenditure on topic A will yield approximately the same benefit as a marginal expenditure on topic B. Under that criterion, in my opinion the expenditures for understanding the new dangers implicit in the development of the potential for biological warfare, for example, far outweigh in importance the expenditures needed for understanding the dangers of financial systems sabotage. In relative importance my guess at the investments called for is that the former requires many billions while the latter requires a few million. Thus, this note may be regarded as being addressed to a small problem in the context of the "big picture." Yet, if the appropriate small expenditures of money and effort are not made on small problems, the losses can be considerable relative to the costs of prevention.

Communication and the Nation-State

The deep changes in the economics and technology of communications and computation are such that quantitative change clearly implies qualitative change. The institutions and ways of yesterday, whether individuals know it, are being swept away by the profound changes implicit in the new technology. The permeability of the nation-state is increasing daily. Thirty years ago central banks were controlling entities to be reckoned with; for better or worse, they had considerable influence over their own economies. Furthermore, if several major central banks were willing to cooperate, they could rule the international economy. Today there are several private fund international arbitrageurs with more financial power than most of the smaller central banks.

The growth of the power of the arbitrageurs and international firms has come with the new flexibility and cheapness in communication and computation. Billions of dollars can be moved around the world in a matter of seconds. Interest rate swaps based on differences of a few basis points can be identified and commercialized between parties many thousands of miles apart. Thirty years ago these opportunities did not exist.

A Brief Historical Introduction

We tend to take key aspects of our society's communications, such as language and money, as givens for all time. The key communication and computation methods needed for an advanced financial system are not that old, however. The history of the emergence of gold as a means of payment, followed by formal coinage, followed in turn by a shift to paper encompassed only 3,000 years, with the emergence of paper confined primarily to the last 300 years. The following historical sketch provides an appreciation of the intermix of societal, political, legal, and technological conditions that set the stage for the great benefits and future potential dangers involved in possible sabotage of the modern financial system.

With the emergence of the economy, barter involved physical exchange of needed goods for goods. Some time between 2000 and 1000 B.C. the switch to payment in gold started. Around 1300 B.C. hard evidence of exchange for gold appears.

The early precursors of paper instruments grew with the extension of law, transportation, trade, and technology. The warehouse receipts in early Babylon and Egypt were not originally financial instruments because they were not negotiable instruments. Eventually the warehouse receipt could become negotiable. The loan contracts of Babylon clearly predated the invention of coinage but already were used to finance inventories for international trade. It was probably in international trade that the first glimmerings of price system appeared.

The growth of the use of coinage may be viewed in terms of the minimization of the need for individual trust. With gold coins of full value, trade involved exchange of value for value, where the government and its laws served to guarantee and enforce the value of the coinage. The individuals did not need to know anything about each other as long as one was being paid in coin of value. There is an old New England saying, "in God we trust, all others pay cash." That, of course, implies that you trust the cash. As the currency was debased, however, the trust had to be in the government and institutions, not the metals.

Probably the earliest clearly defined paper financial instrument was the bill of exchange. Its origin is not clear, but by the mid-fourteenth century it was well established and facilitated trade between distant cities by making it unnecessary for individuals to risk the transportation of gold over large distances. Trading in bills of exchange represented another step in the increasing financial abstraction of trade. Symbols of wealth, rather than wealth itself, were being exchanged.

The decades around 1700 mark the takeoff into the modern financial world of ever-increasing communication and paper or other abstract financial instruments. The Amsterdam and London stock exchanges came into being around 1700, having developed from the changes in financing joint ventures: nonnegotiable shares in a single ship voyage became negotiable shares in the voyage and then became shares in many linked voyages. The accounting for the several ventures allowed for accrual accounting methods, thereby introducing timing differences. These developments were important precursors in separating ownership from management by introducing high levels of anonymity in trade and far less transparency in accounting, thus lessening the ability of a nonmanager to interpret the economic health of the enterprise.

The growth of technology has continued with breakneck speed. Vast changes have occurred in the production of both coins and paper. It is difficult to have a hyperinflation or to ruin a currency if the means of production are extremely slow and the technology for producing either official or forged money is difficult. The first inflation via debased coinage is attributed to the Romans, but paper and printing make the possibilities for inflation far broader. The honor for the first paper-based inflation goes to the finance minister of Kublai Khan.

The mid-nineteenth century saw the explosive growth of the corporate form of business enterprise. The corporation had its early history during the Roman Empire. There was a considerable gap in its evolution until both its for-profit and not-for-profit forms developed in England, culminating in the limited liability shareholding form with greatly separated ownership and management, as characterized by the current major corporations of Europe, America, and Japan.

The markets for the paper of these enormous aggregations of capital have grown exponentially along with the telephone, telegraph, and ticker tape. Now with the computer revolution, the possibilities for even more abstract representation, exchange, and transmission of symbols of value have increased.[1]

What is the operational significance of all this? The complex interaction of technological advances in communication and calculation has completely transformed the nature of risk assessment and credit and trust evaluation and the speeds at which more and more impersonal trade can take place. Vast communications networks and data files cover the globe, connected so that a transaction or a transfer can be made halfway around the world at a speed quicker than the recipient's ability to read the output.

Means of Payment

Before we consider specific possibilities for financial sabotage and warfare, we might review the changes that have taken place in the means of payment as society has adjusted to new technology and organizational structure. Table 1 covers from around 1690 to 1875, showing the decreasing significance of specie and the quick rise and fall of the importance of the banknote.

Coins and small bills in the United States now account for probably more than 99 percent of the individual transactions (such as paying for a bus fare or a hamburger) and considerably less than 1 percent of the dollar value.

In spite of modern technology, different societies have highly different attitudes and customs; thus, table 2 shows a considerable divergence among different nations. The major means of payment in the United States by dollar volume is now electronic funds transfer. The checking account of 30 years ago is being challenged by credit cards, accounts in mutual funds with check-writing possibilities, debit cards, and other special payment systems. Each and every one of the systems depends on a specialized set of information considerations. Large firms that do a large volume of business with each other over periods of time no longer need a commercial banker for much of their bridging finance; it is becoming easier and easier to net out their trade by bilateral specialized accounts.

Table 1.   Stock of Money and Means of Payment
(in percentages)

Period	Specie	Bank note	Deposits	Bill of exchange	Total
1688–1689	50.8	10.0		40.0	100.0
1750	37.5	12.5	12.5	37.5	100.0
1775	25.4	15.9	11.1	47.6	100.0
1800–1801	12.1	15.2	3.05	69.7	100.0
1811	7.0	20.9	7.0	65.1	100.0
1821	11.9	21.2	16.6	50.3	100.0
1831	18.1	17.4	24.1	40.4	100.0
1844	16.4	12.9	36.6	34.1	100.0
1855	13.3	7.1	38.7	40.9	100.0
1875	18.1	5.6	70.7	5.6	100.0

Source: R. Cameron et al., *Banking in the Early Stages of Industrialization* (Oxford: Oxford University Press, 1967), p. 42.

People have become more literate. Bodies of national law have increased, and there are some indications of increase in the volume and effectiveness of international law, although it still has a long way to go. Nevertheless, although the speeds of communication and calculation have changed by many orders of magnitude, the same does not hold true for changes in the IQs or moral aspects of individuals. The managerial or supervisory aspects of the enormous communication networks and international linkages have grown larger.

The Problem of Forgery

Recently a smuggling ring based in Lebanon has been discovered flooding the world outside of the United States with many billions of dollars of nearly perfect counterfeited $100 bills. They are produced outside of U.S. jurisdiction, probably in the Bekaa Valley. Is this ring merely a group of imaginative entrepreneurs with high technology trying to make an interesting if dishonest living in competition with our own Federal Reserve System?

Table 2. International Comparison of the Ratio of Currency to Gross National Product (GNP)

	% of GNP cash or currency	Money holdings per capita (US$)	% of GNP covered by money supply (M1)
Belgium	9.9	750.0	180.7
Canada	3.2	399.0	46.8
France	5.1	416.8	75.1
Germany	6.0	577.0	53.0
Italy	6.4	392.0	95.9
Japan	7.6	740.9	150.0
Netherlands	6.5	602.0	68.4
Sweden	6.0	677.0	60.0
Switzerland	10.0	1,545.0	117.0
United Kingdom	4.0	308.0	33.0
United States	4.2	595.5	75.4
Average	6.6		

Source: Survey of Payment Systems prepared by the Bank for International Settlements, 1985.

One of the reasons why the U.S. Treasury and Federal Reserve have made an enormous profit out of printing money has been the history of the $100 bill in the United States. The Federal Reserve management is perfectly aware that much of the illegal economic activity of the world runs on the $100 bill and the fact that it leaves no paper trail. A few years ago the printing of $100 bills cost about $26 per thousand. As they go into circulation, 20 to 30 percent of them disappear to Colombia and Mexico and elsewhere, where they stay in circulation outside of the United States for a considerable time. Given the forgone rate of interest, it is a good business for the Federal Reserve Bank. Unfortunately, as the $100 bill and the $1 bill cost the same to manufacture and have been made out of the same paper, an imaginative entrepreneur can avail himself of a supply of the paper by bleaching $1 bills at a cost of only 1 percent for raw materials for the manufacturing of the final product.

How do we catch international forgers? Furthermore, could the forgers be in the employ of the Syrian or Iranian government, or some other government wishing to join in on sharing the bounty of the Federal Reserve and Treasury?

An Aside on Anonymity and Economy

The $100 bill forging problem is only a simple example of the problem of anonymity. What constitutes enough anonymity is in the eye of the beholder. When most of us pay for a meal using a credit card, we implicitly consider it an anonymous transaction. It is not an anonymous transaction. Paying cash on the barrelhead, unless the paparazzi are present, is an anonymous transaction. That is what makes the $100 bill so fundamentally attractive.

Although many have predicted a cashless society, I suspect that from the viewpoint of cost effectiveness the most efficient means of payment is probably the quarter. A quarter lasts more than 25 years with no paper trail and performs many thousands of transactions for a cost of around 3 cents in its manufacture and initial distribution. If one asks a major bank about check-cashing costs, the estimates will be anywhere between 15 and 50 cents to cash a check (with a sophisticated computerized system). Part of this may be function of the accounting, however, because the splitting up of the overheads of a system used for many other purposes is a difficult trick. Nevertheless, it appears that a system with records and information flows is more expensive than the use of coins for small transactions.

Whatever the respective costs of cash and cashless systems, the value of anonymity to individuals deserves recognition. As the value of specialized mailing lists grows and as databanks proliferate, problems involving the protection of civil rights against Big Brother and the protection of the individual against the increasing intrusion of the modern communications hustler grow.

On Management

The recent failure of Barings through its foreign exchange trading in Singapore, the earlier Chilean copper futures trading problems, the current Japanese banking crises with trading losses of more than $1 billion covered up over several years, and the derivatives market disaster in Orange County are all symptoms of a managerial system that does not match the new technology.

One of the standard pieces of modern financial economics mythology attached to the joys of the competitive markets is the myth of stockholder democracy that is filled with false analogies to the governmental voting system. I have yet to see two candidates stand every two, four, or six years to replace the corporate governance of any major firm, yet simple game theory tells us that competition begins at two, not one. More than 60 years ago, Berle and Means raised basic questions concerning corporate governance.[2] The problems they raised have not only not been solved; they have grown considerably more complex with the growth of multinational firms with dozens if not hundreds of different incorporations. This complexity, combined with the growth of pension funds owning significant blocks of stock in many of the large corporations, offers new possibilities for strategic control of the corporation.

How to Study Money and Financial Institutions

Finance and money matters are frequently presented as some form of arcane mystery. Checks are cashed by magic; credits are rung up by the "black box" called the financial system. Shadowy financiers and bankers gather to create money. Economists invent hierarchies of different definitions of money types. The economic statistics are filled with items that tell us that the M-1 has shot up, but the M-2 and M-3 have done something else.

The basic way to avoid the mysteries of finance is adopt a simple engineer's and physicist's viewpoint. Concentrate on elementary particles, the role of time, and the rules of transformation and conservation. Do not wonder about the mysteries of what government money "really is." Treat it from the analytical point of view as Blue Chips that, by the rules of the game, can be created and destroyed only by the government. Bank money is Green Chips, which can be created and destroyed by institutions called banks that must conform to various sets of rules, which may differ somewhat from government to government. Ask the simple question, "What are the processes for the production, delivery and destruction of each financial instrument?" Be concerned with the apparently mundane technological and legal questions such as what does it cost to produce and deliver an instrument, what are the laws of the society concerning fraud, bankruptcy, failure to deliver, and so forth.

Much of the financial mechanism of our society deals with differentials in risk assessment and apparently minor differentials in costs of delivery caused either by technology or legal considerations. Most of the processes have been designed to cope with usual daily human commercial errors and not to function efficiently under sabotage and attack.

Crisis Scenarios

What are the possibilities for the vulnerability of the financial system? A useful way to approach this question is to consider the stress scenarios we might like to look at. I suggest that there are 10 scenarios worth checking:

1. Cold war

2. Proxy and limited war

3. Conventional war

4. Nuclear war

5. Biological war

6. Local criminal terrorism and profit-oriented sabotage

7. Local liberation or idealistic terrorism

8. International terrorism, jihad-like operations

9. Pathological individuals and local crazies

10. Spiteful hackers and disaffected employees intent on internal damage

A quick survey of these candidates suggests that we need concentrate on only a few. Cold war and proxy and limited war are fruitful scenarios for tampering or other actions adversely affecting the financial system.

In a conventional war, most of the conventional economic weapons are known. Except for some newer ways of disrupting money supplies and extra problems involving multinational corporations, financial warfare does not appear to be of major importance.

When we consider scenarios involving nuclear war, there is a financial component to postwar infrastructure repair. A major biological war might result in less physical property damage, but the postwar reconstruction of financial infrastructure would be one of the minor problems faced.

Local criminal terrorism and profit-oriented sabotage are items that merit consideration. Local liberation movements or idealistic terrorism might indulge in boycotts or in blowing up banks, stock markets, or clearinghouses; but they would probably not be highly organized for systematic sabotage, and overt attack on the financial infrastructure is unlikely except as a gesture.

International terrorism and jihad-like operations are probably not going to generate much in the way of new attacks on any country's financial infrastructure. As with the Lebanese $100 supernote, however, forgery is an excellent way to obtain financing. In particular, the change in communications technology and the increasing permeability of national borders make the financing and coordination of terrorist movements an item of concern.

The new dangers posed by pathological individuals and local crazies are probably mostly manifested in the unprecedented dangers of biological warfare on the cheap, now available at the organizational size of one or two individuals.[3]

The final, and possibly most important, scenario is what I call the spiteful hacker and disaffected employee problem, wherein an individual inside an organization is intent on the creation of mischief and internal damage. It is highly likely that the individual may be a trusted and knowledgeable member of the organization.

In summary, the scenarios meriting serious consideration and investigation are 1, 2, 6, 8, and 10, with the last possibly being of most concern, and proxy war and international terrorism being candidates for the next more important.

Some Specific Areas of Vulnerability

Limiting our concerns to the more relevant scenarios, we see at least nine fairly obvious means for attacking and damaging the financial system:

1. Subverting currencies

2. Destabilizing markets and causing panics and runs

3. Physically attacking communication nodes

4. Breaking financial institutions

5. Blocking assets

6. Swindling and theft

7. Generating false information

8. Corrupting credit and other files

9. Financing dissident groups

Empirical evidence appears to indicate that it is relatively hard to subvert a currency. The Japanese and the Germans tried in World War II. The Germans had a project on forged money based in the Sachsenhausen concentration camp, but it did not have great impact. The history of major forgeries has not been impressive. Possibly the most interesting case is the current forgery of $100 bills noted above. The new technology for money-making is changing fast, however. The Australians recently have substituted plastic for paper money using an advanced coding method. The problems in forgery of currency involve the speed of technological change in the production and the distribution system. The dangers appear to be highest in proxy and limited war, where there is a national protector and a bureaucratic system to aid in distribution.

Financial fiction places high on its list the destabilization of markets and crises that cause panics and runs. The truth of the matter is that although we do destabilize markets on occasion we do not know how we do it. I would be delighted if we could discover how to do it. Computer technology has not offered any major threat.

The opportunities for damaging credit and payment systems seem to offer possibilities for damage on the cheap. Although there may be enough redundancy in the financial system for ordinary error, a serious question that is under-researched is the adequacy of the redundancy in the system under sabotage. Scenarios involving the blowing up of clearing houses and data banks are promising candidates for damage exchange ratios that are highly in favor of the attacker, even if the system is reasonably redundant and recovers fast.

The destruction of financial institutions, like the destabilization of markets, is mostly self-inflicted. It is usually accomplished by bad delegation and poor accounting. The Barings failure provides a good example of bad management. A key problem that has happened with the growth of communications and computer technology is that the speeding up of reaction time is magnifying the effect of bad management. The preventive actions call more for a managerial fix than for a technological fix.

An important financial weapon some years ago that was quite effective was the blocking of international accounts and embargoes. Although we have had some success with Iraq, today the blocking of accounts is becoming more and more difficult. National boundaries are more and more pervious to new technologies.

A large growth industry is probably swindling and thefts. When markets reach billions and even a trillion dollars a day, the volume of trade is such that a program that siphons off the sixth decimal point, rounding error into a special little account, may provide a large source of income.

One of the most important concerns should be the possibilities for the generation of false information. The opportunities for the corrupting of credit and other files are considerable, especially from inside sabotage that would be hard to check. It is spiteful; it is cheap to accomplish and expensive to remedy. Its antidote involves both technology and the quality of managerial controls.

Another item of fairly high importance is the considerable change in the ease with which dissident groups can be financed and controlled. If there is a country on the outside financing covert activity, the mobilization of resources for sabotage virtually anywhere in the world where there is a modern financial system is becoming easier with new technology.

The hot and cold wars of the future are tending more and more to have high information and disinformation contents. They involve striking at systems and their interconnections. Unless we opt for several of the more obvious scenarios of self-destruction offered by nuclear and biological warfare, the emphasis will be more on paralysis than on destruction. The growth of the intercommunication of international financial and other structures offers enormous gains in productivity and flexibility. Nonetheless, the very dependence on complex systems and the high information content introduce new dangers unless the redundancy and robustness of the systems can absorb attack. The levels required for the survival of a state are in general higher than the levels that emerge in the growth of these systems for individual commercial purposes.

As the deep changes wrought by the communications and computer technologies are felt by our society—and globally—we will be faced with analytical challenges, perhaps most notably those related to risk assessment. Posing questions and puzzling over some of the most salient issues is the necessary first step.

Notes

1. The New York Stock Exchange was formed on May 17, 1792, under a buttonwood tree; the first million-share day was reached on December 15, 1886 (1,200,000 shares). Around 100 years later, on October 20, 1987, trade was 608 million. By 1990 the estimate of direct and indirect stockholders was more than 51 million. In 1994 the value of all stock was around $4.45 trillion and bonds $2.37 trillion. Currently the foreign exchange markets are over $1 trillion a day.

2. A. A. Berle and G. C. Means, *The Modern Corporation and Private Property* (New York: Macmillan, 1932).

3. Martin Shubik, "Terrorism, Technology and the Socioeconomics of Death," School of Management Research Paper, Yale University, New Haven, Conn., 1995.

5

Information Warfare and National Security: Some First Amendment Issues

James B. Ferguson

As the federal government has become increasingly concerned about "information warfare," it has considered a number of controls on the publication of encryption data. In March 1995, for example, the Clinton administration determined that export controls should remain on the dissemination of most types of encryption technology to certain restricted nations.[1]

These efforts to impose restraints on the publication of technical data give rise to several First Amendment issues, all of which involve a clash between two values of unquestioned importance—national security and freedom of speech.

In resolving conflicts of this kind, the Supreme Court traditionally has relied on a general "balancing" approach that focuses on the specific circumstances of each case. Through this approach, the Court has sought to accommodate competing interests by weighing the importance of the speech in question against the strength of the government's regulatory concerns. This balancing occurs within a framework of general rules or "tests" that define and allocate the burden of proof. For example, in a modern version of Oliver Wendell Holmes's well-known "clear and present danger" test, the Court has held that the government must demonstrate a "compelling" justification for any restraint on fully protected speech.

What is most notable about the Court's balancing method is that it allows the justices to accommodate worthy but conflicting interests in a way that allows both interests to survive, at least to some extent. Under this method, the Court first determines how much protection should be given to the speech at issue and then decides whether the government's regulatory interest is sufficiently weighty to justify the challenged restraint.

This two-step approach provides a useful analytical framework for assessing the constitutionality of national security controls on the publication of encryption systems and other kinds of technical information. In the first step, we will determine how much protection should be given to technical speech as a discrete category of First Amendment expression. In the second step, we will outline the analysis the Court is likely to use in evaluating the strength of the government's national security concerns.

First Amendment Fundamentals

Like other guarantees in the Bill of Rights, the free-speech clause of the First Amendment stakes out a zone of individual freedom by identifying a specific activity to be protected against unwarranted governmental intrusion. The enforcement of such guarantees is left to the Supreme Court, the branch of government removed from public accountability and vested with the power to invalidate official acts that encroach on the protected freedoms. This power of judicial review, however, carries the risk that the Court will frustrate the democratic process by freely substituting its own preferences for the enacted will of the public's elected representatives. Accordingly, under prevailing constitutional theory, the Court's power is properly exercised only when its decisions are rigorously based on principles derived from the text of the Constitution.

These larger considerations have often guided the Court in deciding cases arising under the free-speech clause of the First Amendment. Rejecting the notion that all speech is absolutely immune from official regulation, the Court has adopted what might be described as a "hierarchical" view of the First Amendment—a view that asserts that "not all speech is of equal First Amendment importance." The Court has thus held that different categories of speech warrant different levels of constitutional protection. For example, in a series of recent decisions, the Court has held that (1) "political speech" warrants a full measure of constitutional protection; (2) commercial advertising warrants only a limited measure of protection; and (3) "sexually explicit" speech warrants virtually no protection at all.

In light of this hierarchical approach to the First Amendment, the question arises whether encryption systems and other types of technical data warrant the same full measure of constitutional protection accorded other categories of speech. Although the Supreme Court has not yet decided, the issue has attracted the attention of legal scholars, some of whom have criticized the notion that technical data are a form of fully protected speech.[2] The critics' argument is *not* that as a matter of policy the government should embark on the wholesale regulation of scientific and technological expression. Rather, they argue that, as a matter of constitutional law, the Supreme Court must base its decisions on principles rigorously derived from the text of the Constitution and that under such principles the First Amendment cannot be construed to protect the entire class of scientific and technological expression.

In making this argument, the critics draw on a widely shared perception that encryption codes and other types of technical data really do not fit into the traditional categories of First Amendment speech. The critics thus argue that the free-speech guarantee is intended primarily to protect the speech of advocacy, opinion, and dissent—the free expression of individual beliefs in the public discussion of public issues.

This conception of the free-speech principle is part of a well-known "democratic" or "politically based" theory of the scope of the First Amendment. As described by that theory, the sole purpose of the free-speech guarantee is to promote the well-being of democratic institutions by protecting the "free discussion of governmental affairs." The theory holds that a self-governing society cannot function effectively unless the voting public is well informed on all matters of public policy. The theory also holds that government officials often have a strong motive to mold public opinion by restricting the information upon which citizens may draw. For these reasons, according to the theory, the free-speech guarantee has as its sole function the prohibition of all governmental efforts to regulate the public discussion of public issues.

If these premises are granted, it follows that the free-speech guarantee applies only to official acts designed to suppress political speech or to censor information relevant to issues of public policy. Under this standard (as the critics are quick to point out), many forms of scientific and technological speech do not qualify for the full protection of the First Amendment. The critics do acknowledge that a scientific paper or technical publication can have a direct bearing on questions of public policy. In most cases, however, according to the critics, scientific and technical papers do not have any real "relationship to existing issues of public policy," and the government's efforts to restrict the publication of technical speech do not reflect a desire to control individual thought or public opinion. This is especially true of most national security controls on technological data, including encryption systems and other cryptological publications:

The government may adopt security policies limiting disclo-
sure of scientific and technological information notwith-
standing adverse side effects on scientific progress and self-
fulfillment and remain consistent with the view that the
foundation of the First Amendment is denial of the government's power to try and control viewpoint. First, little reason
exists to suspect that a national security regulation having
these side effects actually was intended to distort scientific
debate. Second, a valid national security purpose can be
linked only tenuously to illicit thought control. No plan can
be found to shape ideas in the abstract nor to control viewpoint to prevent "undesirable" behavior. Rather, the assumption in this discussion is that persons, groups, or nations
already are committed to, or are threatening to use force
against our society. The scientific and technological information represents a means to an end in the same sense as a
weapon.[3]

On this view, then, the imposition of national security controls
on technical data does not violate the First Amendment because
it is not part of a governmental effort to regulate individual
thought or public opinion.

Significantly, however, the Supreme Court has declined to
accept the "democratic" theory as the sole rationale of the First
Amendment. To be sure, the Court has long emphasized that free
speech is crucial to a democratic society and that political speech
warrants the highest degree of constitutional protection. Rather
than confining itself to a single First Amendment value, however, he Court has relied on a broader, more flexible approach
that holds that the First Amendment serves at least three principal values: (1) an individual interest in self-expression; (2) a generalized social interest in the free flow of information and ideas;
and (3) a political interest in enlightened self-government.[4]

It seems clear that scientific and technical communications
contribute to each of these values and thus warrant as much protection as political tracts, literary works, or any other variety of
speech. Indeed, a system of free scientific expression not only
enables scientists to draw on the work of colleagues but also tests
the validity of hypotheses against current data and opposing
views. In these ways, it promotes the discovery of scientific truth
and fosters the intellectual advances that contribute to the collective wisdom.

In the case of purely technical data, however, more difficult questions arise. For example, does technical information having *only* military uses (e.g., weapons design) warrant the same degree of constitutional protection as political speech or basic scientific knowledge? The Supreme Court may well answer in the negative; it has previously held that other, less conventional forms of expression do not stand on the same constitutional footing as more traditional varieties of speech. For example, the Court has held that commercial advertising occupies a "subordinate position in the scale of First Amendment values" and thus warrants only a "limited measure" of constitutional protection.

Most forms of technical knowledge, however, are subject to a wide range of uses, some of which have military value but most of which contribute directly to the material welfare of the community. This point is clearly illustrated by encryption systems, which have a wide variety of applications in the private sector. Given the obvious social value of such technological achievements, the Supreme Court may well hold that the broad category of technological knowledge warrants a full measure of constitutional protection, while noting an exception for information that is subject only to military applications.

Once this larger question is decided, the Court will not assess the social value of the technical data at issue in a given challenge to a governmental restraint. Rather, it will simply note that the information in question falls within the category of fully protected speech and will then turn its attention to the government's countervailing interest in regulation. At this point, a crucial issue will arise: Given the strong constitutional presumption in favor of free speech, just what burden of proof must the state carry to justify its imposition of restraints on the information? Or, to put it in legalistic terms, what standard of review will the Court apply to the government's stated justification for the challenged restrictions?

Determining the Standard of Review

To determine the relevant standard of review, the Court will focus on two broad questions. First, is the individual whose speech the state is trying to restrict an employee of the government? If so, the Court will apply a mere "reasonableness" standard to any governmental restraints imposed on government employees in an effort to preserve the secrecy of the data. Thus, for example, in *Snepp v. United States*, a well-known case involving a book published by a former Central Intelligence Agency employee, the Court broadly upheld the state's power to impose "reasonable restrictions" on the dissemination of governmental information obtained by government employees. In addition, the Court pointedly noted that this general principle applies "even in the absence of an express agreement" between the government and the employee.

In like manner, the Court will probably sustain any reasonable restraints imposed on the dissemination of information resulting from the government-funded research of private parties. Indeed, in such a case, the government's restraints will likely be upheld on either of two grounds: (1) the state, by financing the underlying research, acquires a property interest in the resulting information or (2) the researcher, by accepting the public financing, agrees to restrictions that might otherwise be constitutionally impermissible.

On the other hand, if the government attempts to regulate the dissemination of nongovernmental information by private parties, the Court will apply a far more demanding standard of review. Indeed, on the evidence of the so-called Pentagon Papers decision (*New York Times v. United States*), the Court will uphold the restraint only if the government can show that a "grave" and "irreparable" harm will almost surely result from publication of the data in question.

Under this standard of review, the government clearly is faced with an exceedingly difficult task. Nevertheless, the Court has indicated that in some "exceptional" cases, principally in the area of national security, the government's interest in regulation may be sufficient to warrant a direct infringement on fully protected speech. The remaining question, therefore, is: Just how will the Court assess the importance of the government's concerns to determine whether they are adequate to justify an abridgment of First Amendment freedoms?

Weighing the Government's Interest in Regulation

As noted above, even "fully protected" speech can be abridged if the government can demonstrate a "compelling" reason for regulation. In weighing the state's argument on this score, the Court will look to a number of critical facts.

First, in the case of alleged national security data, the Court undoubtedly will require some showing that the information at issue is not currently available from a third-party source. If such a showing can be made, the Court will then turn to an assessment of the state's interest in regulation. In particular, the Court will evaluate the gravity of the alleged harm that the state is seeking to avert and the likelihood of its occurrence.

In the context of encryption systems and other types of "militarily critical" technologies, the first inquiry would assess the magnitude of the harm that would result if a potential adversary used the data to acquire the relevant capability. The most serious danger would arise from technical capabilities that could alter in major ways the current balance of international military power. This category would include technologies that directly conferred on a potential adversary a new offensive capability or an effective countermeasure to U.S. capabilities—for example, a technology that enabled an adversary to cripple the command and control system of the United States. The category would also include technologies that exposed the United States to new threats by providing a smaller adversary with a destructive power that it had not possessed before.

These are examples of sudden and disastrous giveaways. There are other capabilities that, if acquired by a hostile nation, could result in a number of lesser harms to U.S. security. Most significant is the wide range of militarily useful technologies that could enable a foreign adversary to add incrementally to its current military strength by (1) directly improving the performance of its weapons systems, (2) enhancing its communications network, or (3) increasing its ability to compromise U.S. military capabilities—for example, through information warfare.

A less immediate harm would result from technologies that enabled a foreign adversary to improve its military research and development. The most significant are technologies associated with the use of the computer for correlating experimental data with theoretical models. Other well-defined technical methodologies are used to "guarantee reliability, explore the limits of design, and reveal new phenomena that can affect the next generation of weapons."[5]

A slightly different harm to national security would result from technologies that enabled a foreign power to upgrade its manufacturing capability in industries of military importance. For example, microelectronics and computer technologies are important in the development of in-flight guidance systems, while precision ball bearings are important in the production of missiles and other military hardware.

Turning to the question of the likelihood of occurrence, the Court will address the probability that a third party will use the information at issue to develop the new capability. This line of inquiry will consider both the complexity of the technology and the skills of the receiving nation. The need for the inquiry arises in part from the fact that the impersonal transmission of technical knowledge is rarely an effective method of transferring technology. As a general rule, the normal channels of intellectual communication convey only the broad outlines of technical design and theory. What is usually not published or codified is the body of associated know-how that constitutes the art of the technology, typically including methods of operation, organization, and manufacturing procedures. This is particularly true of emerging technologies with few previous applications.

Accordingly, the Court's inquiry into the likelihood of occurrence will focus on the ability of the receiving nation to absorb the knowledge at issue and put it to use. For example, if the receiving nation has a high level of technical expertise in the relevant area, the government could show with virtual certainty that the receiving nation will put the information to an immediate military use. If the receiving nation lacks any of the needed skills or resources, the state could show only a possibility that the knowledge will be put to a significant use in the foreseeable future.

Together with the gravity of the threatened harm to national security, the Court's finding on the likelihood of occurrence will generally determine whether the state's interest in regulation is sufficient to warrant the restriction of First Amendment rights. Assume, for instance, that the government can show that a potential adversary has sufficient skills to compromise U.S. information security by acquiring a U.S. breakthrough in encryption technology. On these facts, the Court will likely agree that the government's concerns are sufficiently compelling to warrant an abridgment of First Amendment freedoms. This will probably hold true, moreover, even if the government concedes that the potential adversary will eventually acquire the capability anyway because the maintenance of a military lead time can be highly advantageous. On the other hand, if the threatened harm to the nation's security is less serious, the state's case will be correspondingly weakened, and all the more so if the receiving nation is shown to lack the requisite skills or resources to absorb the technology.

What is most striking about the Court's method of First Amendment adjudication is that it takes into account virtually all of the commonsense perceptions that have informed the general policy debate on the government's effort to impose national security controls on scientific and technical knowledge. Indeed, if the Court applies its standard analysis to this issue, it will not only give due weight to the value of scientific freedom but also examine critically the nature and magnitude of the threatened harm to national security. In addition, it will address a variety of other considerations, such as the technical skills of the receiving nation and the reasonableness of the regulatory technique. By incorporating each of these factors into a method of adjudication that formally allocates the burden of proof, the Court's approach provides a well-defined analytical framework for accommodating the claims of individual freedom with the legitimate interests of national security.

Notes

1. Louise Kehoe, "Crime on the Line," *Financial Times,* March 3, 1994. See also John Fialka, "Pentagon Studies Art of 'Information Warfare,'" *Wall Street Journal,* July 3, 1995; Peter Wayner, "Should Encryption Be Regulated?" *Byte* (May 1993).

2. See, for example, Robert D. Kamenshire, "Embargoes on Exports of Ideas and Information: First Amendment Issues," *Wm. & Mary L Rev* 863 (1985); Lillian R. Be Vier, "The First Amendment and Political Speech," 30 *Stan. L Rev* 299 (1973); Robert Bork, "Neutral Principles and Some First Amendment Problems," 47 *Ind LJ* 1 (1971).

3. Kamenshire, "Embargoes," 880.

4. The following discussion is drawn from my earlier work, James B. Ferguson, "Government Secrecy After the Cold War," 34 *BCL Rev* 451 (1993); James B. Ferguson, "Scientific Freedom, National Security and the First Amendment," 221 *Science* 620 (August 12, 1983); James B. Ferguson, "National Security Controls on Technological Knowledge," 10 *Science, Technology & Human Values* 87 (1985); and James B. Ferguson, "Scientific and Technological Expression: A Problem in First Amendment Theory," 16 *Harv CR-CL Law Rev* 519 (1981).

5. Department of Energy, 45 *Fed. Reg.* 65, 152.

6

Law, Civil Society, and National Security: International Dimensions

Henrikas Yushkiavitshus

There is a clear political will in the industrialized countries to support and encourage the development of information networks and systems, which are seen as major factors for boosting the economy, employment, and consumption. Although economic objectives constitute the major driving force, governments are also assigning social, cultural, educational, and scientific goals to new services and information highways. Several of these governmental efforts are discussed below.

In the United States, the National Information Infrastructure (NII) was announced in September 1993. Although the network will be built by the private sector, the government will define the regulatory framework and plans to allocate $2 billion per year for research and development (R&D) and for setting up education, training, health care, and government services applications to run on the NII, including applications sustaining the role of libraries as agents of democratic and equal access to information, and ensuring more effective environmental monitoring. In a speech in January 1994, Vice President Al Gore challenged U.S. industry to connect all of the country's schools, libraries, hospitals, and clinics to the information highways by the year 2000. In his keynote address to the International Telecommunications Union World Telecommunication Development Conference held in Buenos Aires in March 1994, he called for the establishment of a Global Information Infrastructure for international action

> to determine how every school and library in every country can be connected to the Internet, the world's largest computer network, in order to create a Global Digital Library. Each library could maintain a server containing books and journals in electronic form, along with indexes to help users find other materials. As more and more information is stored electronically, this global library would become more and more useful. It would allow millions of students, scholars

and business people to find the information they need whether in Albania or Ecuador.

The European Union's Fourth Framework Programme for Research and Development for 1994–1998 envisages a $3.8 billion component to support the development of a new information infrastructure. This will cover R&D in communications and related technologies, as well as distance learning, a university and research center network, health care, and other services of public interest.

Gerard Thery's report to the French government, "Les autoroutes de l'information," foresees a number of advances in this area: new electronic publishing opportunities for French newspaper and book publishing companies; new audiovisual activities combining television and telecommunications; and the renewal of the great tradition of French public service in education, medicine, libraries, and museums.

In Japan, the Nippon Telegraph and Telephone Corporation intends to wire every school, home, and office with fiber-optic cable by the year 2015, at an estimated cost varying between $150 billion and $230 billion. The Telecommunications Council of the Japanese Ministry of Posts and Telecommunications in its report entitled "Reforms towards the intellectually creative society of the 21st century" asserts that information technologies will enable a comfortable lifestyle reflecting a shift away from material wealth to the spiritual quality of life, will promote mutual cultural understanding between Japan and other countries, and will help address environmental problems efficiently.

A report by Canada's Ministry of Industry on the Canadian information highway states that the "information highway will stimulate the development of an enormous range of education, training and lifelong learning applications that will provide access to courses, libraries, museums, specialized databases and other people regardless of location."

The G-7 Ministerial Conference on the Information Society in February 1996 stressed that the smooth and effective transition toward the information society is one of the most important tasks that should be undertaken in the last decade of the twentieth century and that "countries in transition and developing countries must be provided with the chance to fully participate in this process as it will open opportunities for them to leapfrog stages of technology development and to stimulate social and economic development." One outcome of this meeting was agreement on a number of pilot projects in various areas, including cross-cultural training and education, electronic libraries, electronic museums and galleries, environment and natural resources management, global emergency management, and global health care applications.

At the same time, there is a tendency to marginalize some already existing traditional systems of information, especially in the media domain. For example, the budgets for Radio Liberty and Radio Free Europe have been reduced. Considering the interests of national security and the flow of international information, I think this is a mistake by U.S. policymakers.[1] Glasnost is the only principle that works effectively in Russia today. Regrettably, one cannot say that about principles of a market economy or national product growth. It seems premature to weaken independent information sources when, as a result of disillusion, anti-American feelings are growing among intellectuals and even among the population at large.

There is certainly a clear desire to use the power of the new technologies; but as futurist Arthur Clarke wrote, it is always necessary to separate desire and reality. He said: "Our time has been called the information age, but information is not knowledge, and knowledge is not wisdom. And there is something beyond all of these that is even more important: foresight. It is a rare and often unpopular talent. . . ." At the risk of being unpopular, let us try to foresee what new technology can bring and speak not only about the challenges, but also about the dangers.

Dangers and Challenges

The principal tenet of the information superhighway concept is to provide universal access to services that have thus far been available to only a few and to open up vast opportunities for the accessing and sharing of information and thereby for the empowerment of men and women in every aspect of their lives, for increased democratic participation, and for greater communication and understanding across frontiers. There is, however, a considerable danger that the information revolution will increase the gap between developing and developed countries, and generate new gaps within countries and societies, between the rich and the poor. High technology may well, once again, outrun social justice.

If we look at the basic telecommunications infrastructure in developing countries, we discover that less than 2 percent of the

World Bank's lending and less than 3 percent of regional development banks' lending goes to telecommunications projects. We must not be in a hurry to blame the banks or international agencies, however. Analysis shows that many governments use the revenue from state-owned telecommunications to finance other activities. Despite the fact that investments required for setting up modern telecommunications structures—the basic "conduit" technology for information highways—are relatively modest compared to other development sectors, priority assigned to communication projects is very low, both in assistance programs and in national development plans. In view of their deep penetration in the social fabric and of their large reach, the establishment of such conduit technologies for information access and exchange could be an extremely cost-effective way for less developed countries to boost their development and rapidly bridge the North-South gap.

The challenge facing the international community with regard to the emergence of global information and communication technologies is considerable: while these technologies are designed to provide universal access to information facilities, they could reproduce at a higher technological level the inequalities among different social groups and nations, leading to new types of exclusion, both within nations and at the international level.

Unequal access is not the only danger. Information highways, like any other highways, can go in different directions. Some of them could lead to the domination of certain cultural patterns and languages. Today, more than 90 percent of databases on the Internet are in English. Other databases, instead of leading to a monolithic worldwide culture, could give a fresh impetus to cultural identities. In fact, both phenomena may well occur at the same time. The "global village" can accommodate the existence and proliferation of "tribes." There are televiewers in Paris who watch only Russian television via satellite or only television in the Arabic language, and televiewers in the United States who watch only Spanish language channels. From this point of view, the issue is one of exchanges between various communities and of diversity rather than of identity.

Some fear the weakening of social and interpersonal relations because, ultimately, new multichoice services would satisfy leisure, learning, and work requirements: man/machine could become the privileged relation, to the detriment of the social fabric. Fears are also expressed as to the "brainwashing" effects of new technological innovations, such as virtual reality, which may lead to escapism from the real world. These views are, however, somewhat controversial because many see computer networks as introducing a new social fabric linking people with common interests and problems independent of location and helping to reduce the social isolation of the modern city.

Major ethical and legal issues such as privacy of information are posed in a more acute way by increased access to interconnected networks and databases. A recent book by Claude-Marie Vadrot and Louisette Gouverne, *Tous Fiches,* describes how our every movement is tracked by the use of credit cards, highway gates, telephone calls, telephone cards, hidden cameras, and so on. George Orwell's Big Brother has a much less sophisticated system. The problem is not easy. A wave of terrorism is sweeping across the world. We want security, but we also want privacy. How much are we ready to trade off? The right of individuals to have access to personal data concerning them is becoming more and more important. We are all in databases, and if we are lucky, the information is correct.

There is also the problem of information security and informatics crimes: just imagine electronic vandals sending a virus through information highways, racing through computers and software. Multimedia technologies also considerably affect copyright issues: how can authors' intellectual property rights be preserved in this moving environment, where artistic integrity and moral rights are endangered by new technological possibilities of mutilation, modification, and worldwide distribution of distorted work through information highways?

Things get really serious when it comes to personal, institutional, and national security because new information technologies offer immense possibilities not only for progress but also for crime. Almost every day one can read in the papers of yet another criminal "genius" who hacked his way into the computer system of a company, bank, or even the Pentagon. Thousands of pirated software programs are available on the Internet. As regards transborder communications, governments today are increasingly marginalized by transnational production and trade giants, as well as by the Mafia, which is often far better equipped than the police. For example, it becomes incredibly difficult for law enforcement bodies to detect cases of money laundering, let alone seize crime-generated millions that can be instantaneously wired into numbered accounts in some remote part of the world.

Many recognize that the biggest threat to national security today is international terrorism, which more and more often makes use of communication and information technologies. How can we effectively fight this new (and, this time, common) enemy, without resorting to the extreme of total and permanent surveillance?

This is just a brief overview of some of the potential dangers of the information revolution. It is important to know them, but it is even more important to know how to avoid them.

Some Suggestions

The starting point, to my mind, should be the raising of awareness, especially among concerned decision-makers. By doing so, we can hope to promote the creation of information policies and strategies that will take into consideration all existing challenges and potential problems.

The adoption and enforcement (as far as possible) of appropriate national laws and international agreements, as well as the close collaboration of all concerned national authorities, can certainly contribute to making our relations in cyberspace more orderly and civilized. Here the United Nations Educational, Scientific, and Cultural Organization (UNESCO) hopes to play a catalytic role, promoting international reflection and exchanges of experience on this issue. Nevertheless, we should not overestimate the capacity of the law to define and regulate every aspect of life in the information age. We know that attempts to create any kind of "curtains" are not effective, and possibilities for control and restriction will apparently continue to diminish in the future. In this context, education and promotion of ethics acquire a renewed significance, particularly for the professional providers of information. The elaboration of professional ethics, by professionals themselves, should be promoted; there are already models such as the medical code of ethics, which can be summarized in three simple words—do no harm. Eventually, however, everyone will become both provider and consumer of electronically distributed information; hence, the importance of general education. Every child learns (often the hard way) that knives and matches are useful but potentially dangerous. It should be the same with the information increasingly available through high-tech communication. When a child grows up and gets a car, he or she learns that there are things one should not do on a highway (even if the police are not watching). I think we should start to lay the groundwork for education that will allow our grandchildren to move around safely on the information super-highways.

All these, as well as other issues relating to rights and obligations of network users that would be too long to enumerate here, pose new challenges to existing regulations and practices.

The Role of UNESCO

UNESCO's mission, as defined in its constitution, is predicated on the belief "that ignorance of each other's ways and lives has been a common cause, throughout the history of mankind, of that suspicion and mistrust between the peoples of the world through which their differences have too often broken out in war" and "that the wide diffusion of culture, and the education of humanity for justice and liberty and peace are indispensable to the dignity of man." The task assigned to UNESCO in the United Nations system is to contribute to "advancing the mutual knowledge and understanding of peoples, through all means of mass communication," "to promote the free flow of ideas by word and image," "maintain, increase and diffuse knowledge," and "to give fresh impulse to popular education and to the spread of culture."

New usages of technologies and global information networks are multiplying and expanding the opportunities for the pursuit of this task. Adequately used, information and communication technologies constitute powerful means for furthering education and learning, access to knowledge, intercultural relations and understanding, and tolerance and peace and for preserving cultural heritage, national identities, and languages. It is not true that technology always imposes uniformity. Book-printing technology ended the monopoly of Latin and Greek languages in science and art. It led to preservation and development of many national languages. In short, new applications of information and communication technologies could become instrumental for supporting a truly human-centered development.

In this context, as the agency of the United Nations responsible for intellectual cooperation and covering the fields of communication, information, and informatics, UNESCO has a twofold basic mission:

- to promote usages of information and communication technologies and information highways for information sharing, public debate, democracy, and the advancement of education science and culture; and

- to encourage the development of communication and information technologies, information highways, and telematics services in developing countries.

Information highways must not simply provide newer and more powerful channels for electronic consumption of commercial goods and services. Culture, education, and science cannot surrender to the automatism of economic forces. Major technological breakthroughs must be shared by all and should not lead to new exclusions between and within societies.

This mission embraces many areas in which UNESCO should be active. These include ethical and legal issues, such as information privacy, human rights, and intellectual property rights, to which I referred above. Cultural heritage, cultural identity, intercultural dialogue—all these topics are becoming important in the new environment. They also include content and diversity of information services and products and the role of the media, libraries, archives, cultural institutions, and educational systems in the new technological environment. Other issues such as artistic integrity and moral rights are also important.

For most of the twentieth century, humanity lived in a shadow of a great political confrontation, when every important decision on both sides was weighed on the scales of ideological struggle and economic competition, and when "supreme political considerations" prevailed over all the others. The end of the cold war has offered the world a unique chance to free itself from this stifling dominance. It would be a mistake to replace the "great political criterion" of the old times by a multitude of petty "considerations" that would again prevail over common sense and the desire to live together in peace in our small world—a world that is no less vulnerable for the fact that it is endowing itself with information technologies. If, as I hope, common sense wins, resulting in true international cooperation, it will greatly facilitate solving all the world's problems, including the ones related to the information revolution.

Note

1. In this case, I express my personal point of view and not that of UNESCO.

7

The Information Warrior

John W. Rendon Jr.

I am not a national security strategist, and I am not a military tactician. I am a politician and a person who uses communications. In fact, I am an information warrior.

My job as a public relations practitioner, and as named in the paternity suit of strategic communications, is to review the important and changing role communications in general, and the news media in particular, play in today's world in the development of national security policy. I have three general topics:

- First, the evolution of the news media and public policy development in the context of the changes in our society;

- Second, the effect of this evolution on the policy process in today's environment, from both a policymaker's and an operator's perspective;

- Third, some impressions about the future of the news media and policymaking environment;

The shift to participatory journalism and real-time reporting has brought about significant change. In contrast to the past, journalists are now *inside* the theater of operation before the engagement of forces. For example, in Somalia in 1992, the night landing of U.S. Marines was not without eyewitnesses. Fortunately, the troops were greeted by reporters' klieg lights and not hostile fire—or both.

That can be contrasted, however, with the tragic downing of a helicopter inside Somalia and the death of a brave U.S. soldier and his body being dragged through the streets.

Now, move that mental picture 7,967 miles and eight time zones west to Port-au-Prince, Haiti, where the U.S. naval vessel *Harlan County* was about to dock. Here the demonstrators actually cited the Somalia events in their chants and public talking points. Reuters reported, "The mob beat foreign journalists and chanted 'Go Home, Yankees,' threatening, 'we're going to make a second Somalia here.'"[1]

The Role of the News Media in Public Policy

The Past

To understand the current environment, we must cast ourselves back to the sixties.

In the early sixties a majority of Americans read two newspapers each day—one in the morning and one in the evening. The mail was delivered twice a day. The United Nations had 115 members. Edward R. Murrow of CBS News set the standard for broadcast journalism (and, ironically, was forced into retirement). He and his colleagues went to the story, covered it, and in many respects put viewers there. When television news covered Vietnam, it took two days to get the film edited and back to the United States for broadcast.

Time passed, and we moved through the seventies; but changes continued in the way Americans lived. Family dinner was generally at 6:00 p.m. but gradually evolved into family members eating when hungry (the ever-increasing visits to McDonalds or Burger King or both). News and information reached us through one of the three television networks, if not already through the morning or afternoon newspaper.

Then, cable television and satellite communications changed the American experience. Through the decade of the eighties, just as fast food replaced set dining times, when our minds were hungry we ate, now by turning on (and tuning in) Cable New Network (CNN) to catch news when we wanted it.

This period of American history also saw a functional realignment of institutional power as a legacy of Watergate, Vietnam, and the race riots of the sixties. Reporters became analysts or experts on subjects, and our world became more complex, as reflected, for example, in the fact that the United Nations grew by 20 percent to 137 members. In a 1976 document entitled "CBS News Standards," John A. Schneider wrote the following:

> The advent of television saw the development of a new set of journalistic techniques and a rapid expansion of broadcast journalism. And as the reach of television accelerated, so did its impact on the way the public learned about the world in

which it lived. As television news became the primary source of news and information for the American public, the need for consistent standards became increasingly apparent.[2]

Alas, this concern about consistent standards is no longer apparent. Moreover, I have not met many real reporters in more than 10 years, although I have met plenty of participants, experts, and analysts.

By the mid-1980s, the majority of U.S. households were getting their information from television news; newspaper subscriptions declined and papers often went out of business.

In addition to these structural changes in the American media, changes in television licensing also significantly altered basic television coverage. Local stations had less need for network feeds and more need for their own news. Newspapers closed, and low-power television and independent stations opened.

News directors justified capital expenditures of equipment by doing more live news reporting from their vaunted "death stars"—mobile television broadcast and production units. Everyone began to think pictures.

During this period, network television news divisions were forced to be profit-making entities. CBS had to produce profits; and the network news division with the legacy of Murrow and Walter Cronkite was forced to deliver better ratings instead of better reports. Television news departments came to the attention of the accountants and finance departments; content and quality were replaced by cost containment and profit.

News and information were rapidly becoming news and entertainment. A novel word entered the U.S. television lexicon and described the product produced by the three major network: "info-tainment." Money, money, money became the predominant concern, even at the expense of truth and fairness. The news standard became "Controversy breeds coverage."

The Present

Two hundred years ago it would take one month for the news of a treaty to reach troops engaged in combat. Now, more initial information about international events is passed by the news media than by official government reporting. Today, real time is unreal. Poised as we are now on the threshold of a new century, we find ourselves in an arena where time, technology, and travel drive our decision-making process.

With new technology all of us can travel from Chicago to Cairo (or Cairo, Illinois), from Great Britain to the Great Wall of China all in the flash of an instant, in the change of a channel. What does this mean?

Look at the way news and information—in particular, television news—have changed the way our decision-making processes work. For this we need only to look back five short years to the Gulf War.

The good news for CNN was that it became the network of record for most of the world's major events. The bad news for CNN is that everybody watched it.

As a result, other news organizations began to follow suit, instituting 24-hour news programming. Today there are more than 12 24-hour news platforms. In Russia alone, 200 new broadcast platforms have emerged in the past four months. In the summer of 1994, 10,000 satellite dishes were being smuggled into Iran and sold each week.

Today, a majority of Americans get their news and information from television. For those concerned about content and the need for our public to understand the intricacies of a more complex and unstable world, the following may be dismaying: the 22-minute news broadcast by the networks—the primary source of information for the American public—is the equivalent of the newsprint found on the front page, and only the front page, of most newspapers.

A full two-thirds of the U.S. population now has cable television. The average American household has a television set turned on more than seven and one-half hours per day. They live on it, through it, and from it. In some respects the television set has become a non-Internal-Revenue-Service-approved dependent.

Trends

Against this background, five other events or phenomena were occurring.

1. Foreign governments began to use the media to send messages directly to governments and in some cases directly to the American people.

2. Getting it first became more important than getting it right. The news hole that news organizations had to fill once a day or once an edition was now ever present. News will take anything. Today the news hole for network news is 22 minutes long. For CNN it is updated almost hourly. Competition for air time gradually eroded content.

3. Ratings have become all important. As a result, some news organizations have chosen to fill some of their programming with news talk shows, which place a premium on dramatic portrayals or rhetorical violence rather than content or quality. In many respects, these shows have slipped, in my opinion, from news and information to news and entertainment.

4. The phenomenon of distant participation, the contemporary version of live "soap" news, is increasing in demand. For example, people across the nation sat virtually glued to their television sets to watch the bombing in Baghdad and again to watch O.J. Simpson drive a white Bronco down the highway. People did this in order to have an asymptotic relationship to participation, close but not quite touching. This phenomenon of distant participation results in huge rating spikes. Numbers of viewers, and hence, revenue, go through the roof, causing the news organization to have a stronger interest in live or breaking events.

5. The sheer quantity of information has become overwhelming. The increased demand for news and information greatly exceeds the capacity of news organizations to independently scan, evaluate, chase, obtain, and report news from around the world. Covering the Gulf War cost vast amounts of money. Many news organizations closed bureaus.

The craft of journalism is also changing: today's journalists carry a laptop and travel with a satellite communications unit and a portable telephone. They will access Lexis/Nexis to find out everything written or reported on a subject, form opinions, access wire reports, and cover the story while passing their stories through their R-11 jack.

Although, equipped with new technologies, reporters also have even more to cover. This is reflected, for example, in the fact that today there are 184 members of the United Nations—a 60 percent increase in less than 30 years.

To further illustrate, after a meeting of the United Nations Security Council, Jed Duvall of CNN asked Madeleine Albright, U.S. ambassador to the United Nations, "The government decides what to do in the world by watching television?" The ambassador replied, "Well, there is no question that television has become the 16th member of the Security Council because television brings the horrors of the breakdown of peace and stability to the table."[3]

Media Risks

There are, as might be expected, some risks with real-time reporting, especially as it relates to the policy process. CNN provides decision-makers in both the public and the private sector with instant access to news and information—however inaccurate they may be.

The Danger of Being Wrong

Unfortunately, the established reporting requirements and procedures have not kept pace with developments outside government. They are outdated and largely obsolete. So, absent a good and accurate source of information, all too often the policy process is jerked from one area to another in large part because of contaminated or inaccurate information.

Real-time news operates about 90 minutes ahead of CNN and the other round-the-clock news organizations. Look closely at CNN and you will see (and hear) that a substantial number of CNN stories begin with the words: "As Reuters or Agence France Press is reporting." Lack of an ability to assess a situation independently and then to verify the facts has made the international news items suspect.

Alas, as noted above, getting it right has been eclipsed by getting it first. This rush to reporting can have serious consequences because most sidebar discussions in Washington begin with the words: "What did you make of the CNN report on . . ." or "Did you hear what Rush Limbaugh said last night?"

Example of Incorrect Reporting

In May 1991, while President Guillermo Endara of Panama was traveling in New York, I was sitting in the staff room of the Plaza Hotel providing communications consulting to our client, the Government of Panama. CNN broke a story that there had been a coup d'état in Panama. I, being the diligent staffer, called the U.S. Secret Service control room and asked if the president was still in power. Their radioed response confirmed the president was in power and currently addressing an editorial board of the *New York Times*. Next, I called the two vice presidents to see if they were okay. The conversation went something like this:

"Are you okay, Mr. Vice President?"

He replied, "Yes, are you okay?"

"Yes, I'm okay. Can you talk?"

"Yes. Are you sure you're okay?"

I explained about the report from CNN. He understood, checked the street outside his office, and reported everything was fine.

Afterwards, I called CNN and explained who I was and why I was calling. They commented that they had received information from "their person" that there had been a coup attempt, but that it was not successful. I gave them one news cycle (30 minutes) to correct the story. They did.

I thought we had earned our supper by stopping a report of something that had never happened from causing damage or driving someone to try. I was wrong.

For the next three days, senior members of the Panamanian delegation and I received a constant stream of inquiries from numerous allied governments and their policymakers. Much to our dismay, the false report had an afterlife.

There is a difference between truth and news. It is unfortunate that in today's media and information environment, an item needs only repetition to become credible.

Lessons from Today, Plans for Tomorrow

In 1994, the young, articulate, and charismatic president of the United States addressed the nation to define U.S. strategic interests in Haiti. Immediately after the president's televised address, Dan Rather of CBS News went live from Port-au-Prince and asked General Raoul Cédras what he thought of the president's speech. Cédras replied that Haiti would not be defeated and would fight.

Rather: "General, what is your immediate reaction to this?

Cédras: ". . . I am rather prepared to fight with my people."

Rather: "And prepared to die?"

Cédras: "Every soldier, while he enters the armed forces and signs his papers, signs that there is a possibility for him to lose his life."

You may recall that more than 30 years ago, another young, articulate, and charismatic president addressed the nation regarding vital interests in this same region. Now imagine for a moment what would have happened if Dan Rather—or, at that time, Walter Cronkite—had asked Nikita Khrushchev the same questions. We might well have ended up with a nuclear war.

Real-time reporting and the change from reportorial journalism to participatory journalism have changed the way we do our public and our private business.

Policymakers are not the only ones driving policy. The media are also driving policy. Most recently, in Haiti, the young army lieutenant who intervened in front of the international media to break up the beating of a Haitian citizen in the hands of Haitian police helped drive the policy process back in Washington.

With these recent examples as backdrop, there are six observations I think are of value:

1. Alvin and Heidi Toffler's Third Wave of change is truly upon us, making change the only constant. Thus, flexibility must be an acceptable strategy.

2. The world will get smaller and with this decrease in size will also come an increase in technology in the hands of a few elites driving education, business, and government.

3. As the world becomes generally more democratic, the methods of preserving power will shift from the use of military power to control civilian populations to the use of news and information to persuade voting publics into valid power retention or change in power. The news media and other forms of strategic and tactical communications will be at the center of this persuasion.

4. The recent rapid increase in countries and cultures has resulted in a virtual explosion of local television broadcast platforms and a parallel dearth of (and, thus, dynamic demand for news) information and entertainment programming.

5. As easy as it is to gain access to the current real-time news cycles, the United States should stand vigilant against corruption of the news and information process by forces opposed to the United States.

6. Finally and probably most important: If policymakers in general, and the United States in particular, do not actively engage in the use of strategic communications (perception management) to drive their national security policy, opponents of that policy will drive it and distract the U.S. government from its objectives.

Notes

1. Reuters, October 12, 1993.

2. John A. Schneider, "CBS News Standards," document written for CBS News personnel, April 14, 1976.

3. Madeleine Albright, in an interview with Jed Duvall, *News*, Cable News Network, "Do TV Images Control Public Support for Policy Issues?" February 13, 1994.

8

The View from the White House:
A Public Policy Perspective

Michael Nelson

We all know that the Global Information Infrastructure (GII) is a top priority of the Clinton administration. The vice president in particular is spending a lot of time trying to adapt old, outdated policies to the digital world and promote the development of a "seamless" network of networks that will provide information to any point on the planet. Many of you are probably familiar with the speech he gave in 1995 in Buenos Aires on the GII, describing how it is going to affect every aspect of our society, industry, economy, international relations, environment, and so forth.

The administration is convinced that the GII is going to be a very powerful force for democracy, for sustainable development, and for peace. We are also convinced that there are many unknowns. We do not know how the technology is going to evolve; we do not know which businesses and applications are going to grow up around the GII. We have very few ideas about the new legal challenges that we are going to run into. We cannot even figure out who has jurisdiction in cyberspace, which is very important when we are trying to enforce laws—national laws—on intellectual property protection, pornography, national security, libel, and so forth. We also can only vaguely guess at how these new technologies will be abused by hate groups, by organized crime, and by terrorists.

I would like to divide the issues before us, as I see them, into "good news" and "bad news"—the opportunities and the challenges.

We must assume that the GII is going to grow at an even faster rate than it has been, that more and more information about individuals—more and more personal information—will be stored in electronic form and be more accessible over the GII. There will be more on-line services, and they will be more central to our daily life, in business, at home, in school, and in government. We also assume that strong encryption will proliferate, that one will have the ability to use the system anonymously, and that there will be increasing amounts of criminal activities on the Internet. We must also assume that there are no magical solutions for the security problems that we all know are out there.

Some of the issues that are before us, of course, are ones that will have an impact on our national security and the way nations relate to each other. In some countries, no doubt, information technologies will be used for monitoring citizens, controlling their movements, controlling thoughts, and controlling their freedom of expression. We have seen already how propaganda can be used in the modern media. The fact that television technology is spreading so quickly and becoming so affordable makes propaganda a much more powerful weapon. In both Bosnia and Rwanda, for example, hate radio has been a very powerful motivator of ethnic warfare.

We are also going to see terrorists and criminals using the Internet and electronic media and relying on encryption to cover their tracks. Because of the greater availability of encryption, we are going to lose some of the intelligence that we are able to gather today. I do not particularly like the term "information warfare" because it focuses too much attention on the military threats to the GII, but there are clearly real issues that deserve more work.

In the White House, we are increasingly concerned with the growing information gap and the possibility that the new digital technologies and the GII are going to increase tensions between developing countries and the developed world as the latter uses the GII to increase its wealth and power. Freedom of information on the Internet could also weaken some of the links that tie together communities and even nations, replacing geographic communities with virtual communities in cyberspace, communities of interest whose members communicate on-line with each other. The GII might accentuate the clash of cultures within countries as new information and foreign media come into traditional societies. We could see the kind of turmoil that we saw in Iran under the shah. In some countries, as more varied media become available, we could see the polarization of society if different parts of society rely on different (often biased) sources of news and information.

It is also clear that these technologies are going to challenge completely our fundamental assumptions about government and its role. The "information revolution" is a decentralizing revolution. All this technology will give more power to citizens, more information, more access, more ability to organize with other people. I have been meaning to print up some bumper stickers that say "Data to the People." I think that is the new motto in cyberspace, the motto for the cyber-revolutionary. That is what it is all about. This administration welcomes that revolution because at the base of American democracy is information— giving information to citizens, so that they can make intelligent decisions.

In his speech in Buenos Aires, the vice president likened our democracy to a massively parallel supercomputer, where there are thousands of individual processors (i.e., citizens) all capable of making their own decisions. Then those decisions are combined through the electoral process and the legislative process to determine national policy. Of course, the leaders of some other countries will not be very excited about "Data to the People"— they are not very excited about decentralizing, and they will soon find that they will not be able carry on as they have in the past. They will not be able to control the information that flows to their citizens. They will not be necessary or be able to control the telecommunications networks that the information goes over—particularly as more and more global satellite systems are launched and more and more companies start investing in other countries. We are going to see a lot less control by governments.

Intellectual property will be much harder to control because laws about intellectual property that one country imposes will not necessarily apply elsewhere in cyberspace. It may not even be possible to control currency. Anonymity is another challenge, not just for national security, but for law enforcement.

There is a lot of rethinking that needs to be done in the United States and around the world. We do not have a lot of time: It is very clear that technology is moving forward at an ever-increasing pace and that there are some real problems out there. The encryption debate that I have been involved in is just one small example of new technologies changing our assumptions of what our government can control—and where new technologies and new solutions to new problems are needed.

Of course, countries that cannot adapt and cannot find new solutions are going to be left completely in the dark, left behind as we move forward into the "information economy." No country wants to be in that situation, but staying with the trend, using the new technologies, will require major changes in government policy and mindsets.

The administration is optimistic that we can use the GII to promote peace, democracy, economic growth, sustainable development, cooperative research, and cooperation at all levels of governments. The first bit of good news is that we all see that this is an incredibly powerful tool for economic growth. It is also a very powerful tool for sharing information and fostering democracy around the world. The thing that I am very excited about, and that the vice president is very excited about, is the fact that we can use the Internet to foster people-to-people contact. I call it *digital diplomacy*: people, not only at the top level but at the "working level," are able to communicate very effectively across borders—not only State Department to Foreign Ministry, but Agriculture Department to its counterpart, the National Aeronautics and Space Administration to its counterpart. We will see much more integration, much more cooperation, much closer cooperation.

The administration's GII initiative is promoting the development of these technologies and the global network they make possible. We are working with the World Bank on promoting the use of information technology (IT) in development. We are working to link different institutions in different countries. Institutions like the U.S. Information Agency (USIA) and the Voice of America are using their assets in new ways, using new technologies to reach out to more people.

I think the good news is every bit as important to national security as the bad news. We tend to focus on the bad news: the threats to our assets, both digital and physical, and the possibility that there will be a military engagement. I think that it is equally important that we focus on waging peace. Some of the aforementioned technological changes are critical in this regard.

The biggest problem that I see in this whole business is that we do not have anybody in charge, we do not know who is responsible for what piece of this. I like to joke that in Washington it usually takes about two days to figure out what the problem is, about two months to figure out what a plausible solution is, and about two years to determine who actually implements it. I think that we have entered the second phase in this area. We are still searching for good solutions.

We need to think about how we are going to get this job done. Who is going to get their hands on the problem? Who is going to represent the government? Who is going to work with industry? Who is going to make things happen?

When you look at the whole issue of national security and IT, you see dozens of problems and dozens of agencies that need to be involved.

I think that part of the problem is the "information warfare" metaphor. Because my job description includes metaphor management, I would like to talk about that a bit. We talk about information warfare and everybody gravitates toward the Department of Defense (DOD) and thinks, "Okay, that is their job." Information warfare is actually only a small piece of the question, however. We also have to talk about computer crime, which involves the Department of Justice. We have computer security—that is the National Institute of Standards and Technology at the Commerce Department. There are digital cash and electronic money—that is the Treasury. There is digital diplomacy—that is the State Department and USIA. There is intelligence gathering—that is another set of agencies. In the end, we have almost everybody involved in this.

How do we get the leadership that we need? The first thing that we have got to do is get the top leaders of relevant agencies up to speed. We have slowly been introducing key players in the administration to the reality of what this technology is doing. It is taking time. Of course we are lucky in that we have a vice president who understands the issues and uses the technology, so we are making progress. To date, however, we have not factored IT into the general national security equation.

To summarize, I think I can say that we need a holistic approach; we need to look at the good news and the bad news, we need to look at both waging war and waging peace in cyberspace. We need to do what we can to find some better metaphors, so we do not have to always use the phrase "information warfare," which tends to focus on military attack and ignores the terrorist threats, computer crime, and a number of important pieces. We also need to avoid focusing exclusively on DOD and ignoring the commercial side, which is actually where most of the problems—and most of the solutions—are. Industry will have to take a bigger role here and be much more concerned.

I suspect I have said nothing that has not already been said, but from the perspective of the administration, I think that we have some real opportunities here and a chance for the United States to get this right.

9

The Ten-Foot-Tall Electron: Finding Security in the Web

Larry Seaquist

What are we to make of this information revolution? Is it more than computers growing together in an international web of intelligent interconnections? Is it more than microprocessors growing inside our simplest everyday appliances? The technologies are dazzling, almost certain to change our lives and communities as much as the automobile and the printing press.

I recently spent two wonderful hours in an exhibition mounted in Washington, D.C., by the Library of Congress in collaboration with the Bibliothèque Nationale. Among the many remarkable books on display was the first book printed in France. It was produced, as I recall, in about 1440 by printers who had imported the very new technology of the printing press learned from Johannes Gutenberg in Germany. The exhibition noted the alarm of the French sovereign that printing could undercut royal authority. Printing was dangerous. Printing crossed borders easily. Printing was subjected to *official concern* (emphasis by the French king).

These fearful reactions to new communications technology seem to be a pattern. Perhaps there is a human propensity, part of our evolutionary survival equipment, to identify the risks before seeing the opportunities.

Friend or Foe?

As many of us have seen, discussions of the new information revolution have quickly turned to dire forecasts of the coming electronic wars (e-wars). Everyone seems to have a favorite scenario, usually fashioned either around a genius (and teenage) hacker or a high-tech SMERSH systematically bringing modern life to a halt. In the forefront is the Pentagon's official enthusiasm for the new dangers of the so-called information warfare (IW). Already capitalized, IW has been elevated to the college of "Ws"—a cardinal form of warfare. Like Gutenberg's books, IW crosses borders, bureaucratic as well as political. "Infowarriors" are now at work in each of the military services, in the defense think tanks, and among many supporting contractors—a brand-new military-technical industry like the others that cluster around tank warfare or missiles or warships, but larger in ambition and intertwined with all those other forms of fighting. The electron: a Big Danger!

Clearly, some of this shiver of fear about the IW specter has to do with the end of the cold war and the loss of a superpower opponent. A seemingly universal adversary, able to attack deep inside one's own computer systems from anywhere on the wired planet, could be a worthy replacement for the threat of World War III posed by the massive military of the Soviet empire. I wonder, too, if some of the attractiveness of e-war stems from its accessibility. Formerly, barriers of physical qualification and life-long training restricted access to the military professions. Now, anyone with a keyboard and a modem can join the clan of electronic warriors. Geeks can be as macho as fighter pilots.

To be sure, there is a real threat. Computers are vulnerable, and hackers are sometimes ingenious in their attacks. Nonetheless, we need to step up to these risks without expecting an electronic Pearl Harbor.

Should we not address these security issues in a larger context—a framework broader than cyberwar? Like the revolution of the printed book, the computer-telecommunications revolution is propelling some profound changes in our societies and in our politics. The threat from teenage hackers may be less significant than the remarkable grasp of quite young children for surfing the Net. What we are calling the information revolution may be something going deeper, to the roots of human social and political structures.

We ought to test our fears of cyberwar at these deeper levels, to look at "security" in its broader sense of human security in the civil society. We risk missing the real significance of the information revolution with our view blocked by a ten-foot-tall electron of our own devising.

The Information Core of Life

The celebrated Marshall McLuhan may have been one of our more misleading visionaries. His quip "the medium is the message" suggested that information was a hypnotic externality for us as rather empty and manipulable individuals. The very fine construct explained by John Arquilla and David Ronfeldt in this book more usefully parses "information" into three categories. In addition to messages and the various media through which those messages pass, Arquilla and Ronfeldt identify information about "self." This information, like the codes of human DNA, the Constitution of our government, or an architect's drawings of an office building, is the information that organizes and structures ourselves, our environments, and our communal lives.

Although the boundaries between "self," "media," and "message" can be indistinct, some information comprises the messages being sent and received via various media channels, some information is about the sending and receiving channels themselves, and some is being exchanged within the self as it manages its internal and external interactions. We can use this tripartite division to reconsider the fears of information warfare on a broader, strategic scale. If we move above the electronic battlefield to the broader realm of our interactive societies, what are the risks and what are the opportunities that might lie ahead?

The Message Is Trash

The trends are toward multimedia, hypertext, and more primary, direct-from-originator-to-you messages—and toward inaccuracy. Massive improvements in computing power now enable multimedia messages that blend text, audio, video, and graphic data. Among the developments ahead are holographic constructs in which all those media might present the "reader" with dynamic, three-dimensional "messages" vastly more rich and complex than those available in printed text or in radio-TV formats. Hypertext links take us beyond our linear reading or viewing into the additional realms of ideas and information that attach to any one word or incident—a kind of four-dimensional reading. Also, of course, there are more messages: vast and still increasing quantities of information pour out on us.

Where is the infowar threat in these floods of "information"? There has always been a lot of information, but now it is hooked up, on-line. Some is edited, as the information in a good newspaper has been filtered through the balancing judgment of a good editor. Much of what fills the airwaves and cables, however, is raw, unedited stuff: some data, some local opinion, a lot just junk—infosmog. If the cyberworld were subject to the Clean Air

Act we would all be required to attach catalytic converters to our modems.

With such massive, richly linked, and increasingly unmediated message deluges becoming our daily norm, it seems implausible that infowar-spawned signals—purposeful junk—will have a strategic impact. Perhaps they might if focused on limited tactical-operational audiences, but not on the whole, global infosphere. The "message" of a large nuclear detonation seems likely to remain more strategic than e-bullets.

Still, we might worry about the side effects of infowar campaigns that deliberately corrupt public information. The major risk, it seems to me, is the acceleration of the current damage to our collective lungs from infosmog. To continue the weather analogy a bit longer, this is a vastly more serious, if less dramatic, challenge to our civil society than the lightning bolts of computer attacks on other computers. It reminds me of Mexico City—a huge, bustling megalopolis imprisoned in a massive blanket of bad air. Life—vigorous life—goes on, but life expectancies are reduced and cancer rates are increased. Mexico City is diminished. Is it any different with dirty information inhaled into our collective lungs, our civil societies?

Like a factory spewing toxic fumes on the neighbors, a special kind of information pollution deserves worry: deliberate misinformation such as that of negative politics. Political scientists report recent studies showing that although negative campaign ads do swing votes they also have the effect of depressing voter turnout and increasing voter turnoff. The studies suggest that attack-ad campaigns for political office have the effect of reducing the relevance of those offices by eroding public confidence in our own political institutions. This is information warfare on ourselves.

I am going to jump over the traditional fields of military perception management and psychological operations, noting only that the traditional objectives of misleading others by feeding them doctored information can now be addressed with even more powerfully constructed multimedia messages. The methods may be better, but the game is timeless: "Make a noise in the east; attack in the west" is the ancient advice of Sun Tzu.

There is, however, another side effect of military image-mongering that may be a particularly dangerous consequence of the military embrace of IW. I nominate this danger for special attention. Just as we had to take extreme care not to be contaminated by our own nuclear weapons, we may have to take extraordinary measures to protect our own professional integrity from contamination by our message-war devices.

Recall that in the traditional, Clausewitzian framework, political objectives were sought by the violent force of arms. These force-on-force encounters could be real or threatened—battles or deterrence—but the strategic calculus always started on the battlefield. The core competence of military professionals lay in the hard skills of the warrior. That has changed.

Now, it seems, the prized skills of the military are image management. Uniformed message-managers, the ubiquitous public affairs officers and spokespersons, engage not the enemy but the press in the daily struggle for spin control over military operations, current and contingent. The result, in my view, is the corrosion of the integrity of military professionals. The military's self-management of its image corrodes professionalism and public accountability just as negative campaigning and poll-chasing corrode the political process. Indeed, the two phenomena are clearly twins.

In sum, one of the security risks of the information revolution is that the military professions will dissolve into mere image manipulators as we embrace the new information technologies and techniques. I am not a lethality Luddite, dismayed by the advent of electronic bullets. I am leaning forward in my Web site-equipped foxhole. I do worry, however, that this is the time when we need a renaissance of the military professions, not their devolution into uniformed advertising agencies. Lethal technologies and the people willing to use them are proliferating. This is not a time when we can substitute a handful of computer geeks and a few press officers for the discipline and accountability of military professionals. We need to develop the info-equivalents of the methods we used to enable ourselves to work safely around nuclear radiation hazards. Corrupt information is just as carcinogenic as plutonium.

Let us move now from messages to the changes in media. Does information warfare portend a strategic threat to the global networks of media?

Webbiness

Like rabbits, media proliferate. Day by day more channels and new techniques move more and more information in transactions that are increasingly two-way, interactive. Formerly the media dispensed information in an almost one-way process: Newspapers were delivered, movies shown, broadcasts transmitted to us with little save letters to the editor we could do to respond directly. Now we can talk back, and we can tailor the channels from both ends. Senders can deliver information packages shaped to the particular interests of individuals and special groups; receivers can exercise the passive but powerful interactivity of selection, tuning out those media not of personal interest, calling up those that are.

Infoworriers fret that the media are key vulnerabilities—the strategic jugular veins of the cyberworld. I do not think so. First, "the media" are much too vast to be a "target." Individual channels and nodes may be, but not the dense jungles of networks growing everywhere. Remember our rich history of failures in past media interdiction campaigns: the U.S. failure to close the Ho Chi Minh Trail, the German failures to interdict shipping in the Atlantic in two World Wars, the Soviet failure to block outside radio news broadcasts, the shah's failure to choke off the ayatollah's cassette tapes. Occasional, local, and short-term successes may happen, as may lots of near misses, but there will be no sustained strategic successes. The overall, global array of media channels, nodes, inlets, outlets, and methods is growing into a dense web vastly more robust than the Ho Chi Minh Trail complex. I think it quite unlikely that info interdiction will be more successful. Indeed, it seems certain to be even less effective, at least on the strategic level.

Let us go back to the word "web." Here is a new phenomenon that reinforces the point. The World Wide Web is becoming something quite different from a traditional communications or logistics network. Roads and intersections, communication channels and nodes are linear, point-to-point interconnections. As Stuart Kauffman at the Santa Fe Institute observed, there is a point at which a growing network of interconnected nodes becomes a complex, "living," organic whole.[1] Notice also that the nodes and even whole regions of the global skein of electronic interconnections are being equipped with more and more powerful computing qualities. The Web is much more than a tangle of phone lines. The Web is an organism with more chips than people. The ratio of silicon to humans is growing exponentially.

My own view is that this sudden appearance of intelligent webbiness is the true heart of the information revolution—the prime mover of what we will come to see as a profoundly new stage in our political arrangements. On balance, I believe this evolving civilization will be more secure, more civil. Peace and security have always been suspended between the contending human proclivities for the violent exercise of power and the civil harmony of the community.

There are reasons to hope that the information revolution, manifested as an emerging global webbiness among individuals and their communities, will buttress civility more than it will empower corrosion and destruction. One of the primal human urges is to communicate. Young people in all our cultures show an astonishing appetite for the computer. Their instant, interactive expertise signals that the information revolution, rather than forcing a slide down into an Orwellian regime of global thought control, will turn out to be a natural boost to individual empowerment and global democracy. Do we not all agree that the Internet is dangerous to dictators?

Let us move from the media to consider the information underpinnings of civil society and its vulnerability to information warfare.

The Information Center of Gravity

As John Arquilla and David Ronfeldt so brilliantly point out, information is more than messages flowing across the media. Just as the information coded in our genes determines the nature of each of our bodies and at least part of our personalities, so societies and organizations have sets of virtual codes that determine the architecture of our collective lives. Geneticists probing the human genome now identify three basic kinds of instructions in our DNA sequences: codes that set the physical arrangement of some 256 different kinds of cells; codes for processes (the biochemical functions that churn along minute by minute); and switching codes—instructions for those processes to stop, go, or change speed.

Enter the infowarriors, rubbing their hands with glee at the prospect of e-attacks straight to the heart of an opponent's society. Here we come to the heart of the infowar versus infosecurity question: Will increasingly exotic forms of electronic disruptions to banking systems, air traffic control networks, and so on lead to a time when one group can threaten destruction of the core structure and functions of a target society? Or will these capabilities prove to be less lethal?

We must seek two kinds of counsel, one technical, one metaphysical.

Attacks on the core of a community or a nation—to use the genetic metaphor, attacks on the structures, processes, and controls of civil life—would be attacks with strategic ambitions, the e-bullet version of strategic nuclear warfare. In the infowarriors' vision, a society and its government could be brought to their knees by the destruction of keystone systems. They warn that, lacking banking, transportation, and other systems, its complex fabric torn, its vital functions disconnected, the target society would be compelled into submission.

Balderdash. Double balderdash. E-attacks have none of the comprehensive destructive potential of, say, megaton nuclear barrages or the Black Plague. The fibers of our society are much too robust for such fantasies to turn out. The risks are declining by the day as new computers and telecommunication installations enrich and diversify our societies. We may experience a rash of electronic potholes in our socioeconomic streets, but we will not see our societies atomized into dysfunctional bits. We may experience damage tactically or locally but not strategically in the sense of the electronic stake-in-the-heart that the e-warriors seem to find so much pleasant fear in imagining.

I find this assessment less in a calculus of system redundancies than in our history. Over the millennia of conflict, humans have proven to have an astonishing capacity for resilience under fire. At this writing, the Russian army has just obliterated a small town in Daghestan harboring a band of Chechen rebels and their hostages. Most of the rebels and most of their hostages walked away from the rubble, organization and political leverage intact. Is there any e-attack capable of crushing a community so thoroughly as the firepower that leveled that town in the Caucasus, yet failed in its strategic objective? Seemingly not. Indeed, next to the now nonexistent town, the attackers seem to have suffered the most military and political damage, outdone by human grit.

I propose we leaven the scenarios of computer Götterdämmerung with a measure of disbelief. Yes, we do need to be prepared to fight electronic battles and to wage information-boosted campaigns. We need to think through how information systems are dissolving the boundaries of the battlefield that have partitioned civilian from soldier. Still, I suggest we not chase once again the chimera of the ultimate, society-killing weapon.

What should we be doing? We should be exploring the positive, measuring the opportunities as well as the risks.

Capacity-Building

If information can destroy, it can also create. I suggest that we need to invest at least as much enthusiasm and money in our development of the civilization-building capacities of the information revolution as we devote to its destructive potentials. Is the Internet a powerful force for democracy and tolerance? Will these massive, intelligent media webs forestall dictatorships? Yes? Then we ought to be helping wire the Bosnian society back together again with infotools as much as with the tanks of the First Armored Division. Let us tackle some of these real-world problems. IW as it seems to be conceived by the infowarriors is too bloodless, too sterile. Let us look over the top of the computer screens to the problems of human societies. If the information revolution is worth our time—and I insist that it is—then it must have some relevance to our daily challenges. Let us get on with IC, the information civilization. Now there is a tall order.

Note

1. Stuart Kauffman, *At Home in the Universe* (New York: Oxford University Press, 1995). See especially chap. 3, "We the Expected," for his discussion of autocatalytic sets—what I call webbiness.

Part II

Conflict in the Information Age

10

Resilience and Vulnerability in the Information Age

R. James Woolsey

In Neal Stephenson's novel *Snow Crash,* the hero and protagonist (who, as Stephenson fans know, is, of course, named Hiro
Protagonist) has to prevail both as a hacker in the virtual reality
Internet, the metaverse of the novel, and as the world's best
swordsman in a world of the future—in which the anarchy of
the real world has in many ways surpassed the anarchy of the
virtual one. Hiro Protagonist must win, one might say, on both
Surf and Turf against the wonderfully evil Evangelist Minister
R. Bob Riff and his allies, both in the world of violence, sword-
play, and aircraft carriers and in the world of ones and zeros.
Both worlds are dangerous and interact with one another, but if
anything, the virtual one is more rational and forgiving. Leaving aside the outrageous, hilarious, and bizarre features of
Stephenson's metaverse and his physical world of the future,
there are some troubling resonances in his visions.

The Internet may be anarchic, but then we look at Bosnia. I
am not speaking only of the mothers of Srebrenica, who are still
weeping from last week, when their daughters were raped and
their husbands and sons had their throats slit, or only of the
mothers of Zepa this week, or only of those of Gorazde perhaps
next week, or perhaps of Sarajevo some time after that. Certainly
there are other horrors in the real world: in Rwanda, Chechnya,
Somalia, and, for that matter, Oklahoma City; but I want to stay
with Bosnia for a moment because it illustrates quite dramatically a point that I think ties the security implications of the
information revolution together with the implications of other
revolutions that modern society has produced. The citizens of
Sarajevo lived for years in a society that was, in a number of
ways, advanced and pleasant, not radically unlike our own. It
was not at all resilient, however. It was not resilient in part
because its multiethnic tolerance and sophisticated culture were
to some extent a patina thinly covering some ancient hatreds—
hatreds that were easily fanned by a demagogue. In this it may

well have been more vulnerable than most societies. I think it was certainly more vulnerable than we are here in the United States and in much of the West today. It was also not resilient in, for example, the design and the method of heating its buildings, in the structure of its food and water supply, indeed in much of the wherewithal of modern life.

Now, I hope that Sarajevo's fate does not prove to be a model for the rest of the civilized world; but in its lack of resiliency, I am afraid that it is not unique at all. Our own modern evolving world of massive information flow and interdependency is increasingly mirrored in the admittedly somewhat slower flow and interdependency of all goods and services. Our dependence on Gulf oil, for example, is again increasing. In transportation, we stockpile things less and less now. Goods are manufactured "just in time" for precise delivery, assembly, or consumption. International trade, banking, investment, and many aspects of modern life that have been significantly changed by the information revolution have thereby enabled us to increase our comfort and our productivity. Nevertheless—and this is a key point—this interdependency also increases the ability of those bent on destruction to do to us what the Serbs have done to the citizens of Sarajevo: to disconnect many aspects of their lives from that which makes them work. This is true whether we are talking about the electricity that powers elevators for high-rise apartments or trucks for the delivery of food.

Natural disasters are bad enough in a modern, interdependent world of this kind. In the words of Albert Einstein, however, "Rafinierte ist der Herrgott, abcr boshaft ist Er nicht." I would roughly translate that as: "God may be sophisticated, but he's not plain mean." In other words, when you are playing against nature—or, in a sense, against God—by trying to build a suspension bridge or fly to the moon, there is no crafty opponent trying to make your problem worse. In a World Trade Center or an Oklahoma City bombing or, to some extent, in many types of attacks that could be launched on information systems and on our interdependent society, however, there have been, there are, and there will be calculating opponents who are trying to use the interdependencies to maximize destruction and damage. Presumably most of them are not going to be as dumb as the member of the World Trade Center conspiracy who went back to the rental car agency for his deposit on the car used in the bombing.

In all of these vulnerabilities in our information systems, energy systems, transportation systems, and others, I am not so worried about our vulnerability to direct action by nation-states. There could be exceptions, but nation-states taking action that can be traced to them have much to lose. Just as Saddam Hussein was deterred from using chemical and biological weapons in the Gulf by various potential actions, by us or by the Israelis, and just as the Soviets had much to lose in the cold war and were deterred even during very difficult moments such as the Cuban missile crisis, I believe that our military reach, together with that of our allies, is sufficiently great to deter or, if necessary, to defeat states that take direct and traceable efforts to exploit these vulnerabilities. If we utilize even a share of the technical and educational advantages that the United States and countries that are close friends and allies of ours have available, we should be able to deter and defend against the most severe threats to our information infrastructure and the other interdependent systems on which we so heavily rely. I think that this is also the case for deterring and defending against the overt use of nuclear weapons by a rogue state, such as North Korea.

I do not mean to make these problems sound trivial. I have spent much of my life thinking about them and trying to deal with them. Nor do I mean to suggest that deterrence and defending against, say, ballistic missiles armed with weapons of mass destruction in the hands of a rogue state are a piece of cake. Deterrence takes will and nerve, and to make it effective one cannot let one's nation get a reputation as a patsy. It also takes resources, both military and civilian; making decisions about resource allocation is much of what the Department of Defense is engaged in on a day-to-day basis. Those who are working on the more tactical and offensive side of information security, information warfare, and related issues—for example, figuring out how to fight the next Gulf War—are very usefully employed in the nation's service. In my view, however, that is not the toughest or the biggest or most troubling problem.

At the other end of the spectrum, we simply have to make the investments to protect information networks from things like the smart, single-hacker threat. As Assistant Secretary of Defense Emmett Paige, Jr. has said, our focus on the speed and ease of information transfer has left us vulnerable to a number of types of penetration and disruption by individuals, even with respect to defense-related information. This is not to speak of subjects that many are far more expert in than I—for example, protecting the information infrastructure for managing banking, writing social security checks, controlling air traffic, distributing energy, and the rest from clever and malicious individuals. We must get started on this. It will take many years and many billions to build in as much protection as we can, consistent with our needs to have a free and open society and the ready use of this information. In my judgment, this sort of task is hard, and it is harder because we have not given too much thought to it until very recently; but it is not impossible.

The toughest problem is that posed within the United States or any other civilized country by small, dedicated, even fanatical groups—groups that may well be financed but perhaps not wholly controlled by a nation-state. For example, Iran—operating through the MOIS, its intelligence service—finances but may not fully control Hizballah and a number of other Islamic extremist and terrorist groups. Such groups may have access to far more money and technology than any renegade individual. They may well have access to the best that the market can provide—to the technical sophistication that is necessary to mount a clever and coordinated attack on some particularly crucial part of our information infrastructure or to assemble and use a bacteriological weapon. I believe that this latter combination—a small, fanatical group and a bacteriological weapon—is the most severe problem in the area of weapons of mass destruction.

Such small groups present the most demanding threats for another reason. It may well be impossible to deter them. Their supporters in a foreign state, such as in Iran, may either be well hidden by the state or even be acting independently of the leadership of their state. The activities that they undertake may be plausibly deniable, or at least the terrorist group may think that they will be plausibly deniable. If they think that we are willing to accept, for example, that the government in Belgrade bears no responsibility for what went on recently in Srebrenica, they may well think that we will believe almost anything—that many things may be plausibly deniable. False flag operations, as they are called in the intelligence business, are a very real possibility. Iraq, for example, might undertake terrorist operations through proxies and blame Iran, or vice versa.

Such dedicated, sometimes fanatical, terrorist groups are the most dangerous threat to the information networks and to the rest of society's infrastructure, I believe, for a third reason. Because of our decentralized federal governmental structure and the existence of a vigorous private sector, it is often a very good question in many dangerous circumstances to ask: Who is in charge? If you are asked, for example, who is responsible for the physical and the information network security for the computers in New York that control many of the electronic fund transfer networks—which transfer hundreds of billions of dollars a day—who would you say is in charge? The police who stand around on the street corners outside? The companies themselves? The Federal Reserve system? New York State? The City of New York? The federal government?

Some well-planned terrorist group efforts in the information arena could also have crime for profit as their motive. Other terrorist acts may be driven by ethnic or religious hatred. The problem with these types of groups—whether one is talking about introducing a virus into the computer network that handles air traffic control or covertly spraying anthrax throughout a large U.S. city—is that they may well be able to assemble a small but critical mass of smart people and enough money to pursue some particularly fanatical objective.

Far and away the greatest danger of any of these types of concerns that we have been discussing is, in my judgment, biological weapons. Such weapons are far easier to assemble and to use than nuclear weapons, for which fissionable material is still somewhat difficult to obtain. Biological weapons are far less bulky than chemical weapons. Anthrax has 100,000 lethal doses in a gram. It persists in sunlight, unlike many other biological weapons. It takes, in most cases, several days to take effect so that a perpetrator of an anthrax attack could be long gone before we knew an attack had occurred, and the perpetrator could perhaps leave a deceptive trail.

I know of only two ways to obtain warning and threat assessment and to be able to do something to thwart small terrorist group efforts. One is to spy on them. Anyone who suggests that the Federal Bureau Investigation can effectively spy on domestic groups without developing an informant inside the group itself, or that the Central Intelligence Agency can be effective overseas without recruiting agents inside the foreign terrorist group, is naive in the extreme. This may seem to be an obvious point, but I do not know how many times I have read editorials, particularly over the course of the last two years, claiming with great assumed moral force that one ought to be able to learn what groups composed entirely of very dangerous people are doing by some method other than to spy on them—as if one could learn what Hizballah is doing by recruiting an agent inside, say, the Rotary Club in Beirut.

The only other way to learn what groups like this may be doing, whether domestic or overseas, is to intercept their communications. That means, at least to the U.S. government in possession of an appropriate court order, that such groups' communications cannot be unreadable. If you want to find out what they are doing, that in turn means—in the face of modern, commercially available encryption—requiring the escrow of a commercial cipher key and permitting access under proper legal safeguards to that key by the U.S. government: the so-called Clipper chip solution. This is one of the ways that freedom in our society and the private use of communication networks by all of us have to be limited, at least in my view, if we are to both protect ourselves against serious threats to security, such as terrorist groups, and maintain basic freedoms that we want to maintain.

You may not agree that terrorism by knowledgeable groups, homegrown or foreign-based, against information networks or by using biological weapons is a potentially serious problem. If you do take such threats seriously, however, I think you need to admit that obtaining warning about and thwarting such terrorism can really only be done in these two ways: by effective espionage (domestically, by recruiting informants) and by communications intercepts.

I suppose a third option is to shrug and say, with Otto von Bismarck, that the Lord God looks after fools, drunkards, and the United States of America. Still, it is said that even divine intervention helps those who help themselves. On this Earth, I can think of no practicable weapons against terrorists other than the two that I have described.

Groping at different parts of this huge elephant—the information revolution and national security—is worth doing. Trying to put the overall problem in context and trying to make hard calls about freedom versus privacy versus infrastructure are both very difficult and very important. This is probably the toughest security question facing the United States and the rest of modern society. I do not think that anyone should despair at not finding quick and easy answers.

I have not spread much cheer, but I will not apologize for that. Ultimately what we have to do is push the federal government to show some leadership, to turn the creativity of the United States and its friends and allies loose on the problem. We and our allies in this century have won three world wars: two hot, one cold. None of that was easy either. We can pray that we will stay ahead of those who would exploit our current vulnerabilities without our needing some wake-up call that is terribly damaging to us. Even if that type of wake-up call comes—a biological weapon in a World Trade Center, or something horribly damaging to our information infrastructure—even if we have to dig ourselves out of a terrible hole, figuratively or literally, I would still take some heart from Carl Sandburg's line in *The People, Yes*: "This old anvil laughs at many broken hammers."

11

The War after Byte City

Michael Vlahos

It was the greatest military power of its day.
Always the innovator, its technologies of war
        were the newest;
Its command and control the best of the best.
Its ability to mobilize national resources
        was matchless;
Its traditions the envy and admiration of all,
And surely, imitated by all.
It was the world's military superpower,
And it owned war.

But now peace was everywhere.
Its great armies, mobilized for decades,
        were drawn down.
What had been the center of grand strategy,
        the cockpit—Central Europe—
Was now a portrait of like-minded states.

So the great nation refocused,
Turning its military toward new roles.
It built a mobile deterrent force:
A rapidly deployable army that could be rushed
To quell a regional contingency (or two!)
        and restore stability.
It reshaped its military forces
Around a core, professional force
That could be used flexibly to achieve
        the larger, strategic goal:
The preservation of a stable world system.

Of course, I describe France in 1860.

But there is something familiar there for us. Like France then, we are today's *grande nation,* and we have been for some time in this American century. Like France then, American culture has set world fashion, and our English is the world language. We too seem set now in a long peace. Does a passing historical resemblance tell us anything about the future of our own national security, or the future of war itself?

Although France may have been, like us, the military superpower of that era, it was the defeated superpower in 1815. Yet, in the long peace after the wars of Napoleon, France regained a military preeminence only briefly lost at Waterloo. By 1860, France again seemed astride the earth like a god of war:

- Who wrote the doctrine of war everyone used? Henri Jomini.

- Who was the innovator? The French developed the first breechloading rifle—the *Chassepot*—the first shell gun— the *Paixhans*—the first machine gun—the *mitrailleuse*—the first ironclad battleship—the *Gloire.*

- Whose army had real global reach? With successful offensive and peacekeeping operations just recently concluded in Spain, Italy, Algeria, and the Crimea, the French army would soon sortie even to Mexico too.

France in midcentury was a world power, using its military power to balance and manage world order. France was pledged to preserving a world system and nearly 50 years of stability. Like the United States today, France in 1860 was the status quo power in a world where the status quo, stability, and the old system itself . . . were about to end.

And end they would in a big bang for France.

Ten years later, the *grande nation* would begin a historical reeling from which it would never recover. War with the German Federation would humiliate the French, destroy their reputation for war forever, and end also their long certainty of national greatness.[1]

This fate could never happen to us. *Of course not.* Like all analogies, this one is imperfect and, in mixing military metaphors, manipulative even. *Of course.* Still, as different as they are, two times and two peoples and two ways of war, France then and the United States now share the same strategic problem: Big Change.

France did not lose in 1871 because it was stupid or unlucky. Certainly, its war technologies and combat experience were superior to Germany's. France lost in 1871 because a revolution had swept Europe, and that revolution changed war. The French military and their ruling national elites had not kept up. They had missed the revolution in war.

If you could go back to 1860 and tell this to French ruling elites, they would be offended. They would protest: "We have the world's most modern military machine. Look at our record of innovation: superior French science and engineering have changed the face of war!" So everyone thought. You could see it in every newspaper—just look at Daumier's grisly cartoon *Triumph of the Needle Gun.* New gun, new ship, new war.

If you went back and talked about a revolution in war, people would nod their heads: "Yes, there is a revolution: the ironclad revolution at sea, and the breechloading rifle and needle gun on land. Yes. These are revolutionary weapons." Everyone thought that revolutions in war are about new weapons.

It was the Big Change in ordinary life, the life of people in society, that had changed war, however. The new artifacts of daily life were the bringers of revolution in war . . . like the railroad. The railroad was the tool of Europe's transformation, the agent at the heart of industrial revolution. The railroad had brought whole pastoral worlds to the new cities of brick and iron.

The railroad could also bring whole cohorts of young men to the new killing grounds of the needle gun. Between 1815 and 1870, industrial society created industrial war: war by mobilization, war by train timetable. In 1860, that war had not yet been fought, however: it was still theory in the mind of Moltke. New war had been enabled, but not enacted. France's elites were free for a time yet to pursue old wars with modern cosmetics, wars still won by quick offensive maneuver and long-service veterans, without apprehension that this way of war was already dead.

And the French elites could still believe the future of war was theirs: as long as they stayed ahead of all others in weapons technology and kept their warrior ethos stoked hot. There were no worries here.

This is the point of comparison: We are in the midst of an economic upheaval equivalent to the industrial revolution in its capacity to transform our lives. Like the industrial revolution, this metamorphosis will reach up to politics and to war and remake them as well.

But America's ruling elites have defined a world system that does not allow for the possibility of Big Change. Like the French plutocrats of the 1850s, the old, cold war establishment is pledged to preserve the old paradigm at all costs. This establishment defines the United States as the status quo power, its sacred word is stability, and its imperative verb is to manage.

The military component of this ruling class sees U.S. military power as the ultimate world management tool. War is defined as combat operations in pursuit of stability. Some in the national security subculture talk quietly about a revolution in war, but they describe this revolution as did the French military innovators of the 1850s: a revolution in weapons.

This, then, is the four-point hypothesis:

- The world economic revolution is a true Big Change, what old German philosophers would call a phenomenon of world-historical significance. As it transforms individual societies across the world, it changes the very patterns of relationship between societies—what we call the world system. Thus, economic revolution changes the world system as well as the world's societies. Here, change comes first as systemic breakdown. New norms—perhaps a new system—will evolve later.

- Economic revolution will bring upheaval to world cultures as old ways of life are torn apart. Upheaval will encourage new belief systems as people seek new meaning out of the shock of Big Change. Change will hit different peoples in different ways. Culture and environment will shape different demands for new meaning around the world. New bodies of meaning that arise—whether we call these religions or ideologies—will look different, act differently, and, most important, see big differences between each other. New differences will lead to new human conflict.

- New war will serve the needs of new meaning. The new ideologies and religions born of economic revolution will use the new tools of revolution to win. Industrial war used the new tools of railroad and telegraph, assembly line and spreadsheet to serve the war visions of the new ideologies: mass democracy and its competing *-isms*. New war will be as determined and as opportunistic—and new meaning will have no ties to old war.

- We, the status quo power, greatest of the old powers, will not only still be fighting old war, but still be *thinking* old war. The successful bureaucracies of old war will continue to refight old victories and continue to dress future combat in the cool desert camouflage of far battles long won. We will still have the world's best high technology, and our people will have the combat experience and the military professionalism. But our mythic reputation, first built on a good war fought eight or nine decades before, will be both our glory and our curse, and we will await our Sedan.

Let's look at this hypothesis point by point.

A Time of Upheaval

Of all world cultures, America believes in the sanctity of progress. We like to say that this has been a Century of Progress, meaning, by implication, that progress is a gradual, incremental thing, accommodating itself to the world it finds, changing it in polite if not always comfortable ways, giving us time to familiarize ourselves with the new. Every wrench has been buffered by its careful insertion into our lives. We did not jump from vaudeville to color television. It took decades.

A Surprise for the United States: Discontinuous Change

Yet, this is not a time of progress: it is a time of revolution. Change, instead of stretching the fabric of reality, is about to rip the canvas. But we are not prepared to see revolution for what it is.

Part of our problem is that we have disarmed our own language. In our vision of progress, we have used the word *revolution* as a commonplace. It has been used as an accent, a spicing for product debuts: television was a revolution, the atomic bomb was a revolution; and so was the jet plane, then the VCR, Dolby sound, and the microwave oven. These were products that amplified and altered our lives, but in no way did any of them fundamentally change our *way of life.*

We have forgotten what revolution is. We are about to be reminded.

The Second Surprise: It Is Our Own Doing

The Big Change is not happening out there. We are making it happen right here. We are bringing discontinuous change to ourselves.

The United States, the premier status quo power, is now that very status quo's undoing. We are the dynamic force actively dismantling the old paradigm, the old world system.

We are the system breaker. We are the makers of revolution, like Britain's self-made industrial revolution of the last century. We are bringing the new railroad to American life, and, like the railroad, our new net will transform first our lives and then the life of the world.

As the railroad created a new network of cities and an urban, industrial society, so this new network (or the net after the net after today's World Wide Web) that we are laying will replace the urban, industrial world with a new city, a new gathering place for American life: Byte City.

What Does Byte City Mean?

For American business and the American way of life, it means the following:

- There will be no distance—as well as no time—to transactions. This is happening now.

- There will be no distance, no time barriers as well, to meeting and working in Byte City. You will be able to meet anyone, anywhere, anytime, with the fidelity of digitized life. It will not be videoconferencing, and it will not require headgear.

- There will be a new standard of value, defined by the marketplace. People will set value for knowledge, directly, person to person.

- The pressure for openness and transparency of transaction will be absolute.

There will be a new economy, built on knowledge services. There will be an explosion of productivity and a whole new workforce. Work will take on wholly new patterns: commuting dies, for example.

It will be a new way of life for most Americans. There will also be end to the old workforce and to the old jobways, the old rhythms of life built around manufacturing and the servicing of the machine.

This change will mean dislocation, anxiety, fear of the future. It is happening right now, but it will get much worse. Many will do very well in this new world, as they are right now, but many will not.

We are at the beginning of an upheaval the likes of which we have never known. Nor have our parents, nor theirs, nor theirs.

It means this for American politics. The last Big Change overthrew not just regular people's way of life, but how all life was organized, how whole countries were ruled. As millions of Americans find themselves in the fearful, rollicking slide of Big Change, stripped of old meaning, they will demand new meaning: What is my status in society? How do I belong? What is my worth? What kind of life can I expect for my family, what kind of future for my children?

These questions, when asked collectively, will tear apart American politics as we have known it. The surge of change will spell the end of the New Deal, cold war elites, already under siege. The world these elites still represent will have nothing to say about The Change, but all of it will be seen to have failed.

The technologies of the new net, of the not-yet-apprehended Byte City, will make it possible for regular Americans so long disenfranchised by machine politics and plebiscitary democracy to gather and talk and act. They will gather not to nominate petty demagogues, for they will need no telegenic spokespersons, but to move, to speak, to be felt directly: as groups of citizens.

Economic revolution transforms the U.S. economy. Like the last revolution, this change increases everyone's wealth, but not everyone's happiness. The stress of social adaptation will mean a protracted period of inward-turning by the United States. As economic revolution liberates great national energies, these passions unleashed demand resolution. Like America after the Civil War, there will be very little energy to spare for the rest of the world . . . except that the revolution itself becomes our connection.

What we create here creates demand there. Everyone wants it; it is the spellbinding new world, the promise of a better life for billions still tied to sweatshop and factory, and silver billions more for elites that can bring its wonders home.

Like Britain then, we export the agent of transformation: our new city high on that hill in cyberspace. The violence of our Big Change crashes and redoubles itself on them.

How Big Change Hits the World

The Cultural Dissonance of Revolution

There are reasons why we might expect that our economic revolution will hit others harder than it hits us. The forms of our revolution, as they are developed, tend to fit our cultural norms and belief system. America is a chaotic culture; it likes chaos, and even more important, it thrives on chaos—or apparent chaos. Beneath the spectacle others see of us, there is the same working pattern here of human culture everywhere: custom and taboo keep us all in line.

The Byte City spectacle will alternately thrill and repel other cultures. It will thrill individuals with its seemingly infinite possibilities. It will threaten their ruling classes in their guts.

The new economy the United States is building directly attacks the entrenched hierarchies of the industrial world. Pseudodemocratic elites whose rule depends on control of information will be confounded by the absolute transparency of Byte City. A social welfare system jointly created by elites and manufacturing workers cannot be sustained in an economy where value is determined not by job status and time in job but directly—by what one actually offers the new marketplace.

Thus, the elaborate industrial paradigms of Europe and Japan cannot long survive the advent of Byte City on their shores. Nor, given U.S. market intimacy and the intimate demand of their own people, can it be kept out.

The problem is in adjustment. The United States has already adjusted to structural dismantling of manufacturing society. The United States has made the big investment in the new enterprises of revolution. Also, the United States carries much less of a social welfare overhead than the G-7's other six.

Consider the European Union (EU). In each European society, more than 50 percent of gross national product (GNP) goes to government; majority support for the welfare state is built in. Keeping the social welfare world means squeezing the

productive sectors, however: in France, marginal tax on business was just increased from 85 percent to 93 percent! Yet, even
this would still work if there were enough productive enterprises to sustain the overhead. European economies need the
new enterprises of the revolution, but these are so regulated that
they have been strangled almost to death. EU GNP equals that of
the United States, but . . .

- The value of its software is only about 20 percent of U.S.
  software.

- The EU has 47 percent of global manufacturing exports,
  but only 7 percent of the world computer market.

- None of the world's top 5 computers is European.

- None of the world's top 10 semiconductor producers is
  European.

- In the Euromarket, the top 4 computers are American
  made.

- U.S. job growth was 33 percent between 1976 and 1990; in
  Europe job growth was 8 percent, and 97 percent of this
  was in the public sector.[2]

Europeans buy U.S. knowledge products and knowledge
services: the EU runs an $18 billion trade deficit with the United
States in software. Smart Europeans who want to save on long-
distance calls phone a service in Oklahoma that places their
European calls: they save up to 50 percent that way. They are
becoming parasites of America's revolution.

Europe's elites still believe that high value-added manufacturing, like Mercedes cars and Italian shoes, can finance the
industrial welfare state. But there are no jobs in Europe, and only
so much value-added. The real value-added is here: in the
United States, 50 percent of new capital investment goes to electronics and information systems; in semiconductors alone, value
in terms of total capital investment shot up from 7 percent in
1990 to 23 percent today.

Right now, real unemployment in Germany is close to 30
percent, the truth masked by so many unemployment percentage points stashed in perpetual job-training programs: 40 days
guaranteed vacation cannot fig-leaf a job world that rations
work. In France, where unemployment is officially 13 percent,

the reality is also closer to a third if the marginally employed are counted. New French folklore fastens on the numbers of three-generation families who have never held a job.

As it barrels into this world, America's economic revolution brings social revolution. The stratified industrial economies of Europe and Japan (yes, Japan; 87 percent of Japanese workers are in globally uncompetitive companies that receive some form of government subsidy) are not prepared for the trauma that we are even now bringing to them. The old, developed world is as brittle as the thin civilization of late imperial Rome, its ruling elites as dogged as eighteenth-century Chevaliers facing the Great Fear and, yet, as helpless to stop its insatiable onrush.

And what happens to the Third World? What happens to those still industrializing, still half-locked in the last revolution? If so much disruption awaits those of the G-7, those who should be ready but are not, how much worse will it be for those who still daily deal in famine and industrial pollution?

To spectral witnesses like Bob Kaplan, the future belongs to the Third World's masses of misery, where the driving force is not economic revolution but human and environmental degradation. In his tortured landscape, cyberspace is the toy of neomedieval privilege, of a postindustrial caste secure in its pristine monasteries.

We can be sure that the agonies of Abidjan will not soon be relieved by America's virtual public squares—the vision of Byte City. In Victorian times too, the industrial revolution brought no succor to the slave markets of Mali. Today's transformation, like the last, begins in a single place and then fans out, staking its claim over the historical reality it has created.

These are like Victorian times in another way. Third World elites routinely, eagerly, spend their pampered youth in American universities. As the architecture of a new world takes shape here, ruling elites everywhere will rush to plug in. So the net that transforms American life will pull in the gangsters and warlords and languid princelings of Kaplan's forlorn anarchy.

And entrepreneurs. The economic revolution will make wealth everywhere. As for the programmers of Bangalore, the new net will be a way out and up for go-getters who need not get up and actually leave. But these new enterprisers will be working in America. They will be less inclined to pay homage to physically local rulers, and so ruling classes initially delighted will then clamp down hard.

From a Singapore Telecom exec in the know:

My government doesn't care, it isn't listening in to our citizens on the net; but I'll tell you one thing: Lee Kuan [Yew] et al. freaked out when they were told that there were 3,000 unlicensed electronic bulletin boards on the island! That's why we now have a national website. And [surprise] everybody posts there before they post out. But we don't listen in.

As Kishore Mahbubani, Singapore's permanent foreign secretary, told me: "We don't want America's decadence, but [to control] there are other alternatives to *Pravda*."

Mechanisms of control will be everywhere; and not all will fail. The industrial revolution that brought democracy to Britain brought new paternalism to Germany: workers got protection, but old Junkers kept political power. Through the wash of peoples we call the Third World, there will be as many responses to the new as there are cultures and tribes.

Those places lost today will likely stay lost. But many places full of energy—like India and East Asia—will grow in huge surges.

What is missing from analysis is how people respond to such creative destruction. Kaplan controls humanity's outcome by reducing all our options to a narrowing circle of choices in a world aching just to survive. But economic revolution means expanding choices: more stress, but more hope too and fertile ground not for old, but for new religions.

The New Religions

Economic revolution takes time to do its disruptive work. The transformation of American life doesn't happen tomorrow, or next year. It isn't ushered in by *Windows 95*, or forced into our living rooms by set-top-box interactive TV. The world we are building may only reach initial maturity—meaning an up-and-running infrastructure—20 years from now. Its impact on the world will take still longer. We can anticipate Big Change hitting Japan a bit before Europe, but both places closest to us will be upended no later than a decade after we take the first hit.

The great uncertainty rests with cultures other than our own. Even if social revolution in Europe is a calamity, it is difficult (although not impossible) to imagine the rise of a new ideology there that would in its fulfillment of new meaning demand the rejection of all things American.

It is far less difficult to imagine such an outcome among cultures that historically have found fault with America. Those cultures that have suffered from contact with the West, and those that believe especially that the United States has inflicted on them a lasting degradation of identity, will be receptive to new constructions of meaning that celebrate all differences between us—and them.

Even places that have been sympathetic to the American Crusade since 1945 may respond with dismay to the theater of chaos that economic revolution stages—for all the world to see—in early next-century America. Their dismay with us could have far more historical consequence than the sum of all their current frustrations.

Kaplan's terrible "Coming Anarchy"—like Freddy Krueger's *Nightmares* observed in adulthood—translates into a sordid, but not necessarily threatening, world. There are lots of unhappy people out there, but their sad slide means they have less and less with which to make us truly unhappy. Our national security problem becomes our choice to be depressed by contemplating such unhappiness.

Revolution, however, gives us a real problem. It not only makes things more interesting, it also makes them more threatening. Revolution means the United States has re-created economic life, but at the cost of its former world leadership and the world system it led. U.S. allies from the old paradigm have been undercut, ironically, by their former leader, whose economic revolution has sliced their elites' authority off at the knees. Europe and Japan, plunged into an economic clearance sale, have in pain and anger reorganized their societies and their politics. And those 1980s dynamos of growth, Dragons and Tigers, have exploded in their own dynamism.

Year 20xx: There Are New Religions Abroad

New religions claim new allegiance. Industrial revolution created anomie; anomie demanded meaning. And meaning came: positivism, Marxism, socialism, communism, bolshevism, fascism.

We called these attempted new organizations of humanity ideologies. Nonsense. They were new religions. What is always distinctive about new religions is their passionate conviction that their truth is the only truth. A world that creates several new religions at once is a world eager for combat.

How the New Make New War

No New War without New Meaning

There is no point looking at the world as it is and then trying to leap to the next war. We get stuck immediately in tortured excursions that try to make of today's regime in Beijing or New Delhi an adversary we could face in combat with a straight face. Such exercises bring new meaning to the term "suspension of disbelief."

It gets harder the farther out we go with the same director and cast—like a never-ending sequel to an old Defense blockbuster: *DPG XXIII, The Final Agony.* Planning tells us to take today's snapshot—with all current trends holding—to some arbitrary, even-numbered date called "the planning horizon." This gives us Beijing or New Delhi with $x+y$ number of weapons more than they have today but Washington with the same, disbelieving face.

There will be no new war without new religions . . . just as there can be no revolution without a disruption of meaning. That disruption has already begun, and so new religions are ensured. It is today's stale, crust-brittle constructions of meaning that are not long to crumble.

You don't believe this? Why are we so shocked by Serbian blood vengeance, Chechen blood vengeance, Algerian blood vengeance, anybody's blood vengeance, but not by our own lack of awareness of it?

Our elites take pride in denouncing these passions as primitive, dismissing them as deviant: If they can't be put down, they should be condemned. These same elites have no sense of the authentic source of these passions—a demand for meaning in a world where stability and order have been ruthlessly stripped away—and these passions' abiding power—to fight starving in the snow at 30 degrees below, to make yourself a living bomb, to head-shot prisoners one after the other, without flinching, because they are The Stranger. We watch, heads shaking, as the edges of civilization slough and scale and feel nothing but scorn and superiority. The shock will come when it all hits home.

The shock at the violence of new religions—unlike our contempt for today's brutal tribal chant—must be the shock of recognition in revolution itself. Part of the experience of revolution is overcoming that shock. Eventually, we will accommodate to upheavals at the center, and they will seem different to us because they happen here, or in places that we have long ago decided are centers of civilizations: not Serbia, not Daghestan; but Japan, France, China, the United States.

Revolution takes war away from the margins, from tribal splatterings at the limits of what we control, and puts it back in the firmament of the center, among close relations, in the heart of the world *metropole*. Revolution so changes the world bourse that nothing else can stay the same.

Conflicting new religions in a world after economic revolution runs its course will be accepted by Americans. We will surely have run a course with many homegrown cults and religions of our own.

But we may be less ready to deal with triumphant, inimical movements that have us directly in their sights.

By less ready I mean less prepared to deal with the fruits of their animus against us. Today, we chafe at the prospect of highly motivated, Islamic revivalist groups doing their worst on us, but compared to the potential power of a great new religious movement, drawing strength from its millions and the surging technologies of revolution, these zealot-clusters are nothing.

If new religious movements, like the Nazis or Bolsheviks of this century, claim the energies of whole peoples—passionate, educated millions—then the new world and its new meaning are really worth worrying about.

War Celebrates New Meaning

We still think of Nazi Germany as somehow keener on new technology than we: better tanks, guided missiles, jet planes; forgetting that we pushed the technology envelope far more in our Good War than they. "German scientists" became cold war slang because of what science and technology meant to the then-new isms. Then we shivered over *Sputnik* because of the meaning Soviets invested in war's technology.

Soviet and Nazi religionists used the sharpest badges of modernism—high-tech weapons of war—to celebrate (and make us believe in) the inevitability of their triumph: hence the

new-wave Panzers and hot Heinkel formations of a Leni Riefens-
tahl newsreel or the intercontinental ballistic missiles grimly
rumbling across Red Square became the totems of new meaning—publicly, flamboyantly celebrated. Hitler's and Stalin's
cults were receptive to new war because new war could be used
to insinuate emotionally the conviction that their vision, their
belief systems, were about to be unconditionally fulfilled.

We have come to see war in stark contrast. We permit ourselves some modest, tame association of war's technologies with
our own belief that mastery of such technology shows a kind of
natural superiority, but then we go and drown this almost-cele-
bration with apologies in advance of its demonstration. We have
done this too in historical retrospect, stripping former celebra-
tions even from the Good War, even on its fiftieth. To us, war can
never again be a celebration. It is at best a profession.

Why does distinction between wars matter? It matters
because war for us serves a very different purpose than war for
them. This is the heart of the difference between status quo war
and revolutionary war; and it is the heart of the difference that
matters much more than the visible things that seem to make
war.

Revolutionary war is not defined by revolutionary weapons,
just as status quo war is not defined by status quo weapons. The
weapons of war, and the way war is made, are vehicles for realizing what this war represents and, in fact, what it is: *Revolutionary
war is the celebration, the realization, of identity.*

This was true for the Hitler cult especially. It is important
also for us to understand how we defeated revolutionary war
then. The United States met revolutionary war—the celebratory
war of the new cult—head-on: with a messianic fervor of our
own. We made of world war a "crusade" (in Ike's words) and
used the power of American movies and American music to
infuse our "war effort" with a religiosity of passionate commitment and fulfillment. The power of mass, religious mobilization
can be glimpsed in the thrill Americans felt when hearing of
Hiroshima. The Good War built up enough messianism to carry
us through a dreary and depressing cold war, 20 years and more
down the road, all the way to Vietnam.

Revolutionary war as enacted by the Hitler cult is worth
remembering because it was done to us. Memory should give us
something real with which to approach the future. Remember
that it is a messy, even unsatisfactory example, but it is an example we all know. It is unsatisfying because the thing that is to be

feared in our future—from the new religions—will not resemble the Hitler cult; but war will have the same, celebratory purpose. For the new religions, war will be essential to their becoming. The very experience of war is realization of the new: you create yourself by destroying the stranger.

This is why it is important to recognize the religious dimension of Nazi, Soviet, (and American) war. If the Good War gave the United States its cold war momentum, the Great Patriotic War did even more for the Soviet regime. It became the treasured, sacred experience of the Soviet state and its peoples. It may have been the only shared element of meaning holding up the rotten Church of Lenin in its last decades.

We, like the old Soviets, finally lost the talisman of the Good War. Vietnam destroyed it, and young generations have all but forgotten it. A half-century of cold war slowly turned its back on the very celebratory war that immediately preceded it: the Good War. The American way of war changed, and those who made it changed. Part of this was blamed on the A-bomb, but there was more than that at work. Things military became tied to a social order: its own caste, studiously, even excruciatingly, niched in the larger hierarchy of those who ran the cold war and cold war American life.

There is no longer an American Way of War in a national, and certainly not in a religious, sense. War has become a toolbox owned by the ruling establishment. For the American overclass, war today is a reverse affirmation of everything that can be lost. This is classic status quo thinking, of course. War is something *not* to be fought, but its tools are always to be *used* in support of that same status quo.

But preserving the late-twentieth-century American status quo is far different from France or Britain preserving the mid-nineteenth-century status quo. The difference is that Americans do not like imperial wars. Therefore, the Washington ruling establishment must manage by demonstration and awe. This means maintaining very high force levels for world management purposes, even in the absence of a major competitor. These forces must be constantly and bullishly in play—in operations other than war—and yet still not used. This helps to explain why any successful war activity is immediately and loudly trumpeted as an advertisement for the national security subculture (which includes defense industry and other civilian constituencies) as a whole. In the face of domestic un-interest, a world management force must be sold to Americans on the basis of a carefully crafted package that combines residual nostalgia for the Good War crusade and a coded message about preserving U.S. military superiority.

We must stay on top [in control] or we will lose.

The unintended emphasis, strangely for the superpower, is on losing. To get the current force levels it wants for management, the ruling elite must insinuate the notion that any retreat from these levels is a historic loss or retreat for the American nation. To send this message—as untrue as it is—these same elites must strike a tone of pessimism, even defeatism.

This mental stance is the starkest contrast to the unbounded optimism of the religionist bound for revolutionary war: *The future belongs to me.*

Why We Stay Stuck In Old Think

The Old Establishment Will Resist Big Change Everywhere

Defenders of the world status quo, the cold war elite is visibly hunkered down in its final Plaine des Jarres command post. America's current national establishment was crowned in crisis. Exigency equaled authority, so the cold war became the perpetual crisis that demanded a perpetual imperial ruling class. And it is a big, messy world out there. Even when the big crisis—the cold war—died, there seemed so many out there to take its place. Change was always out there and always bad, which meant always good for the elite.

But the onset of Big Change within the United States is like "The World Turned Upside Down" (the denouement tune Cornwallis had played at Yorktown). Elites have no authority to defend against, let alone even define, domestic change as a threat to national security. It is simply a threat to their own security: the security of their position.

It is an overclass in need of a rescuing world crisis—not a real crisis, but an emotional situation that renews overclass authority—that limits our imagination and our ability even to prepare for the next (real) war. This would not matter for those charged with America's defense except for one thing: They too are part, an indissoluble part, of that same elite. How did this happen? With the coming of the cold war, the brass moved into their big building in the Imperial City complex. Theirs was the point of the Free World spear, but they were also allowed into the Mandarin Club as the American Empire's warrior-diplomats.

And most important: they gained real political influence in support of a real political constituency—one-third of the federal workforce! They got sucked into Free World rule.

So responding to world change, and a world revolution that is American made, is channeled by Washington's ancien régime into rigid, familiar paths, with the unconscious complicity of America's military societies. The leading corps of these societies see a dense and dangerous thicket for their people, but one they must enter nonetheless. And they seek, with all the nature and honor embedded in their ethos, to bring everyone out on the other side.

Their watch has marked the beginning of that dense and dangerous peacetime. They have taken to cut for themselves three characteristic paths through the thicket, or footpaths to the future, called Readiness, Reform, and (R)evolution.

Readiness. Readiness is a worldview that believes in the robustness of control. Things can be managed, and change can be held down, as long as we have the means. Readiness is the predominant peacetime ethos of the defense world.

One good opinion gives us the flavor of a true on-top, status quo mindset:

> The lessons and revelations . . . of the Persian Gulf War victories . . . mandate that a new style of warfare will be employed in future elective wars. Technology offers the leverage that facilitates the accomplishment of the new expectation imposed by the American public. Our military can win decisively anywhere in the world. It can defeat an adversary anywhere in world [sic!] in reasonable amounts of time. The day of long drawn out warfare has past [sic!]. It can take battle to an enemy and with the proper technology minimizes [sic!] our own casualties. It can destroy an enemy on the battlefield while preserving, should it choose, the country, national treasures and way of life of that enemy.

This quote was chosen because it represents, errors and all, an authentic attitude rather than a massaged, politically disinfected, nearly meaningless official statement.

Readiness defines the current enemy as the always-enemy, because within its reasoning, no big enemy could arise as long as the superpower manages world conflict. Deterrence migrates in this mindset from a relationship designed to maintain a permanent nuclear status quo to a relationship where vicious but

smaller regimes and bigger but more benign regimes are
both deterred from challenging a permanent American world
status quo.

The quote's emphasis on the Persian Gulf War as model is
also a feature of the predominant path. It implicitly freezes war
by codifying modern war as the last victorious engagement. This
has the benefit of freezing as well the institutions, relationships,
and force structure that fought that engagement. Modernity is
carefully contained within the realm of things that do not
threaten institution, relationship, or force structure. So new technology—and by extension, research and development (R&D)—is
channeled into the development of high-tech badges, refine-
ments, or appliqués to existing weapons' phyla.

Reform.   Reform's urge follows cherished American tradition. American military reform—to some extent mirroring contemporary reform movements in American society—seeks to
improve bureaucratic performance by improving efficiency.
Intrinsic to its goal is the demonizing of corruption and ineffi-
ciency. The core belief is that efficiency is the desideratum: the
thing most wanted. Efficiency solves peacetime problems. It
allows us to fight future battles without increasing today's budgets. It is progressive in the sense that it brings military society in
synch with what is considered better and more modern in the
current American spirit of the age. Admiral William A. Owens
thus belongs to the lineage of all American reform and symbol-
izes military society's harmony with all of American society, just
as Elihu Root or Admiral William Sims brought their services in
tune with the progressive spirit of their day.

But this path is more of a response to domestic change than it
is preparation for future war, and it creates its own cultural backlash. The example this time is from a reform briefing by a former
Defense Department official. The chart is entitled "Achieving a
Common Futures-Oriented Framework For Defense Decision-
Makers." The chart correctly—even powerfully—identifies one
of the deepest elements of corruption in the Department of
Defense: the swarm of interest groups whose competing needs
must be resolved before any policy or budget can be made. The
chart shows the thick alphabet soup that must be adjudicated
before even *thinking* about the future can happen. He was fired
for trying to do something about it.

Reform, far from simplifying and sorting out the mess, often
only adds to it. The Joint Staff should have replaced several layers in the bureaucratic pastry, like the service secretariats.

Instead, it is now yet another layer. Unless reform is the central agenda of the highest authority, executed ruthlessly from above and responding to a widespread sense of crisis, indeed, a public outcry for change, it only succeeds in creating yet another internal interest group to be fed. So reform's fulfillment waits, often until peacetime's end, for crisis to make it happen.

(R)evolution.   Military "revolutionaries" within a peacetime status quo elite tend to focus on new weapons. It was true for the nineteenth-century French; it is true for the revolution-in-military-affairs guys today. Why?

For one thing, they cannot even think about bucking the dominant paradigm: preserving the status quo. They would quickly be punished or banished to the most terrible hell imaginable for thinkers—obscurity—if they even suggested that military change means deconstructing the old paradigm itself. But then, even in obscurity, they could at least call themselves (R)evolutionaries.

So focusing on weapons is politically safe. And if technology change, which surely accompanies revolution, is big enough, *then it actually looks like the technology change.* And the new weapons it brings . . . are the revolution.

A public example (because he now publishes openly) of this phenomenon is Andy Krepinevich's "Funding Innovation: Low-Cost Operations for Leveraging the Military Revolution":

> . . . in the 1920s, the U.S. military successfully laid the foundation for success in the next great power competition by "reinventing" itself in response to the geopolitical and military-technical revolutions then under way. During the 1920s and 1930s, the military services positioned themselves to engage in new and different kinds of military operations— strategic aerial bombardment, amphibious assault against stoutly defended positions and carrier-based air strikes. And they did it on shoestring budgets. Denied the opportunity to think "richer" about defense, the military services thought "smarter."

He is right about one thing. They did think smarter—about what was already in play. There was no revolution during the 1920s and 30s. What was introduced in the Great War just got worked on. Airborne assault, armored maneuver, carrier task forces, aerial bombardment, wolf packs—the whole repertoire of the second war was rehearsed in the world's collective military mind after the first; year after year, for 20 years. It was just that some thought more efficiently than others.

But as real war, the second differed from the first merely in embellishment and in efficiency. It was better theater. But there had been no revolution.

Yet how advantageous it is to say that cruise missiles or stealth technology or microprocessors have "revolutionized" war! Self-styled (r)evolutionaries can appear to take on the Colonel Blimps of the readiness mind-set, saying they are cutting R&D and merely building the forces of yesterday, while in reality never threatening either their position or their mind-set.

(R)evolutionaries are in this way much like reformers: they want to make the current system better. To the reformer, corruption translates into the sloth and obesity of the system. To the (r)evolutionary, corruption translates into "old think" about fighting war. But the system—meaning the prevailing paradigm that encompasses the physical, the institutional, and the ideational aspects of a war society—escapes all rethinking.

None of this presumes that those defending any of these three paths to the future are moral invertebrates, corrupt of mind, or alien to honor. They are serious people, the finest we have, whose thinking is leashed by a system that permits them to address only part of a problem, to analyze these pieces in strict mental compartments, and to assemble them at their peril. The system that controls thought is neither conscious nor deliberate; but it is enfolding. It is a complete belief system, the reality-defining component of culture itself.

So when the rhetorician asks, "But where is (R)evolution?" we must answer, "It simply cannot exist." (At any level . . . until the larger revolution spends itself sweeping our old way of life away.)

Here the French analogy, full circle, holds little historical comfort. The French too, like us, had their military trajectories of mind. They had their predominant path to the future, and it, too, was readiness. They had their *jeunes écoles*, product of *grandes écoles*, fighting for reform, efficiency, purity of command and operation. And they had (r)evolutionaries, engineers whose visionary weapons promised to hold the key to future battle. And none of the paths was wrong. An ethos of readiness made the French army the most combat-honed force on earth; an ethos of reform pushed France at last to respond to the Prussian threat; and an ethos of (r)evolution gave the *armée* of the *grande nation* the "techiest" tools of war.

As separate mental footpaths to the future, however, these paths would meet, finally, only at the place of defeat. Reform bested readiness too late; and the big army reforms that followed the shock of Sadowa and Austria's stunning defeat in 1866 only served to throw the French army into confusion. It went into battle in 1870 not knowing itself. It could not possibly know itself in time because it had not taken the time to know war: how war was really changing, how the new world was machining it, reengineering it, so that it became something new.

We have several steps to take before we can begin to know this. The first is seeing the real change, and accepting the irony that we are making the revolution that will transform the world. The second step is connecting a transformation in life to a metamorphosis of culture itself, and then of war, which is culture's creature. The third step is confessing that, although we begin the revolution in life, others—their red dreams not yet imagined—will begin the revolution in war because war will be both their celebration of birth and its realization.

If these recognitions were all we needed to begin the road to the next war, we would already be into the journey. But there are other obstacles, the antirecognitions of denial, that are more intractable, that hold us in place like little trees with long roots.

- Our hallowed record of historical success: Why question it?

- The long time since we met a real competitor: Who is this upstart?

- The comforting feel of ongoing "reform": Been there. Did that.

- The power of our national myth: We will always rise to crisis.

- The talisman of triumphant technology: But we have the Death Star!

So we await our Sedan. To dismiss this prospect, we must dismiss the possibility of a future foe, an equal challenger with evil intent. To dismiss this possibility, we must dismiss the transformative power of Big Change and assert that we can keep control of not only our world system, but what happens to it, forever.

But no one can do this.
So we await our Sedan.
This much is certain:
The only uncertainty is in its outcome.

Notes

1. I am indebted to Dennis Showalter for his insights into mid-nineteenth century France and its army.

2. Much of this Euro-snapshot is taken from a fine interpretation by Gary Geipel and Robert Dujarric, *Europe 2005: Turbulence Ahead*, a 1995 Hudson Institute Executive Briefing. Anecdotes from France today are from Pascal de Jenlis, a true enterpriser who makes, among many things, the Cuisinart.

12

Another View of Information Warfare: Conflict in the Information Age

Jeffrey R. Cooper

The transition to an information age is occurring while we are in the midst of another significant transformation in the military-civil relationship, one related to the shift from industrial-age to postindustrial-age societies. The U.S. military, relying in World War II on the broad national economic/industrial base, was the epitome of the industrial-age military, capable of out-producing any combination of potential enemies. During the cold war, however, in order to maintain its position on the cutting edge of a broad range of critical technologies, the U.S. military took the vanguard position in fostering and developing many of these technologies, created military systems that had no civilian counterparts embodying those technologies, and became dependent on an artarkic network of dedicated, special-source suppliers that could meet its needs without regard to commercial considerations of marginal cost versus benefit of the extraordinary technical requirements. As the costs of these weapon systems soared and their production times lengthened, their numbers decreased at least as dramatically; and these factors have altered our perception of how future wars would be conducted. Thus, this transition from an industrial to a postindustrial military economy occurred in parallel with changing concepts about the character of the wars to be fought: from multiyear, attrition-oriented campaigns, in which the ability to field and replenish mass forces was the key, to shorter wars fought with smaller numbers of inventory weapons and forces, as illustrated by the Persian Gulf War.

This change had a profound impact on the relationship of the military to the national economic base and has equally profound implications concerning the need to secure and protect the nation's strategic rear in order to wage war.[1] Indeed, the distinct, artarkic character of military systems and the limited reliance on civil infrastructure meant that the military could focus its security and protection efforts largely on those elements it controlled;

and this ability substantially simplified everything from protecting military satellite communications to securing key defense industrial facilities. We are now, however, in the midst of yet another transformation of the U.S. military economic paradigm; but this time it is one that is returning the U.S. military, with its new emphasis on dual-use and commercial off-the-shelf (COTS) equipment, to its historic reliance on the entire national economic base. In the command, control, communications, computers, and intelligence (C^4I) world, this change is even more profound as the military moves from developer of cutting-edge technologies and operator of its own systems to one among many customers of an information economy driven by commercial imperatives. As this shift evolves, the military will be increasingly enmeshed in a Defense Information Infrastructure (DII) that is tightly linked to the entire National Information Infrastructure (NII) and to the Global Information Infrastructure (GII). As this embedding proceeds, military concern for the security of the entire information infrastructure will grow apace because its information base will be no more secure than the entire system; and, therefore, the military will once again be tightly linked to the nation as a whole—a mutual interdependence of vulnerabilities.

This transition to a postindustrial society is also fundamentally altering the relationships between wealth and power on the one hand and physical resources and capabilities on the other. Industrial-age societies built their wealth on the collective ability of the organized society to add value by physical extraction, processing, or transportation of natural resources. Postindustrial societies, on the other hand, add value largely by infusing information or knowledge in the physical products or services provided; indeed, even physical processing is largely related to embodying information in the raw materials. In many cases, while these infusions of information remain collective activities, like the preindustrial-age guild crafts, individual creativity now plays a far more salient role than does the ability to marshal and organize resources or numbers of people.[2]

Modern information-age societies may be likened to statically unstable aircraft such as the F-16, the first inventory combat aircraft to demand an active flight control system; these societies require continuous active intervention guided by sophisticated computer-based control systems (SCADA). They do not simply return to rest or to a stable static equilibrium; they rely on a continuous stream of real-time information to maintain control and dynamic stability (like a just-in-time production system) rather than on momentum, inertia, and buffering inefficiencies (like an inventory-based factory process). The advantage is in significantly enhanced efficiency but at the cost of continuous active control; these are no longer societies configured for hands-off flying.

At the same time, even at the tactical/technical level these same technological imperatives of silicon and digitization are substituting relatively ephemeral, software-based control mechanisms that operate through transmission of electrons and photons for traditional cams, springs, and other physical control systems that relied on direct transmission of force. As a result, even the physical systems that undergird existing societies, whether industrial- or information-age, may be far more vulnerable to disruption than was historically true; and these disruptions will not necessarily have to be violent physical acts— whether natural or human. This factor, in turn, does suggest that attacks on the information-based control systems of modern societies extend the reach of strategic information warfare (IW) into a realm not previously obtainable, regardless of whether information was a weapon or target. The combination of the two factors suggests that these new information-age economies may be less inherently resilient to disruption because they will not settle into a statically stable posture.

To accommodate this rich spectrum but still provide the necessary taxonomic structure, this chapter outlines a categorization that looks at potential impacts of the information revolution on conflict (in the broadest sense) at three discrete levels.

Ultimately, we may have no choice but to accept the notion of a revolution in security affairs arising from the information revolution because it will be exogenous to the military domain and drive inward; but in the interim, policymakers do have a large number of choices available as to the emphases they select for exploitation. Making these choices correctly demands that we first understand the phenomenology we are attempting to employ; and, therefore, constructing a rigorous taxonomy appears to be the crucial first step.

Background

Information warfare or IW grows from a number of different but crucial roots of which three in particular stand out—both because of their importance and because of their substantially differing focus. First, dating as far back as recorded history is the strategic use of information to affect or mold strategic perceptions in the mind of the leader. This root emphasized the ability to gain victory without conflict on the battlefield, as advocated by Sun Tzu and others.[3] The second root also has ancient antecedents—in the historic battle between code-makers and code-breakers (and in more modern times, signals intelligence) to protect or to exploit vital communications. This root has a more operational-level focus—such as the use of intercepted Japanese naval communications to win a decisive victory at Midway. Finally, the third root has its origins in more modern times, in World War II with the "Wizard War"[4]—the development of electronic warfare, the means to interfere directly with information obtained or transmitted throughout the electronic spectrum (such as "window" against radar). Although this aspect may also have both strategic and operational utility, it is primarily focused on defeating enemy weapons and systems on the tactical battlefield. As a result of these diverse antecedents, information warfare practitioners today represent a number of extremely strong, distinct constituencies, some with ancient lineage. These multiple constituencies bring not only different perspectives but also distinct cultures to the issues attendant on IW.

In light of these factors, it should not be surprising that the concept of IW carries a wide range of meanings. The resulting lack of an agreed taxonomy (and, therefore, analytical structure) complicates the process of deciding on policy choices and selecting implementation steps—not only for substantive reasons, but for organizational ones as well. The large number of players, including many outside the Department of Defense and other traditional members of the national security community, guarantees difficulties in sorting out the claimants for policy primacy and in orchestrating a coherent set of policies and implementing measures; who decides and how one ensures coherency in execution do not have intuitively obvious answers, particularly in the absence of strong leadership and consistent policies in the national security arena.

The subject of IW is of intense interest today for a number of serious reasons—not only because it has become a veritable cottage industry for otherwise displaced members of the defense community. First, it must be recognized that the United States and some other advanced countries are no longer industrial-age economies but have made a transition to postindustrial forms that are fundamentally dependent on vast volumes of timely and accurate information (rather than on industrial production) to maintain economic growth, efficiency, and leadership. Second, the increasingly frequent public reports of computer crimes, coupled with the potential threats of devastating acts of "info-terrorism," have heightened public awareness of the vulnerability of an economic and societal infrastructure based on evanescent digital information rather than massive physical assets. Third, the Persian Gulf War demonstrated that modern weapons do work; and, at their core, they are dependent for their effectiveness on accurate information delivered promptly.

That demonstration of the effectiveness of advanced information systems in guiding discriminating but extremely lethal combat systems for the battlefield has raised concerns about the vulnerability of modern information-age societies to attacks on or through their information infrastructure. Although some in the United States see in IW the means to establish an almost Roman dominion of global scope, others are concerned that we are the most susceptible (both on and off the battlefield) to these new means of conflict. Indeed, the effectiveness of the United States on the battlefield during the Persian Gulf War has raised concern that our next opponent may, therefore, not attempt to challenge our battlefield dominance but attack our more vulnerable and accessible NII that underlies our entire civil and commercial structure.[5] Together, these factors make it crucial that we address both the dangers as well as the potential opportunities in this new environment.

The interest of the U.S. defense community in IW is the result of another specific concern—the recognition that the information revolution could have dramatic effects on how the U.S. military conducts its professional affairs. The transition to an information-age economy is resulting in substantial disruptions in traditional corporate organizational structures and hierarchies; the same types of upheavals in military command and control structures can be expected as they are adapted to new technologies. Moreover, the increasing dependence of the military on commercial computer and communications systems—as opposed to defense-unique hardware and military-controlled networks—may prove to be a Faustian bargain. Whatever the specific impacts on operational concepts, organizational structures, and command and control relationships, it is likely that these changes will transform the manner in which the U.S. military conducts its affairs.

The far-reaching and deep-seated implications of these factors suggest that we are in one of those periods of fundamental transformation, a shift between major epochs in history—a shift that is being driven by the information revolution and the transition to a postindustrial information age. Historically, these shifts have often presaged similar transformations in the nature of security issues and the character of war. The transformation that occurred after the French Revolution in the character of European security concerns and changed objectives of war dwarfed the narrower changes that Napoleon wrought on the operational and tactical battlefields. The "Napoleonic revolution in military affairs" was more about a shift to total, continental-scale conflict between newly industrializing nation-states over unconditional objectives than about use of artillery or independent corps.

Some commentators today, such as Alvin and Heidi Toffler, are suggesting that we are even now witnessing the beginning of a new epoch in the military domain—a Third Wave in warfare that could complement if not totally replace lethal combat on the battlefield.[6] At its core lies information warfare. Whether IW is the crucial element in this transformation and whether it ultimately fulfills the prognostications of its more outspoken advocates will depend both on its inherent technical capabilities and on *how human decision-makers determine to employ it.*

Within the Department of Defense, current definitions of information warfare begin with extremely broad measures far beyond traditional battlefield combat:

> Activities taken to achieve information superiority in support of national military strategy by affecting the adversary's information and information systems while leveraging and protecting our own.[7]

In addition, the definitions include others more focused on specific aspects clearly related to battlefield activities:

> C^{2}W [command and control warfare] is the military strategy that implements Information Warfare on the battlefield and integrates physical destruction. Its objective is to decapitate the enemy's command structure from its body of combat forces.[8]

The first of these definitions covers the gamut of information-related activities, from strategic to tactical levels, and could certainly include activities directed at the opponent's strategic rear, the exposed civilian infrastructure that provides the base of national power and supports its military capabilities, as well as against its combat-ready forces on the battlefield. It is also so broad as to provide no intrinsic metrics for discrimination or priority among the potential implementation options: Should IW be directed toward victory on the battlefield or undermining and destroying the opponent's domestic foundation, or both? The second definition is so confined to the immediate battlespace that it ignores not only the strategic level of war (which should also be the military's concern) but also the potential role of IW in deterring potential conflicts. This narrow definition also overlooks potential information-related activities other than C²W that are also directly important to the military's combat capabilities during battlefield operations.[9] This definition fails to provide military commanders with the full range of battlefield capabilities that IW could offer, at either the operational or the tactical levels. Neither of these definitions is incorrect, but neither provides a useful basis for understanding or acting upon the complex set of issues and priorities with which decision-makers must contend.

Behind these two definitions lie real differences not only over objectives and means but also about a variety of other dimensions including the *meaning* of information itself. Indeed, one of the fundamental complicating elements in IW is that there is not even a common perspective on what information is.[10] Some analysts propose information itself as the target in warfare; others treat information as the weapon;[11] some see information as a critical resource;[12] and still others see information as a realm (like space) or an environment (the "infosphere"), as a medium for military operations (like airpower). Information could also be considered as a catalyst or as a control parameter in a process; and in both of these cases, information is neither transformed or spent.[13]

Even among those who agree that information is the target, some emphasize the destruction of, or interference with, information itself while others focus on the systems and processes that are supported or enabled by information. Indeed, draft doctrinal papers by the air force suggest that a key new element in information warfare is the ability, related to the rapid adoption of digital electronic technologies, to alter information and therefore actions directly without having to go through the perceptual framework of a decision-maker's mind.

Figure 1.
The Changing Relationship of IW

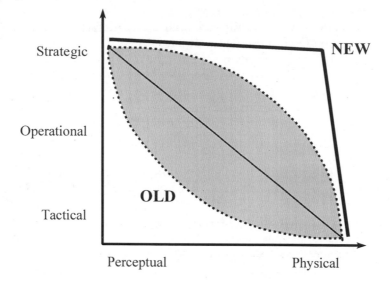

The complexity of IW has confused people and appears to have made sound decision-making problematic because there is so little common ground; we seem unable either to choose objectives that IW should serve or even to determine the role of information. These definitional issues are important because they frame the thinking and guide the measures used to assess utility and effectiveness.

It is therefore important to recognize that information warfare presents an extremely rich and complex structure that includes multiple dimensions of interpretation: definition and meaning of information itself (target, weapon, resource, or realm); level of effect (tactical, operational, or strategic); objective (perception management, battlefield dominance, C^2W, systemic disruption, or destruction); phase (peace, crisis, or conflict); actors (nations, terrorists, or criminals); types of systems affected (military-unique, dual-use, COTS, NII, or GII); as well as fundamental orientation (offensive or defensive). As choices are made along the spectrum of each dimension, every specific combination will result in a different connotation of IW and a different prescription for implementation, each with its own particular focus and priorities.

Historically, the tools of information warfare affected mostly concrete physical effects when the focus of activities was tactical (as suggested in figure 1); conversely, the higher and more strategic the focus, the more the effects were targeted against opponents' perceptions rather than directly on physical systems. For example, tactical IW applications, such as using electronic warfare (EW) techniques to interfere directly with an enemy's missile sensor or guidance, affect the concrete object—the missile. At the strategic level, perception management (PM), even if carried out by classic EW techniques, is more likely to be designed to affect decision-makers' perceptions by corrupting either their data or their reference frames. Thus, at the tactical level, combat is usually conducted by the interaction of physical systems (even with humans in control); but at the strategic level, war is principally about controlling minds.

One new element in the information age resulting from increasing information-dependency and networking of critical communications and control systems is the potential expansion at the strategic level of the ability to cause real physical damage by affecting an opponent's critical information systems that provide the infrastructure for efficient modern societies. Whether information is the weapon or the target (or both), effects on information systems may have profound physical effects as more societies move into this new age.

The structural conditions of the post-cold war geostrategic environment, as well as the expanding definition of national security, suggest that we must be prepared to face an exceptionally broad set of challenges. Key decisions for policymakers will include the roles for IW across this broad spectrum of security challenges. We should expect the nature of a conflict and of a situational phase, whether peace, crisis, or conflict, to exert a significant effect on how IW is viewed and on what actions are implemented in its pursuit. For example, responses that might be appropriate to acts of war could be inappropriate to criminal activities that are financially annoying but not threatening to societies. Addressing IW is especially difficult for the national security community, however, because it transcends the normal boundaries of military affairs and itself begins to introduce a very broad connotation of national security interests, thus blurring the lines between peace, crisis, and conflict.

Part of the IW spectrum deals with IW on the battlefield and another part with state-to-state attacks against the strategic rear. In reality, the IW spectrum is also likely to include actors and

Figure 2.
The New Conflict Environment for IW

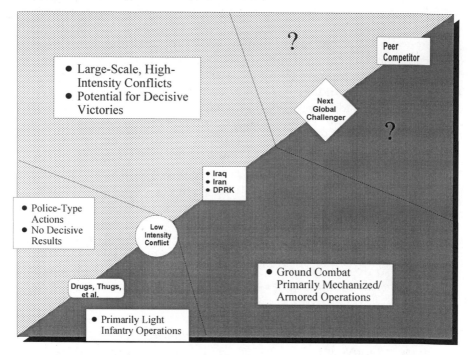

actions not traditionally considered to be military (such as hackers, criminals, and "info-terrorists").[14] Thus, although terrorism has become part of the military's domain over the past two decades, IW concerns may now also extend to criminals looking to purely financial as opposed to political gains because of the extensive damage they can inflict in the globally interconnected environment. Indeed, this ability of a single actor to exert dramatic leverage appears to be part of a broader change in the relative power relationship between the individual and the state.[15] Moreover, we currently lack criteria that would allow us to distinguish and thereby to recognize the nature of attacks that are under way; and, in return, to formulate responses appropriate to actions by hostile states, nonnational terrorist groups, or criminals.

Individuals have always been able to strike at the key organizational and control mechanisms of societies or states by attacks on the individual members of the ruling class, that is, through an assassination whose implications could be grossly disproportionate to the individual's physical powers. Since the age of explosives, however, individuals have also been able to exert physical damage to society at large disproportionate to their inherent physical capabilities. Then the rise of industrial-age states, with their high degree of organization and the bureaucratization (as well as routinization) of critical functions now capable of execution only by large organized units, altered the balance of power between individuals and states. Moreover, with the rise of large mass armies, the balance of coercive power clearly rested with institutions capable of organizing and sustaining mass forces. In their initial modern stages, nuclear weapons, as well as chemical and biological agents, clearly required the capacities of large, organized industrial endeavors to produce them.

Now, however, a range of modern technologies (including IW, chemical warfare or CW, and biological warfare or BW) has clearly amplified the individual's capacity for destruction aimed at society at large, thereby potentially altering the relationship between government and individual power. In the context of the relative power equation, the information revolution has clearly added three significant new dimensions. First, the worldwide interconnectivity of the information revolution has significantly magnified the ability of an individual to reach out and transmit a message to large-scale and dispersed audiences. If the Romans were concerned about Christian evangelism, consider the fundamental threats posed to totalitarian regimes in this new environment. As Jon Katz observes:

> Before the age of print, writes Bennett Anderson in *Imagined Communities*, the Roman Empire easily won every war against heresy because it had better lines of internal communication than its challengers. But by the early 1500s, Martin Luther had published 430 editions of his biblical translations, creating for the first time a truly mass readership. New media are creating a similar diversity. Television, telephones, modems, and fax technology not only leapfrog cities and countries, but are within almost everyone's reach.[16]

Second, the interconnectivity of global communications and the increasing reliance on remotely controlled infrastructure systems have also amplified the ability of individuals to gain access to protected realms that were previously the domains of governments and large corporations. The information revolution has also improved the ability to reach across borders without intermediaries or allies—and strike at a populace's morale or at the moral authority of its leaders—through technologies such as direct broadcast satellites and global communications networks.

Finally, the third new dimension is the ability of an individual (or larger entity) to effect great damage with these new instruments, thereby making the potential implications of their use akin to weapons of mass destruction. Havoc could be wreaked by disruption of critical control systems, such as air traffic control or electric power, or corruption of critical information streams, such as financial transaction data affecting the trillions of dollars that move through it daily.

> It is an invisible but very real war, where Information Weapons of mass destruction are let loose, either in a focused way, to achieve specific results, or indiscriminately, to have the widest possible impact. The victims are not only the targeted computers, companies, or economies, but the tens of millions of people who depend upon those information systems for their very survival.[17]

These changes in the relative power relationship—the ability to wield coercive instruments—between individual and state carry profound implications for the nature and exercise of political power. Thus, while the Tofflers and others are undoubtedly correct that we are moving into an age of "de-massification" that is affecting politics and economics as well as the military,[18] the potential for large-scale or widespread destruction will remain, if not increase; and the tension between focusing tailored effects and violence, on the one hand, and broad societal damage, on the other, can be expected to grow in the decision-maker's calculus.

> The Vietnam war taught us the consequence of winning every battle in the field and losing the information war on the home front. Before the advent of information warfare, propaganda was traditionally targeted through various mass media to influence a mass audience. One key change made possible by the new technologies is the potential for customized propaganda.[19]

Therefore, this change also multiplies the range and number of actors that states must consider as potential threats or challengers; in this information environment, where are the lines between criminal, terrorist, and warlike acts? Moreover, as noted above, the entanglement with issues and interests previously exogenous to national security concerns is increasing rapidly as the defense community integrates into the entire national industrial base and NII.

This change also introduces a whole range of new players not normally central to the national security problem; indeed, just on the government side, civil agencies such as Department of Justice (not just the Federal Bureau of Investigation), Department of Commerce, Federal Communications Commission, Treasury Department, and many others must now be consulted and integrated as these new security issues impinge on their areas of authority. More problematically, this proliferation of potentially major players in the infosphere is not limited to government entities; the U.S. military has already begun to encounter many of these new players (international organizations, nongovernmental organizations or NGOs, private voluntary organizations or PVOs, special interest organizations, and multiplying real-time news media) with its expanding involvement in humanitarian relief and peacekeeping operations. Increasingly, the participation of these actors shifts the locus from the battlefield and the level of conflict to the strategic plane (questions of whether to intervene and, if so, how).[20] Indeed, IW concerns are only one part of a dramatic redefinition of the notion of the boundaries of our national security domain in the post-cold war world.

Complicating this already difficult problem is the rapid evolution (if not revolution) in the nature of the total information infrastructures (data acquisition and storage, computers, communications, decision support systems, etc.) that underlie both military and civilian sectors—a result of the pervasive effects of the information revolution. The military is growing increasingly dependent on information as the core element not only for command and control, but also for the entire range of operations, well beyond the set of special access programs. At the same time, the military is also becoming more reliant on embedded information systems (computers and software) in almost every individual piece of equipment, as well as on massive integrated C^4I systems (such as the Global Command and Control System). These changes are also mirrored in the civilian sector as global telecommunications, and financial systems are introduced side by side with cars, televisions, telephones, and refrigerators that will not run without their embedded information systems. The information revolution is redefining the ways societies—as well as things—function.

As the civilian sectors adopt cutting-edge information technologies, often before the military, the previous reliance by the military on defense-unique C^4I systems and networks is rapidly giving way to adoption of dual-use and COTS systems and networks in which the military is only another customer (and perhaps not even the driving force for innovation). This development significantly alters the types of systems that might be affected by IW, waged even for advantage on the military battlefield. Thus, in this new environment we must be concerned with not only the Defense Information Infrastructure but that of the entire government, as well as the entire National Information Infrastructure and even the Global Information Infrastructure, because all serve as potential entry points to critically sensitive systems. The real impacts of a future with ubiquitous computing, continuous sensor coverage, cheap information, near-infinite bandwidth, high assurance communications, and on-demand encryption have yet to be explicated, much less incorporated into a new paradigm for military thinking.

It would be surprising, therefore, if this revolution did not result in systemic changes to the structures and relationships that we have inherited from the industrial age. The introduction of a widely interconnected and globally networked communications environment, in which companies and national economies routinely control real-time processes and transfer vast sums of resources as well as have access to sensitive information, has redefined the traditional notions of a safe and secure strategic rear. Indeed, as Vice Adm. Arthur Cebrowski has noted, "There is no geography nor sanctuary in cyberspace." Although attacks in the cybersphere do not involve use of physical weapons, their destructive impacts, physical and otherwise, may be no less lethal to nations and societies.

Finally, any taxonomy must contend with the fundamental bifurcation of opinion on the subject between those who emphasize the offensive aspects of IW and those who focus first on protection (or information assurance). Although these facets should be seen as complementary, too often they are viewed as competitors for scarce attention and resources. Those who focus on protection, in fact, concede the awesome potential consequences of the offensive use of IW; but they argue that the United States, as the most advanced information society, is the most dependent on these systems and the most vulnerable to disruption. Therefore, they argue that the most critical need is first to safeguard U.S. information and critical information-related systems from attack, regardless of whether these systems are military or civilian.

A key problem for those focused on protection, however, is that they have, in fact, suggested but cannot yet demonstrate the real consequences as opposed to the theoretical susceptibility or vulnerability to serious disruptions—which is different from recognizing the serious potential consequences to modern societies if destruction of critical systems should occur.[21] Although IW clearly raises the specter of widespread societal disruptions, if not devastation, through attacks on the critical information infrastructures, this threat currently lacks the sparkling clarity of the potential destruction conveyed by nuclear weapons. Indeed, it is important to recognize that there is no "existence proof" that the promised destructiveness of these weapons is real. As a result, it may be difficult to employ strategic IW as a deterrent until these effects are demonstrated with real, and possibly tragic, consequences.[22]

Our reliance on information and on systems dependent on accurate real-time information for our national economic well-being, military power, and effectiveness, as well as our day-to-day individual lives, has dramatically increased in the past decade. The same trends, largely driven by the commercial economics of the information revolution that have accelerated our dependence on these new interconnected systems have, in fact, created a far more robust and potentially more resilient system than existed even a decade or two ago. The breakup of the national telephone monopoly and the collapse of the inhibiting federal regulatory structure; the growth of new television networks (including cable and space-based direct broadcast services); the rapid expansion of cellular, mobile, and long distance services; the explosion of alternate service providers; and the expansion of computer communications networks and the Internet itself all have combined to transform the essential fabric of the information infrastructure that we had known. The vast sums of money tied to the proper functioning of these critical systems would lead one to suspect that, in a properly functioning free-market system, learning from problems and adaptation by evolving to more robust architectures will take place—that measures will be taken to assess and mitigate the most critical risks if only to prevent recurrence. Thus, although the New York Stock Exchange was shut down for three days several years ago because of a fire in an underground cable and computer vault, it would be surprising if appropriate backup systems and procedures have not been introduced to prevent similar systemic disruptions.

A key problem for the offensive-oriented advocates of strategic IW, on the other hand, is that they have not gone beyond the generalized assertions of the potential and potency of IW to do the analytical dirty work necessary to assess these issues in detail—country by country, objective by objective. Thus, there exist no categorizations of effectiveness nor assessments of whether these tools are best employed at the tactical, operational, or strategic level on the battlefield or against the strategic rear of a particular adversary. Thus, the bewildered observer cannot determine whether IW is a potent strategic tool of national power or a modest technical enhancement on the tactical battlefield. Finally, without being able to define or categorize the potential impact of IW, we cannot establish criteria. The debate, therefore, is carried out largely on the basis of anecdote and rhetoric, not by testable propositions supported by facts.

Toward an Analytic Foundation

As noted above, this paper assumes that much of what is common throughout the diverse dimensions of information warfare is the result of new capabilities and impacts provided by the information revolution. Thus, the suggested taxonomy outlined first looks at these impacts of the information revolution on three discrete levels: (1) those affecting the tools of warfare—from appliquéing advanced information technologies on current systems and processes; (2) those affecting the conduct of warfare—by adopting knowledge-based combat in which advanced information systems enable an integrated synthesis of new operational concepts and organizational structures that provide significant increases in combat effectiveness; and (3) those affecting the nature of war—from the transition to the information age that will inevitably alter the objectives for waging war, the entities that conduct it, and its scope and intensity as the fundamental geostrategic environment adapts to the new forces.

These levels clearly form a hierarchy of impacts, from incremental technical enhancements to fundamental alteration of all the dimensions of the geostrategic structure—political, economic, sociocultural, and military. A key in assessing the

Figure 3.
Levels of Impact for IW

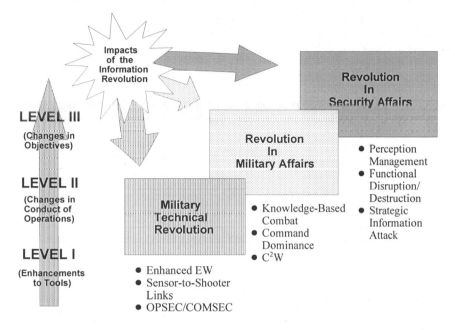

implications of the information revolution for our national security posture is to determine, to the extent that we have a choice, how far up these levels we wish to ascend and exploit it; each successive level requires a greater degree of assimilation of and adaptation to the information revolution in order to capture its potential.

Level I

At this level, the information revolution primarily has an impact on the tools of warfare by overlaying advanced information technologies on current processes, organizations, systems, and equipment. A vast array of individual improvements made possible by enhanced sensors, high-speed digital processing, real-time high-bandwidth communications, worldwide geolocation, and a host of other technology advances has led to increases in the lethality of weapons and significant reductions in the burden of logistics. At this level, only minimal changes are needed to exploit the utility of new information technologies; these enhancements do not require alteration in the way

we conduct our military affairs, but the cost is that we obtain
only an incremental or marginal improvement in effectiveness.
Although these technical improvements may enhance the effectiveness of individual military systems or forces, by itself this
infusion of new technology does not alter the type or character
of the operations they conduct; nor does it necessarily imply
that these improvements will translate into an ability to win
campaigns. Currently most funding for IW-related activities is
concentrated at this level; the army's digitization program is
one prime example. The recent intense concern for protection
against IW threats and information assurance will only result in
even more resources being applied to addressing the existing
threats.

Even major improvements in systems or in overall tactical
effectiveness are not likely to create fundamental changes in perceived military capabilities or in the conduct of operations.
Indeed, one of the benefits of appliquéing new technical capabilities onto existing equipment and concepts is exactly that the
existing paradigm can easily be retained—in reality, the short-
term increases in effectiveness can serve to mask the need for
more fundamental change. To argue that the incremental tactical
impacts at this level can have strategic rather than just tactical
effects requires a logic chain that demonstrates that tactical
lethality necessarily produces strategic victories. For U.S. policymakers, it is unfortunate that there is more evidence that tactical
defeats or the loss of the first battle can produce strategic impacts
redirecting policy (vide 18 dead Rangers in Mogadishu) more
easily than can tactical victories.[23]

Level II

The information revolution also offers opportunities to affect
the conduct of warfare—the overall operational pattern of war.
By adopting new operational concepts and appropriate organizational structures, enabled by new information technologies,
the military could obtain substantial improvements in force
effectiveness and adapt to an environment in which it can no
longer employ the "overwhelming force" paradigm. For example, knowledge-based combat (KBC), in which advanced information systems enable an integrated synthesis of new
operational concepts and organizational structures, could produce effects similar to the impact of blitzkrieg. The U.S. Army
points in this direction with its Force XXI operations, and the

Marines have taken a similar look forward in their *Command and Control: A U.S. Marine Corps Concept Paper*. The purpose of KBC is not merely to know more than the enemy (information domination) but to use the superior knowledge to achieve operationally decisive results from combat by enabling "command dominance"—the ability at the operational level to anticipate and respond effectively, regardless of the opponent's actions; "cycle-time dominance"—the ability at the tactical level to operate inside the enemy's cycle-time; and "phase dominance"—the ability to control relative phase at the time of combat interaction.[24]

Level II impacts go beyond enhancing individual system or force capabilities to employing these new information capabilities to allow real integration of joint forces and operations. Some see a vision of a reconnaissance strike defense complex (RSDC) that would integrate and automate sensors and long-range precision weapon capabilities in order to conduct operations with stand-off strikes. The "system of systems" discussed by Adm. William A. Owens, the vice chairman of the Joint Chiefs of Staff, is also this type of application of new technologies that could engender fundamental changes in operational concepts. The step-function increase in overall force capabilities would be provided by dominant battlespace awareness, a key element of KBC that would result from the ability to bring together and maintain coherence of diverse forces across the extent and throughout the depth of the theater while retaining focus on common operational objectives.[25] These revolutionary capabilities would present opportunities to alter the operational level effectiveness so fundamentally that truly decisive battlespace victories could once again be possible; recovering the ability to win such decisive operational victories on the battlefield would have significant strategic implications.

These benefits, however, cannot be captured by piecemeal adoption of technologies; they demand fundamental alterations in the concepts for prosecuting the operational level of war. For this reason, they are significantly more difficult to introduce and implement than is Level I, especially in an institution that is riding the crest of operational success. These changes, exactly because they are fundamental, threaten all the vested interests and military "rice bowls," from resource allocation, to roles and missions, to the very nature of *command* and how *control* is exercised.

Level III

At this level, impacts from the information revolution would affect the nature of war itself: the objectives for war, the fundamental strategy, the entities that conduct it, and both the scope and the intensity of warfare. These impacts on the nature of war stem not from changes in operational forms or weapons on the battlefield, or changes in the human dimension of conflict. Rather, they stem from basic alteration to the character of the political, economic, and sociocultural fabric in which war occurs—in this case, the transition from an industrial age to an information age. In the information age, in which information or knowledge is explicitly recognized as a key factor endowment on par with the traditional factor endowments of land, labor, and capital (whose seizure or control have been war's historic objectives), information itself may become the objective of conflict.[26] It is at this level that the Tofflers and others have argued that IW, in the form of "netwar," "cyberwar," or "hacker-war," represents a fundamentally different form of warfare than ones waged with primarily physical instruments.[27] If these impacts are real, they clearly portend the most basic changes; and if they are systemic, militaries will be forced to contend with the broad implications of these structural changes in political, economic, and sociocultural factors. Among these changes, for the U.S. military the most salient factors will be the role of the nation-state, the currency of power, the identity and character of IW players, and the objectives for war because they shape both the nature of war and the conduct of warfare.

If the more careful advocates are correct, the key change at this level is to be able to achieve strategically decisive results by operations directly against the strategic rear without having to go through the enemy forces on the battlefield. Indeed, one could argue that this ability will provide decision-makers with a choice between employing new Level II and Level III options in seeking decisive outcomes. As a realm of operations, the infosphere or cyberspace exhibits peculiar properties; despite having a real topology, it has no geography. Physical distances or separations become meaningless; as a result, there are no "denied areas" but also "no sanctuary" in this domain.

Level I activities currently receive the most money but probably the least innovative conceptual thinking (as opposed to analysis). Level III, on the other hand, with its near-science fiction aura and media attention, is the newest and sexiest and not surprisingly is receiving much of the focus, even within the defense community—if both offense and defense are considered—although so far it is mostly promise and little demonstrated performance.

Level II is the place where maximum leverage and benefits could be obtained over the mid- to long term, if conflict between well-armed nation-states remains the norm. Nonetheless, it is the area receiving the fewest resources and least attention. Unfortunately, it is also the level most difficult to implement because it threatens numerous existing constituencies; and these two factors may not be unrelated.

Conclusions

It has been argued here that the term "information warfare" is itself a misnomer, one that covers a broad and extremely diverse array of phenomena linked only loosely by some relationship to information. It would be more useful to consider this array to be one that flows from the "information revolution." The real issue is how we wish to exploit these impacts to affect the characteristics and conduct of warfare. This paper has proposed that, terminologically, we adopt the phrase "conflict in the information age" as the unifying structure. Ultimately we may have no choice but to accept the notion of a broader "revolution in security affairs" arising from the "information revolution" because it will occur outside the military domain and drive inward. In the interim, we have a large number of choices available as to the emphases we select for exploitation. Making these choices correctly demands that we first understand the phenomenology we are attempting to undertake; and, therefore, constructing a rigorous taxonomy appears to be the crucial first step.

Notes

1. This transition should have called into question, for example, modern expositions of Brig. Gen. Gulio Douhet's classic airpower theories and the definition of strategic centers of gravity.

2. Also like the products of the preindustrial artisans and artists, the enhanced value of today's product resides not in its intrinsic physical characteristics but in the infusion of art or information; indeed, what is the value of the physical components of a CD-ROM carrying advanced software.

3. Sun Tzu, *The Art of War*, trans. Samuel B. Griffin (New York: Oxford University Press, 1963).

4. R. V. Jones, *The Wizard War* (New York: Coward, McCann & Geoghegan, Inc., 1978).

5. A number of Third World commentators, in assessing the implications of the Persian Gulf War, noted that any country planning on engaging the United States should not do so on the conventional battlefield but should be prepared to employ nuclear weapons.

6. Alvin and Heidi Toffler, *War and Anti-War* (Boston: Little, Brown, 1993).

7. From a briefing on March 27, 1995, by Barry Horton, principal deputy assistant secretary of defense (PDASD) (C^3I).

8. Chairman, Joint Chiefs of Staff, *Memorandum of Policy (MOP) 30: Command and Control Warfare*, March 8, 1993, p. 3.

9. Unless, of course, it treats command and control (C^2) and C^2W so expansively as to render their definitional utility useless.

10. Indeed, a fundamental split within the IW community revolves around those who view information in a narrow technical (computer science) definition as data and instructions and those who view information as the basic medium for carrying and communicating meaning, in which case both Claude Shannon's work on information theory and Noam Chomsky's on linguistics are at least as relevant as works on computer viruses and "crackers."

11. Air Force Scientific Advisory Board (AFSAB), *Summer Study on Information Architectures*, Summer 1994.

12. For example, the report of the Army Science Board, Summer Study 1994, discussed information as a resource. In the economic understanding of that term, this implies that it is expended during use and that, therefore, there are opportunity costs in using the information when, in many cases, a more appropriate analogy may be that information is a catalyst that is not used up when employed.

13. In these cases, an appropriate analogue for effectiveness of information may be the set of Federal Reserve statistics, such as M1 and M2, that measure the velocity of money and therefore the propulsive effect on economic growth and the economy.

14. A recent incident, for example, involved shutting down the three New York City airports on August 28, 1995 as a result of a telephoned bomb threat against the Westbury Transcontinental On-Route Control Center.

15. I owe this intriguing notion to Maj. Gen. Robert Linhard, USAF.

16. Jon Katz, "Guilty," *Wired*, September 1995, p. 133

17. Winn Schwartau, *Information Warfare* (New York: Thunder Mouth Press, 1994), p. 291. Also see "If War Comes Home," *Time*, August 21, 1995, pp. 44–46, reporting on a government-sponsored wargame highlighting information warfare.

18. Toffler and Toffler, *War*, p. 59

19. George J. Stein, "Information Warfare," *Airpower Journal*, Spring 1995, p. 32

20. As Stein notes, "Information warfare at the strategic level is the 'battle off the battlefield' to shape the political context of the conflict." "Information Warfare," p. 33.

21. The IW analogue to the recent chemical agent incidents against the Tokyo subway system or to the Oklahoma City bombing is not yet in evidence and therefore cannot serve to crystallize or catalyze public recognition that the problem is real. Moreover, despite the tragedy caused by the large number of fatalities in the Oklahoma City case, neither example is a convincing demonstration of consequences fatal to a nation.

22. Almost everyone recognized that significant nuclear exchanges would not simply create local disasters but would be a threat to national or societal survival. Even the extensive damage inflicted by the air campaign against Iraq's infrastructure, however, has not provided a convincing demonstration, an "existence proof," that advanced conventional weapons—despite their obvious precision and lethality—represent a similar threat to a nation's survival. Advocates of information warfare must contend with two absent elements: no single large-scale example of disaster and no demonstration that widespread IW employment would be "fatal" to a nation. Both elements in this causal chain are essential; first, that there is a real possibility of an attack occurring, and second, that the consequences would be as devastating as some commentators have suggested.

23. See Charles E. Heller and William A. Stofft, eds., *America's First Battles, 1775–1965* (Lawrence, Kans.: University of Kansas Press, 1986). Historically, the United States has lost the initial engagement in each war we have fought; fortunately, the expanse of two large oceans and our inherent economic wealth and industrial strength buffered us from the consequences. Even during the cold war, our emphasis was on winning the war, not the first battle. Unfortunately, in the era of Cable News Network coverage and no major "enemy," losing the first battle against a threat perceived as less than to U.S. vital interests may be sufficient for the American public to demand that "the boys be brought home."

24. Jeffrey R. Cooper, *The Coherent Battlefield*, June 1993; and Jeffrey R. Cooper, *Implementing Coherent Operations: A Report to the Deputy Chief of Staff (Operations and Plans), US Army*, September 2, 1994.

25. Jeffrey R. Cooper, *Dominant Battlespace Awareness*, December 12, 1994 (prepared for National Defense University, Institute for National Security Studies).

26. Information is not like land, labor, and capital, which are physical constructs (although today, capital, as a financial instrument, is increasingly represented as transcendental information, while capital, as equipment stock, remains a physical resource). Information is not physical, although it can have physical representation. Information is appropriable; but, like a catalyst, it is rarely consumed in use. These issues, philosophical in nature, have real import for the meaning of conflict in an age in which information is the source of power and economic value-added.

27. See, for example, John Arquilla and David Ronfeldt, "Cyberwar is Coming!" *Comparative Strategy* (April-June 1993): 141–165.

13

Information, Power, and Grand Strategy: In Athena's Camp

John Arquilla and David Ronfeldt

Information has been associated with power, war, and the state since at least the time of the Greek gods. One normally thinks of Ares, or the Roman version Mars, as the god of war. Where warfare is about information, however, the superior deity is Athena—the Greek goddess of wisdom who sprang fully armed from Zeus's head and went on to become the benevolent, ethical, patriotic protectress and occasionally wrathful huntress who exemplified reverence for the state. According to Virgil, for example, Troy would be powerful enough to withstand all its enemies as long as it possessed and honored the Palladium, a sacred statue of Athena provided by Zeus or Athena herself. Understanding this, the Greeks arranged its theft, denying the Trojans the benefits granted by access to the goddess of wisdom. Athena then sided with the Greeks in the Trojan War, where she bested Ares on the battlefield and conceived the idea of the wooden "gift horse" secretly loaded with Greek soldiers. The Trojans, as we all know, made the monumental misjudgment of hauling it inside their fortress walls, over the protestations of the priest Laocoön and the seer Cassandra. The rest is history, and legend.

Ever since, examining the relationship between information and power has attracted all manner of political and military theorists, as indicated by this sampling:

- Sun Tzu observed, more than 2,500 years ago: "Know thy enemy, know yourself; your victory will never be endangered."

- Francis Bacon considered information the key to Elizabethan England's development as a great power: "For the conduct of war . . . in the youth of a state, arms do flourish; in the middle age of a state, learning; and then both of them together."

- Carl von Clausewitz regarded the role of knowledge in warfare as "a factor more vital than any other."

- Michel Foucault, who viewed knowledge and power as inextricably intertwined, considered mapmaking an example of knowing that conveyed juridical, military, and political power: "Once knowledge can be analyzed in terms of region . . . one is able to capture the process by which knowledge functions as a form of power."[1]

What does it mean to believe such statements? Conventionally, it means that something viewed as immaterial and abstract—like a specific piece of information or knowledge—can be put to hard, practical use to strengthen one party over another. The exercise of an actor's power may turn on the possession of such information; it becomes an instrument of power. That conventional view barely begins to probe the depths of meaning in statements that "information is power," however.

In this essay, we offer some observations about the relationship between information and power. Our theme is that information, generally thought to be immaterial, is increasingly seen to be an essential part of all matter. In contrast, power, long thought to be based mainly on material resources, is increasingly seen to be fundamentally immaterial, even metaphysical in nature. As information becomes more material and power more immaterial, the two concepts become more deeply intertwined than ever. These trends may generate some interesting implications for the theory and practice of warfare and for grand strategy in the times ahead.

The assumption that military power and grand strategy will still matter implies that states will still matter and that the international system will remain statecentric in the emerging information age. We believe this to be the case and differ from those who argue that the diffusion of information and the attendant erosion of hierarchy will inexorably weaken states and that a "global village" of nonstate actors may someday even supplant the state system. The information age will surely transform the nature of states in many ways and will probably limit their range of action in many areas unless they cooperate with nonstate actors. Nonetheless, the state will remain vibrant, effective, and desirable as a time-tested form of administrative and political organization for societies, both for those that are still in search of self-determination and sovereignty, and for those, presumably like the United States, that are highly advanced and on the verge of developing additional information-age structures.[2]

The endurance of the state and the state system in the information age will affect the tenets underlying both major schools of international political theory: the realist and the interdependence schools. The statecentric realist school will have to continue recognizing that nonstate actors are multiplying and gaining power, constraining the roles of states in some issue areas. The interdependence school, which has emphasized the rise of nonstate actors, will have to accept that states are going to have significant new political and other instruments at their disposal as a result of the information revolution.[3]

In our view, the "softening" of power and the increasing "tangibility" of information may usher in a new golden age for states. What may be coming to an end, if anything, is not the state or the state system, but rather the empire and imperialism in their classic forms.[4] In the twentieth century, nationalism and other factors, including inherent incompetencies, have dealt a series of sledgehammer blows against empires, the last of which collapsed just a few years ago. The state—in both its nascent and advanced varieties—is the key organization to venture into the vacuums created by the end of the classic empire. There is no orderly alternative.

At the same time, a new model of the state may emerge, probably one that is leaner yet draws new strength from enhanced abilities to coordinate and act in concert with nonstate actors. In this vein, Peter Drucker, after arguing that the classic nation-state metamorphosed into the unwieldy "megastate" in the twentieth century by taking on excessive social, economic, and military duties, concludes that success in the postcapitalist age will require a different model.[5] Other thinkers are also starting to propose that what lies ahead is not the demise but the transformation of the state.[6]

By implication, the skillful exercise of military power and grand strategy may grow in importance in the information age. States are more compact than empires but have smaller margins for error. To do well in the times ahead, they must strive to understand that the nature of information and power, and the interaction between them, may be changing radically.

Three Views of "Information"

Most people think they know "information" when they see it, and any dictionary can provide a working definition. Like any concept that grows in importance, however, it has begun to acquire new meanings and imply new possibilities. It deserves closer scrutiny.

Three general views of information appear in discussions about the information revolution and its implications.[7] Each view approaches the concept differently; each harbors a different perspective of what is important. Two views are widespread: The first considers information in terms of the inherent *message*, the second in terms of the *medium* of production, storage, transmission, and reception. The emerging third view transcends the former two; it speculates that information may be a *physical property*—as physical as mass and energy and inherent in all matter.

Information as Message

The first view is the most ancient, classic, and ordinary; indeed, it is the view found in the dictionary. Reduced to bare essentials, it regards information as an immaterial message or signal that contains meaningful (or at least recognizable) content and that can be transmitted from a sender to a receiver. Such information usually comes in the form of "reports, instructions, and programs."[8]

Figure 1. The "Information Pyramid"

This results in what many analysts call the "information pyramid."[9] (See figure 1.) The pyramid has a broad base of disorganized raw "data" and "facts," atop which sits a stratum of organized "information." The next, still narrower stratum corresponds to information refined into "knowledge." Atop that, at the peak, sits the most distilled stratum, "wisdom"—the highest level of information. A cognitive version would place

"awareness" at the base, "knowledge" above, and "understanding" at the peak.[10]

"Information," then, corresponds to part or all of this pyramid, but the term is usually employed in the latter, expansive
sense. This usage carries some risk of misunderstanding. The
pyramid implies that the higher levels rest on the lower, but that
is true only to a degree. Each layer has some independence—
thus, more data does not necessarily mean more knowledge.
Moreover, critics object sensibly that "information" should not
be mistaken for "ideas."[11]

Nevertheless, the expansive view of information continues
to gain ground and stimulate new insights. In this vein, etholo-
gist Richard Dawkins argues that information comes in varieties:
from discardable old news items to types of information that are
so powerful, so laden with vitality, that they may be deemed
"alive." Thus, the most meaningful information "does not
merely *embody* order; it advances order and maintains it."[12] This
includes not only the biological information in the genetic repli-
cator DNA, but also cultural information (e.g., ideas or fashions)
that gets communicated gene-like in "memes"—a term Dawkins
coined to convey that cultural as well as biological bodies are
based on units of "self-replicating patterns of information":[13]

> Just as genes propagate themselves in the gene pool by leap-
> ing from body to body via sperm or eggs, so memes propa-
> gate themselves in the meme pool by leaping from brain to
> brain via a process which, in the broad sense, can be called
> imitation."[14]

Information as Medium

The second view observes that information relates not just to
the message but, more broadly, to the system whereby a sender
transmits a message to a receiver. This view directs the eye to
the medium of transmission and reception. The key concern is
the ability of a communications system to move signals clearly
and precisely—that is, with low noise, low entropy, and often
high redundancy. In this view, the actual content is irrelevant;
what matters are the encodability and the transmittability of a
message, regardless of its content.[15] This view is more about
communications than knowledge.

This second view gained influence in the 1940s and 1950s
under the rubric of information theory, communication engi-

neering, and statistical mechanics. It was elucidated initially by Claude Shannon, and then by Norbert Wiener, who developed "cybernetics" based on principles of control through feedback. This view then also filtered into the social sciences, helping to stimulate Marshall McLuhan's insight that "the medium is the message."[16] Cybernetics influenced the social and related engineering sciences, particularly with regard to theorizing about decision-making,[17] artificial intelligence, and the design of computers.

Here are two widely praised definitions of information that aptly summarize this second view. The first is by Norbert Wiener, the second by anthropologist-cyberneticist Gregory Bateson:

> Just as the amount of information in a system is a measure of its degree of organization, so the entropy of a system is a measure of its degree of disorganization; and the one is simply the negative of the other.[18]

> The technical term "information" may be succinctly defined as any difference which makes a difference in some later event. This definition is fundamental for all analysis of cybernetic systems and organizations. The definition links such analysis to the rest of science, where the causes of events are commonly not differences but forces, impacts, and the like. The link is classically exemplified by the heat engine, where available energy (i.e., negative entropy) is a function of a difference between two temperatures. In this classical instance, "information" and "negative entropy" overlap.[19]

In similar writings,[20] we see a trend among theorists to equate information with "organization," "order," and "structure"—to argue that embedded information is what makes an object have an orderly structure. As this trend has developed, its emphasis has shifted. At first, in the 1940s and 1950s, information theorists emphasized the concept of "entropy" and were thus concerned with exploiting feedback to improve "control." Now the emphasis has shifted to the concept of "complexity," which has led to a new concern with the "coordination" of complex systems.[21] Control and coordination are different, sometimes contrary processes; indeed, the exertion of excessive control in order to avoid entropy may inhibit the looser, decentralized types of coordination that often characterize advanced forms of complex systems.[22] What James Beniger called the "control revolution"[23] is now turning into what might be better termed a "coordination revolution."

Entropy and complexity look like opposing sides of the same coin of order. About the worst that can happen to embedded information is that it gives way to entropy, that is, the tendency to become disorganized. The best is that it enables an object to grow in efficiency, versatility, and adaptability.

Information and Physical Matter

In the first and second views, information remains basically immaterial in nature, but a third view is emerging that has challenging implications. In this view, information is about much more than message and medium (or content and conduit). It is said that information is as basic to physical reality as are matter and energy—all material objects are said to embody not only matter and energy but also "information." The spectrum for this view runs from modestly regarding information as an output from the behavior of matter and energy; to regarding information as equal in importance to matter and energy in the composition of reality; to regarding information as even more fundamental than matter and energy.[24] Information, then, is an embedded *physical* property of all objects that exhibit organization and structure. This applies to dirt clods as well as DNA strands. New academic fields of study such as information physics and computational physics are emerging around such ideas (while also drawing on the older ideas about information).

One proponent, Tom Stonier, amid a highly speculative, abstruse discourse, sums up the basic idea quite clearly:

> Its main thesis is that "information" is not merely a product of the human mind—a mental construct to help us understand the world we inhabit—rather, information is a [physical] property of the universe, as real as are matter and energy.[25]

A physicist identified with such thinking, Edward Fredkin, reaches further to say that the entire universe is tantamount to a giant computer:

What I'm saying is that, at the most basic level of complexity, an information process runs what we think of as physics. At the much higher level of complexity, life, DNA—you know, the biochemical functions—are controlled by a digital information process. Then, at another level, our thought processes are basically information processing.[26]

The views of information as message and medium persist but are embedded in a view that all matter and energy in the universe are not only based on information but designed to process and convey it. Information is the prime mover. Both order and "chaos" depend on it.

This line of thinking is not confined to physics. Social theorist Kenneth Boulding remarked that matter and energy "are mostly significant as encoders and transmitters of information."[27] In other words, the organization and the complexity of all objects, including social objects, reflect and depend upon their informational content and processing capabilities.

This third view remains odd and unclear but quite intriguing. If it proves a cutting edge rather than a fringe view, it may yet lead to analytic paradigms of as much explanatory power as the first two views. This essay assumes it has some validity; from it we can point out some remarkable implications for military doctrine and strategy, as discussed later.

Parallel Views of Power

Volumes have been written about the concept of power—far more than about the concept of information. Yet, despite those volumes, power is never easy to define—as is the case with information. We do not attempt a definition.[28] Rather, what is notable here is that three views of power can be discerned that parallel the three views of information—but with a reverse twist.

Our characterization is reminiscent of Kenneth Boulding's analysis of the triune nature of power, which he classified respectively into its destructive, productive, and integrative dimensions.[29] The three views we discern treat power as being material, organizational (or systemic), and finally immaterial in nature. Whichever strategic realm one is analyzing—political, economic, or military—has material, organizational, and immaterial ideational bases.

Power as Resources

The most basic view regards power in terms of the possession of resources and capabilities that can be used to coerce or otherwise control or influence a nation or some other actor. These are typically tangible material resources and capabilities like petroleum, weaponry, industrial capacity, or manpower. They may also be less tangible, as in the possession of liquid financial assets or of an office or instrument endowed with legitimate authority. In many respects, this is a natural, even instinctive, view of power and may be the most ancient of the three views.

This view undergirds most geopolitical analyses. As Inis Claude observed, the power of the nation-state consists of "essentially military capability—the elements which contribute directly or indirectly to the capacity to coerce, kill, and destroy."[30] In more formal academic terms, this view has found expression in the widely used "composite capabilities index," which consists of military, industrial, and demographic factors grouped around the size of armed forces and military budgets, steel production and industrial fuel consumption, and total population, particularly the urban portion.[31]

Power as Organization

A second view looks at power in terms of how it is "mediated"—how a people, nation, or other actor or system is organized to use the resources and capabilities at its disposal. This view emphasizes that power is a function or a reflection of the design and performance of a social system, whatever its resource base. Thus, even a nation that lacks many physical resources, like Japan, may still become very powerful, as proved by its rise to the first rank of nations in the early twentieth century.

This view has classical roots,[32] but its proponents are mainly contemporary. The pathbreaking studies of administrative behavior in the 1950s illuminated the fact that power depends on organization.[33] (Some of these studies led the way in showing how organizational designs are basically about the structure of communications channels and information flows.) More recent theorists have repeatedly observed that power does not exist in the absence of relationships; "power is a relation among people, not an attribute or possession."[34] Resources matter in this view, but just how depends on the identity, reputation, location, and other relational attributes of the actor or system that has (or lacks) those resources.

The importance of organization for power is noticeable throughout history. Consider the evolution centuries ago from tribes to states—that is, from kinship to hierarchy as the dominant form of societal organization. States, molded around centralized institutions like monarchies and armies, emerged far more powerful than tribes, which, in their classic form, could barely conduct collective agriculture much less administer conquered tribes.[35] By the eighteenth century, state institutions proved less capable than competitive market actors at processing complex commercial transactions and energizing industrial development. Today, a fourth major form of organization is on the rise: information-age multiorganizational networks. They are proving "powerful"—more so than the tribal, hierarchical, and market forms—for dispersed civil-society actors, like human rights groups, who want to share information, coordinate strategies, and act jointly.[36]

In addition, consider whether democratic or authoritarian (or totalitarian) systems are better designed for asserting power. The debates about this question are increasingly resolved in favor of democratic systems over the long run.[37] Here again, power is seen to depend on organizational structures.

Overall, this view implies that power, much like information, is mediated; power's significance (i.e., its meaning) is affected by the medium of expression, by the system of generation and transmission. Moreover, this view implies that power, again like information, is the antithesis of entropy but potentially subject to it.

Power as Immaterial

The third view moves even further from the resources view. It looks at power as depending on deep psychological, cultural, and ideational structures; it makes "the power of power" virtually metaphysical. Power becomes more like a message embedded in the air than a raw material raised from the ground. Exactly what constitutes power under this third view is often unclear, especially in the more abstract, speculative versions. In the more grounded versions, it is not entirely separable from the first and second views.

In some respects, this too is a classical view of power. It is well recognized that nationalism and ideology may be sources of power. For example, aerial bombing campaigns—a maximalist assertion of material power—have often failed (e.g., Britain, Germany, Vietnam) to break a resolute people's willpower. Among scholarly theorists and strategists, Hans Morgenthau's expansive definition of national capabilities included ideological and morale factors.[38] For Joseph Nye, the current era is one of the "reduced tangibility" of power, and the rise in importance of its "softer" side.[39]

This view of power receives some of its deepest articulations in modernist philosophizing. From a Marxist perspective, Antonio Gramsci's views regarding "hegemonic" ideologies and media fall into this category.[40] From a different perspective, Friedrich Nietzsche built the body of his philosophy on the notion that power was created as an act of will and that this "will to power" lay at the root of prevailing ethical-legal systems.[41] Michel Foucault, as noted earlier, was a major exponent of the notion that ideas convey power, making him in some ways a direct heir of Georg Wilhelm Friedrich Hegel's notions to similar effect.[42]

The appeal of the immaterialist view of power appears to be spreading among speculative thinkers of the information age. Indeed, in many respects, it is a view attuned to the information age.[43]

A Summing Up

These three views of power, rotated against the three views of information, lead to a matrix of possible combinations, as depicted in figure 2. Three cells are notable for this essay. The one where power and information are viewed in their most traditional senses—where power depends on material capabilities, and information is but a useful adjunct—pertains to Mars, the Roman god of war. We identify Athena, the Greek goddess of warrior wisdom, with the far cell where power and information are viewed in postmodern, information-age senses—where information becomes physical and power immaterial, and the two dynamics merge. In between, on the diagonal, is a cell where sociosystemic views of both information and power coincide; this may well be where many people stand today, people who are trying to think about information and power together— and who may not be aware yet of the Athena cell.

A military force whose doctrine is built around an Athenan view should be able to defeat one built around a systems con-

Figure 2.   Views of Information and Power Combined

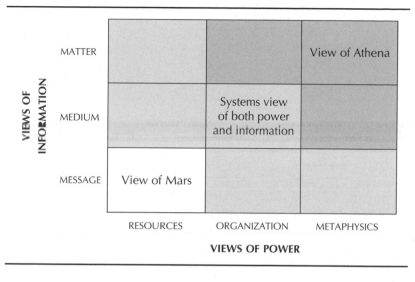

cept; and it in turn should be able to defeat one built around a Mars view. Although we have not discussed each cell in the matrix, in general a cell should represent a stronger approach than any cell beneath and/or to the left of it. This is roughly indicated by the shading—the darker the shading, the more potent the cell. This depiction parallels Martin Van Creveld's view of military history, wherein he traces the evolution of war in terms of its basis first on the tools and materials of war, second on systems of warfare, and third on information-based technologies like the computer.[44]

Which views or blends of information and power one prefers affects how one thinks about the implications for warfare. In the remainder of this essay, we presume that thinking about information and power is moving in the "Athenan" direction, where Fredkin's views may meet with Foucault's. Our intent is to tease out the implications for doctrine and strategy.

Implications for Military Doctrine and Strategy

The U.S. military is in the early decades of its own information revolution, and information warfare has become the cutting edge of a "revolution in military affairs" (RMA). Yet, what information means for military theory and practice is much in debate. The evolution in thinking about information and power discussed above matches up with an evolution that is under way in military circles. Military thinking is moving from a traditional Mars-like view that says information has always been important for particular aspects of warfare—e.g., signals; intelligence; command, control, communications, and intelligence (C^3I); and psychological warfare—and, seeing that those aspects are becoming more salient, is moving toward a new Athena-like view that says information is a bigger, deeper concept than traditionally presumed. Information should be treated as a basic and overarching dynamic of all theory and practice about warfare in the information age.

This is a dramatic, contentious shift. The quest for new concepts has created new analytical problems and new bureaucratic and budgetary tangles—and opportunities. Many leading intellectuals grappling with information-age issues affecting the military—C. Kenneth Allard, Carl Builder, Jeffrey Cooper, Martin Libicki, Thomas Rona, George Stein, Col. Richard Szafranski, and Alvin and Heidi Toffler, among others—have one or both feet planted in the newer, broad view of Athena's camp.[45] Many operators and practitioners, however, remain firmly rooted in the older, narrow view.

Which view prevails may make a difference bureaucratically as well as militarily. In some versions of the narrow view, there is a tendency to make information warfare mean little more than computer warfare and to treat it more as an intelligence activity than as a military activity. This in turn reduces the scope of issues to little more than security and safety in cyberspace. This is an important topic, to be sure, but an overemphasis on it could lead to the notion that one should improve the U.S. government's ability to control society at large, even if this means making society more closed than open under some scenarios. We share John Rothrock's concern that some interpretations of information warfare could

> require fundamental changes in how we understand conflict
> and the appropriate responses of our society to it. . . . Does
> our society want to be the sort that is adept at the degree and
> types of control of information that some of the more enthu-
> siastic advocates of Information Warfare seem to presume?[46]

The Athenan view of information and power implies that it is advisable to develop a broad vision of information warfare, partly because this kind of warfare is inherently multidimensional and partly because a broad vision should prove less susceptible to authoritarian tendencies.

A Force Reformer as well as Force Multiplier

It was said that the new information technology provided a force multiplier for U.S. forces in the Gulf War.[47] Armed with more and better information, the U.S.-led coalition swiftly defeated a large enemy field army in a very short time and at astonishingly low cost in terms of casualties. Yet, putting the emphasis on a quantitative point—the multiplier effect—overlooks a deeper qualitative point: Information is also a force modifier, a force reformer.

Making full use of today's information revolution implies not only adopting new technologies but also rethinking the very bases of military organization, doctrine, and strategy. All this requires reformulation in order to fulfill Clausewitz's exhortation that "knowledge must become capability"[48] in the information age. The information revolution is not simply technological in nature; it has powerful conceptual and organizational dimensions as well. The new meanings of power and information discussed earlier favor the argument that wars and other conflicts in the information age will revolve as much around organizational as technological factors.[49]

There are both entropy and complexity issues here. A doctrinal implication of the Athenan view is that "entropy" replaces Clausewitz's "friction" as a concern in warfare. The latter concept was attuned to the pre- and early industrial ages, when forces, however well-organized, faced inevitable shocks and delays that caused action in war to resemble Clausewitz's notion of "moving in a resistant element."[50] A post-machine age is dawning where friction will no longer be quite the right concept. A key goal will be minimizing one's own vulnerability to disruption and disorganization—that is, to entropy—while fostering it in an enemy's systems. The strength of a system will be a function not only of how much mass, energy, and information it embodies, but also of how vulnerable or resistant it is to "entropizing."

The U.S. military is thinking about this concept. One example is Horizon, an effort to ensure compatibility among all information systems in the U.S. military. According to Lt. Gen. Carl O'Berry,

[Horizon] brings order out of something that until now has been an atmosphere of entropy. For the first time we have taken interoperability to the domain of science instead of emotion. I'm taking the guesswork out of C^{4}I [command, control, communications, computers and intelligence] systems architecture.[51]

As the information revolution develops further, the notion of how complex, or ecologically diverse, a system is in terms of not depending too much on any single form or principle of organization seems likely to grow in importance. A key question is whether hierarchical or networked systems are more robust in the face of disruptive campaigns. Hierarchy is the traditional form of military organization, and a hierarchical core remains de rigueur. Yet, a body of evidence from the wars of the twentieth century suggests that hierarchies, once compromised, often collapse swiftly. The fall of France in 1940 and the defeat of Iraq in 1991 offer perhaps the best examples of this phenomenon. In contrast, the networked organizational style of guerrilla fighters during the same half century suggests the fighters' tremendous robustness in the face of even the sternest countermeasures. The Vietnam War provides the best example of a networked insurgency withstanding everything the U.S. hierarchy threw at it.

The interplay between having complexity but not displaying it harks back to the sage doctrinal dispensations of Sun Tzu, who likens an army to flowing water and advises that

the ultimate in disposing one's troops is to be without ascertainable shape. Then the most penetrating spies cannot pry in nor can the wise lay plans against you.[52]

New Definitions of Weapons and Targets

Information-age warfare implies various shifts in the nature of weapons systems and their targets. One is a shift from using lethal material weaponry (e.g., tanks, planes, or ships) to attack material targets, toward using such weaponry to also attack cyberspace-related targets like C^{3}I and intelligence, surveillance, and reconnaissance systems (ISR) and communications networks that have no firepower but represent an enemy's electronic sensory organs, nervous system, or brain. Another aspect of the shift is the use of nonlethal electronic techniques (weapons?) to disable an enemy's lethal systems or its cyberspace systems that store, process, and transmit information. This use of nonlethal weapons to disable lethal systems may constitute something of a historical watershed, as it allows the possibility of effectively disarming without having to kill an adversary. Previously, nonlethals have been tightly coupled with lethal systems, with the former paving the way for the more efficient use of the latter.

The previous discussion of power and information raises a number of speculative, challenging implications, especially if the increasing materiality of information is adopted as a framework.

This third view of information—that it is a physical property—would treat *all* military systems as being based on, if not composed of, information. This curiously implies that information may be viewed as something that, like mass and energy, can be literally hurled at an enemy. Warfare has long revolved around who can hurl the most mass—as in the aptly named *levée en masse* of the Napoleonic era, or the human wave assaults on the western front in World War I and the eastern front in World War II. In the nuclear age, the emphasis shifted to hurling energy, as exemplified by the shock waves and radiation released by the splitting or fusing of atoms in bombs. Victory depended not only on directing mass or energy to deplete an enemy's war-fighting stocks, but also on keeping that enemy from hurling mass and energy at oneself, and on being able to absorb and recover from whatever mass and energy it did hurl.

If information is a physical property, then in the information age winning wars may depend on being able to hurl the most information at the enemy while safeguarding against retaliation. This notion would affect how we think about all manner of weapons systems. Compare, for example, round shot fired from an eighteenth-century smoothbore cannon, to a shell fired from a modern rifled artillery barrel, to a new wire-guided antitank missile. How do they rate, relatively, in terms of mass, energy, and information? The mass of each may be about the same, but the energy each represents differs greatly. More to the point, each consists of different materials organized in dissimilar ways. Each sums up a very different set of sciences and technologies. Thus, each represents a radically different embodiment of not only mass and energy but also information to hurl at an enemy. The one that represents the most information—the missile—is the most effective. As these systems exemplify, a historical progression has occurred in the amount of information that can be hurled by weapons.

The Athenan view of information and power implies targeting whatever represents or embodies the most information on an enemy's side. In a war, this means ascertaining and attacking the most information-rich components of an adversary's order of battle; to do otherwise may be to court defeat. An example appears in the Falklands War, where the Argentine air force (FAA) chose to attack the British warships that were most capable of hurling mass in shore bombardments, seriously neglecting the transports that moved mass, energy, and information supplies. Some observers hold that this targeting mistake cost Argentina the war.[53] This point also applies to operations other than war. For example, an implication for counternarcotics operations is to attack traffickers' electronic funds transfers and other financial transactions, rather than trying to chase smugglers or eradicate drug crops that represent lower information content.[54]

Three decades ago Marshall McLuhan concluded, in his own way, that hurling information at an enemy made sense:

> Since our new electric technology is not an extension of our bodies but of our central nervous systems, we now see all technology, including language, as a means of processing experience, a means of storing and speeding information. And in such a situation all technology can plausibly be regarded as weapons. Previous wars can now be regarded as the processing of difficult and resistant materials by the latest technology, *the speedy dumping of industrial products on an enemy market to the point of social saturation.*[55]

The Rising Importance of Social and Human Capital

The Athenan view implies an increased importance and capability for hurling messages and memes at an adversary's society through propaganda, psychological operations,[56] "public diplomacy,"[57] "knowledge strategies,"[58] and even "neo-cortical warfare."[59] As the information age advances, many if not all dimensions of international interaction may be subject to information-influencing strategies. An information offensive aimed at an enemy might seek to deter and dissuade a belligerent society without having to destroy its armed forces. In this, strategic information warfare would resemble prior systems, from strategic bombing to countervalue nuclear targeting.

The oft-voiced notion that war is moving toward a largely automated and robotic future is overstated.[60] From the Athenan viewpoint, the information age will raise the value of social and human capital, as man remains the purest, richest information-hurling system. In the words of pulp cinema icon John Rambo, "the mind is the greatest weapon." The rising importance of human capital clearly applies to the skillful training and deployment of information-age warriors.

The importance of human capital may be seen not only in the technical skills of warriors, but also in the continued surfacing of "true believers" ready to act indiscriminately and murderously in the name of some blind faith. To take a term from Dawkins, such fanatics and martyrs amount to "memoids"—people who are so possessed by a meme that they can justify any deed, while feeling that neither their own nor their opponents' survival matters as long as the meme goes forward.[61] In a sense, a memoid's power as capital for his or her cause, and for hurling information at an enemy, stems from total possession by a belief system and accompanying attitudes.

New Assessment Methodologies Needed

If these speculations are worth pursuing, a generation of new assessment methodologies is needed. The challenges for development may include new methods for analyzing the "information quotient"[62] of weapons and other military systems, for describing an "information order of battle," and for analyzing an enemy's intentions, capabilities, and vulnerabilities—in short, for doing a net assessment. It may turn out that a new language must be devised, lest we overburden that already overused term "information." If the concept of information continues to gain significance, a new academic discipline may be advisable.[63] New centers and schools are already being established for the U.S. military that will help address such challenges. The question might also be addressed as to what an "information war room" would look like.

As we in the United States grapple to define our own concepts, we should keep an eye on how information may be defined in other societies and cultures that are trying to gain advantages from the information revolution. To some extent, our nation should aim to identify concepts to which others can relate and that may thus serve as bases for future alliances and other forms of cooperation, where relevant. We should also seek knowledge of others in order to develop early warning signs of potential adversaries, including nonstate adversaries, who may invent concepts that are unusually difficult for us to counter. This may be particularly the case with "neo-cortical"[64] or psychological and cultural aspects of warfare.[65]

Game Analogies: Chess/**Kriegspiel** and Go

As in the past, war and other modes of conflict in the information age will continue to bear resemblances to the game of chess, but such conflicts will increasingly take on characteristics of the "double-blind" chess variant *kriegspiel*, and of the oriental game *Go*. A refinement of chess and *kriegspiel*, so that one's own side has sight of both one's own and one's opponent's pieces but the opponent can see only his own pieces, offers an analogy for military "cyberwar," or conducting military operations according to information-related principles. A similar refinement of *Go*, so that, again, one's own side sees all pieces but the opponent sees only his own pieces, is an analogy for social and other types of "netwar," or conflict and crime at the societal level wherein the protagonists use network forms of organization and doctrines, strategies, and technologies that are information related.[66]

In chess, each side lines up its pieces in assigned positions on opposite sides of the game board. Thus, the two sides face off across a front line. Then, each side maneuvers in ways that are generally designed to fight for control of the board's center, to shield one's valuable pieces from being taken, to use combinations of pieces selectively to threaten and capture the opponent's pieces, and ultimately to achieve checkmate (decapitation) of the one-and-only king. Warfare before World War II was often like this and, indeed, frequently continued to retain this linear flavor up through the Persian Gulf War.

For the age of cyberwar, a modified *kriegspiel* analogy is more apt. *Kriegspiel* is based on chess, but the game is operationally distinct. Each player has his own board and arrays his pieces as in chess. A screen to block vision stands between the two boards, manned by a monitor (referee). Thus, once the game starts, each player knows where he has moved his pieces but cannot see where the other side moves. The monitor signals when contact has been made. Then, whoever is next gets to choose whether to take the contacted piece or make another move. He does not see what piece he may take until he has taken it, and it is handed to him by the monitor. Throughout the game, each side speculates but rarely knows which of the opponent's pieces are where. The game revolves around information vacuums and uncertainties. A premium is placed on deception. Indeed, a player who opens with classic chess moves and strategies—e.g., controlling the center—is likely to lose. The edges of the board may become more important for maneuver than the center.

The aim of cyberwar is for our side (the United States) to play chess—to have full sight of our own and the opponent's pieces—while forcing the opponent to play *kriegspiel*, at best knowing the location only of the opponent's own pieces, and maybe not even that. In this analogy, both sides start with similar mass and energy—the same set of pieces—at their disposal. We, therefore, have an enormous informational advantage—what David Gelernter calls "topsight" [67]—and because of this, each of our pieces is well informed. This advantage means we should not require as many pieces to win; we might even be able to achieve checkmate without taking many of the opponent's pieces. The Gulf War was, in some respects, rather like this and marks a watershed in the transition from traditional attritional warfare to a new generation of information-age warfare.

The game of *Go* provides a better analogy for netwar. This game starts with an empty board. It looks like a vast, gridlike chess board with lots of tiny squares. Each side takes turns placing pieces called "stones" anywhere on the board, one by one. The stones are placed not in the squares as in chess, but on the points where the grid lines intersect. All stones are alike—there is no king to decapitate, and no queen or other specialization. Once placed, a piece cannot move; it can only be removed if surrounded and captured according to the rules. In this game, taking pieces has secondary importance. The goal is to surround and hold more territory than one's opponent. Once emplaced, a piece exerts a presence in that part of the board, making it easier for the player to place additional pieces on nearby points in the process of surrounding territory. As a result, there is almost never a front line, and the major battles are less for control of the center than for the corners and sides (because they are easier to box off).

Thus, *Go*, in contrast to chess, is more about distributing one's pieces than about massing them. It is more about proactive insertion and presence than about maneuver. It is more about deciding where to stand than whether to advance or retreat. It is more about developing web-like links among nearby stationary pieces than about moving specialized pieces in combined operations. [68] It is more about creating networks of pieces than about protecting hierarchies of pieces. It is also less linear than chess. Thus, *Go* is more like social, criminal, and revolutionary forms of low-intensity conflict than like full-scale military war. It might even be said that the forces of North Vietnam and the Viet Cong played *Go* while U.S. forces tried to play chess.[69] Finally, in line with this notion of *Go's* tie with irregular warfare, the game's tactics are very unforgiving of efforts either to build fortifications or to seize unclaimed territory. Bastions or redoubts are subject to implosive attacks that bring them down from within, while "ground-taking Go"[70] is entirely predictable, allowing a smart adversary to ambush these strung-out forces, defeating them in detail.

The metaphoric possibilities for netwar deepen if one imagines combining *Go* with the key characteristic of *kriegspiel*: the screen that obstructs sight. Again, presume that one side has full knowledge of its own and the opponent's array, but the opponent can see only its own pieces until contact is made with an opposing piece. The dynamics of *Go* differ from those of chess/ *kriegspiel*, but the point still stands: Both sides start play with virtually equivalent mass and energy at their disposal, but the side with topsight has far more information. Thus, it should win handily over a blinded player and require (or need to risk) far fewer pieces to do so.

It might be illuminating to run experiments about this point, not only to test its validity, but also to see whether a minimum essential force size can be defined that invariably wins at chess/ *kriegspiel* or *Go* as long as its side has topsight and the other side is blinded. The experiment could vary the amount of information available to either side, in order to see what types and thresholds of information may make the most difference. To refer back to the "information pyramid," it might be found that a game will turn in favor of whoever has better knowledge and wisdom, as long as both sides have full view of the board. The more one side is blinded, however, the more the game may turn on simply who has the most data and information in the narrow senses.

In addition, it might be illuminating to identify a series of cases where apparently small, weak military forces effectively defeated or defended against what appeared to be much larger, stronger forces. The offensive skill of the Mongol "hordes" of Genghis Khan (which were anything but hordes) comes to mind, as do the strategically defensive campaigns waged by the Royal Air Force and related elements in the Battle of Britain, and by hard-pressed U.S. Navy forces up through the Battle of Midway during the Pacific War.

There are always many explanations why a smaller, weaker force wins—but a crucial constant may be superior intelligence and communications, be that because of fast scouts on horseback (the Mongol case), breakthroughs in radar and cryptography (the British and American cases), or other technological and organizational innovations. Indeed, a historical study could help illuminate not only the importance of the information factor, but also the extent to which it depends on correctly combining the technological and organizational dimensions of innovation. Such a study, along with the gaming experiment proposed above, might offer lessons for whether and how the United States could move to develop military forces that may seem lighter and leaner yet are more effective than those of any potential rival in the information age.

Implications for Grand Strategy

According to tradition, power considerations drive strategic choices, and grand strategy consists of the "knitting-together" of a nation's political, economic, and military resources and capabilities in pursuit of its overall aims.[71] Indeed, the major dimensions of grand strategy have long been the political, economic, and military ones—anything else has been deemed secondary, significant only as it affected the major dimensions. Information and related technologies and systems play mainly a supporting role in this tradition.

Even while information is generally deemed a subsidiary factor, it sometimes has transformative effects. Examples abound throughout history. With regard to political power, one need only look at the effect the printing press had on society. Aside from being a catalyst of the Renaissance, the printed word succeeded in empowering individuals and states in ways previously unknown.[72]

In economic affairs, the letter of credit, well known and widely used in Roman times as an instrument for conveying information about the creditworthiness of a borrower or purchaser, allowed for a range and velocity of commercial transactions that exceeded anything seen prior to its invention. Partly because of this instrument, the eastern Roman empire, which focused on the accumulation of wealth and the construction of extensive financial and trade networks, outlived its western counterpart, which denigrated commercial affairs in favor of conquest, by a thousand years.[73]

An early example of information serving to enhance military power was the appearance of the written word, a few millennia prior to the invention of the printing press. This innovation enabled the preparation of complex orders and the delegation of tactical and, eventually, operational command functions. As a result, larger armed forces could be mobilized and deployed effectively in combat. Extended operations by larger forces made the command and control function ever more important, a trend that continued with the advent of the telegraph, telephone, and radio and remains unabated in the current revolution in military affairs.[74]

Thus, the political, economic, and military building blocks of grand strategy may depend increasingly on information to realize their power potential. From its historically subsidiary position, information is now being moved into a transcendent, if not independent, role.[75] As the information revolution progresses and its conceptual and policy implications expand, information is increasingly seen to have overarching, transforming significance for all the dimensions of power and strategy. Once again three views emerge: the traditional one, that information is a subsidiary aspect of the three major dimensions of grand strategy, is being succeeded by the contemporary view that information has transcendent, overarching effects on these dimensions, while a third view gaining strength is that information (and communications) should be developed independently as a fourth major dimension of grand strategy. These three views connect to the matrix in figure 2. For example, current thinking about information as having modifying effects on the traditional dimensions of strategy corresponds to the middle cell on the diagonal between the Mars and the Athena cells. As power and information become more fused under the Athenan view, it may become a moot point as to which drives strategy. Indeed, as this fusion occurs, it may become advisable to move toward the view that information is a distinct dimension.

In our view, information should now be considered and developed as a distinct fourth dimension of national power—an element in its own right, but still one that, like the political, economic, and military dimensions, functions synergistically to improve the value and effects of the others. Table 1 provides a glimpse of the various ends and means of grand strategy, taking

Table 1. American Grand Strategy: Ends and Means

Dimensions	Ends	Means
Political	Spread of democracy	Treaties, alliances
Economic	Growth of free markets	Sanctions, subsidies, trade, GNP increases
Military	Two-war capability	Armed services
Informational	Open access and connectivity	Telecommunications, the media, public diplomacy

its cues on ultimate aims from President Clinton's doctrine of democratic enlargement.[76]

Given the explosive growth in the means of communication in recent years versus the inherent constraints on the use of either force or economic coercion, it may well be that policymakers will increasingly want to resort to information strategies before or instead of more traditional approaches to statecraft.[77] The preference for informational means may be even more pronounced in situations dealing with friends or allies, as opposed to adversarial crises. One can see the difference in the Persian Gulf region, where hostility to the Iraqi regime has led U.S. policy to rely on economic and limited military pressure to try to compel a democratizing change. In contrast, Saudi Arabia, a close but nondemocratic U.S. ally, faces neither economic nor military pressure to liberalize, and political pressure is muted. Informationally, however, the United States has supported the sale, by AT&T, of a cellular communications network of enormous bandwidth. This could give Saudi citizens hitherto unknown capacities for interconnectivities, both domestically and internationally, that may unleash vibrant democratizing possibilities.

With regard to inferences to be drawn from table 1, it is important to point out that, while one might pursue, say, some political ends by political means, it is not necessary to proceed in such a symmetrical fashion. For example, the political goal of democratizing Haiti was pursued by means that included strong elements of economic and military coercion.

Similarly, the ability to win two regional wars nearly simultaneously will rely, no doubt, on a variety of means in addition to

U.S. armed forces, including financial and manpower contributions from allies, as occurred in the recent Gulf War. U.S. strategy has, in recent years, focused on the use of economic leverage in pursuit of political ends. The limits of economic power can also be glimpsed, however, in the frequent failure of sanctions as a tool of coercive diplomacy. The stout resistance of the impoverished, from Cuba to North Korea, suggests important constraints on this aspect of grand strategy.

Finally, we also hypothesize that, in its integrative functions, information will serve more usefully, and be less attenuated, than the other dimensions of national power. Thus, where a good economy is not always connected to a first-rate military, the likelihood that armed forces endowed with dominant informational capacities will perform poorly is remote. Examples of the often weak connections between political, economic, and military means abound. With regard to the economic-military connection, many prosperous nations and empires from Rome onward have suffered military decline despite their wealth, leading to their defeat by economically backward opponents.[78] Information, however, has integrative effects on the political, economic, and military aspects of power that are both robust and persistent.

The other side of this notion is that, as beneficial as information is, the lack of it may have equally serious negative impact on state power. With this in mind, we turn briefly to the cold war as a period that allows for some testing of this hypothesis. Given its recent conclusion, this case certainly meets the standards of relevance to the analytic issue at hand. Also, it affords a "tough test," as both leading actors—the United States and the Soviet Union— had throughout their rivalry large economies and militaries and stable political institutions. To understand fully the collapse of one and the triumph of the other, one must become aware of the deep and enduring effects that information had on the national power and grand strategies of both rivals.

The Cold War as an Information-Based Conflict

The cold war affords a laboratory for assessing the relationships between information and national power. For more than 40 years, an "open system" rich with information—the United States—strove to prevent the domination of the international community by a "closed system" whose grand strategy was often aimed at preventing the generation and dissemination of information. The protracted struggle between these contending systems resulted in triumph for the nation whose levers of power and suasion enjoyed the higher information content—politically, economically, and militarily.

At the political level, for example, the United States mobilized for the long struggle by disseminating information and debating it openly. The decision to pursue a strategy of containment occurred after extensive public discussion, including the notable exchanges between George Kennan and Walter Lippmann. Indeed, Kennan's "long telegram" became the principal instrument for mobilizing the national will and guiding overall policy.[79]

Throughout the cold war, U.S. political strategy held to the notion that the truth would, as the Bible suggests, "set you free." Thus were born the United States Information Agency, Radio Free Europe, Radio Liberty and Radio Martí, among others. The Soviet Union, on the other hand, adopted a contrary political strategy: It restricted access to information and to technologies like the typewriter, both at home and abroad. If information could not be suppressed, propaganda and other dictatorial measures served to control and reshape its meaning in ways congenial to the Kremlin's interests. As the cold war played out, openness proved a more viable instrument of political power, while efforts at suppression only postponed the eventual eruption of demand for information. The policy of openness, or glasnost, enacted during the tenure of Mikhail Gorbachev, came too late to prevent the political implosion whose effects still bedevil Russia.

In the economic realm, similar forces were at work. The United States led an international coalition of states in pursuit of commercial openness, principally via the General Agreement on Tariffs and Trade. To counter this promarket system, the Soviet Union cobbled together a competing system, the Council on Economic Cooperation (COMECON), that aimed at the centralized control of all economic information and transactions throughout the satellite states of the Soviet imperium. Because the two systems had little to do with each other, their economic competition offers a clear test of open and closed information systems in the economic sphere also. The outcome of this "test" is well known. The open, informationally driven system brought its bloc a level of economic prosperity unrivaled in history. The closed system presided over the deepening impoverishment of its denizens, fomenting their eventual revolt.

In the arena of military competition, a similar pattern emerges. The United States and its allies developed flexible doctrines, strategies, and weaponry that emphasized the importance of information. This drive reached its apotheosis with the advent of precision-guided munitions (PGMs), which were seen as a way to defend against a conventional Soviet attack with superior numbers. Meanwhile, the Soviet Union pursued an overall strategy based on massing the greatest amount of firepower possible. This meant bigger weapons, including nuclear missiles, whose destructive power, it was hoped, would offset the vitiating factor of their relatively greater inaccuracy. In the conventional realm, the Soviet style relied, in traditional fashion, on attrition, even within the context of adopting many of the tenets of mechanized warfare.[80] The one protracted conflict in which the Red Army did fight during the cold war, in Afghanistan, featured the defeat of Soviet brute force strategies by an indigenous resistance, the mujahidin, who turned the tide of victory with the information-laden Stinger missile.

Afghanistan aside, the cold-war nuclear rivalry provides perhaps an even better contrast of the two styles. The United States strove for highly accurate delivery systems and actually reduced megatonnage substantially (by more than 40 percent) during the last two decades of the cold war. This accuracy also allowed for the development of a "counterforce" nuclear strategy that provided, possibly, a way never to have to implement a declaratory policy that threatened to hold Soviet civilians hostage to big, inaccurate, city-busting warheads.[81] The Soviets simply could not match U.S. advances in accuracy and had to maintain larger, more destructive weapons and a declaratory policy of all-out nuclear war.[82]

Finally, it is important to note that information also facilitated synergies *among* these basic dimensions of national power and grand strategy. A notable example appears in the market system's ability to foster, along with business wealth and investment capital, a multitude of innovations in defense technology. The Soviets, on the other hand, generated less capital with their suppressive central control mechanisms and innovated little. Thus, they could sustain the competition neither quantitatively nor qualitatively.

As the information revolution gained strength in the closing decades of the cold war, the "open" societies of the West proved better suited than the "closed" societies of the East to take advantage of the new technologies and to adapt to the challenges they posed to established concepts of sovereignty and governance. Moreover, the deliberate fostering of information and communications flows proved a powerful instrument for compelling closed societies to open up. Thus, U.S. Secretary of State George Shultz, writing in 1985 before the revolutions of 1989 proved the point in Eastern Europe, observed that

> the free flow of information is inherently compatible with our political system and values. The communist states, in contrast, fear this information revolution perhaps more than they fear Western military strength. . . . Totalitarian societies face a dilemma: either they try to stifle these technologies and thereby fall farther behind in the new industrial revolution, or else they permit these technologies and see their totalitarian control inevitably eroded. . . . The revolution in global communications thus forces all nations to reconsider traditional ways of thinking about national sovereignty.[83]

If the Soviet regime risked pursuing the new technologies, Shultz and others predicted (correctly) that its leaders would eventually have to liberalize the Soviet economic and political systems.[84]

It is important to recognize that the U.S. grand strategy of openness during the cold war had many closed aspects as well. For example, in the late 1940s and early 1950s, vigorous efforts were made in the United States to prevent the diffusion of communist ideology, much as the Soviets tried to keep liberal ideas from gaining a hearing or a following. By the mid-1950s, however, the United States grew aware of the ethical and political bankruptcy of this policy and began to change course, fostering an open competition between the rival political ideologies. In the economic sphere, as much as the United States was open to its allies, it remained closed to its enemies, actual or potential. This policy mellowed only at the margins and persists today in such policies as the continued embargo on Cuba. Finally, with regard to military matters, advanced technologies were consistently treated in "closed" fashion. They were classified in the hope that the diffusion of knowledge could be precluded. Although this effort failed in the nuclear weapons area, it succeeded, to some extent, in the realm of computerization, information systems, and, most notably, radar-evading Stealth technology.

Despite these aspects of closed approaches to information (about ideas, markets, or weapons), the overall U.S. approach remained devoted to openness. From the increasing willingness to compare and contrast ideologies, to the creation of the greatest free-trading economic regime the world had ever seen, to the development of interoperable military systems for common use among allies, the United States fostered the free movement of information in all its incarnations. There was even a sustained effort to share information *with* the Soviet Union, to help promote stability and change. From the "hot line" that allowed for clear communication in crisis to the transparency of information about nuclear arsenals, there was a strong belief, apparently on both sides, that openness was a condition well attuned to the needs of the bipolar international system.

In sum, the U.S. triumph in the cold war was not only a victory for our political, economic, and military systems and strategies, but also for our overall approach to information. Information variables affected all the major dimensions of power—political, economic, and military—in crucial ways. This was a key, overarching difference between the Western and Soviet systems.[85] Should one infer from this success in the cold war that the same strategy of openness is necessarily the right one in the emerging new era?

Openness Reconsidered

Openness—the open society—is an ideal that permeates U.S. interests and objectives, including all the political, economic, military, and informational ends and means discussed above. It is so potent an American ideal that George Soros lucidly proposes "that we declare the creation and preservation of open societies as one of the objectives of foreign policy. . . . I propose substituting the framework of open and closed societie for the old framework of communism versus the free world."[86]

One could extrapolate from the foregoing that the decisive role of information in the cold war, linked to a grand strategy of openness, should serve as a model for U.S. grand strategy in the post–cold war world. Indeed, the current doctrine of "democratic enlargement"[87] appears to grow logically from the opportunity provided by the dissolution of the Soviet Union. In terms of its power relative to others, the United States enjoys a position of preponderance unlike any in its previous experience. Also, in the ideological realm, a broad-based strategy of openness has close links with the most essential aspects of twentieth century American political and philosophical thought.

The strategy of openness that won the cold war may not be the same one that will be best serve U.S. objectives and interests in the emerging era, however.

In the post–cold war era, the inherent stability provided by rough parity between two superpowers has given way to a period of flux and uncertainty. While the dissolution of the Soviet Union has left in its place a less powerful Russia, and the United States has seen some diminution of its absolute military and economic power, a variety of states, great and small, are rising to recast the structure of the international system. In East Asia alone, for example, Japan and China show every sign of movement toward great power status; and even the smaller states, such as Vietnam and the Koreas, have robust capabilities.

Does the shift from a stable bipolar to a volatile polycentric world imply taking a new approach to openness? Should we not be more guarded than we were, or at least become guarded in ways different from what we were in the cold war period? In any era, the informational aspect of grand strategy may consist of a skillful blend of open and closed sectors. The challenge for the post–cold war era will be to find the informational mix appropriate for a much "fuzzier" international environment, one in which the very meaning of "openness" may have to be reconsidered.

In the political realm, for example, the tenets of political liberalism once served as a rallying cry to oppose Soviet expansionism. Now these ideas, which form the core of the rhetoric of democratic enlargement, might be received as a subtle form of American ideological imperialism. To any number of state and nonstate actors, this may seem quite threatening, encouraging them to balance against us.[88] Thus, one might expect, in response to current U.S. political strategy, a variety of opponents to rise. A few examples would include China, as the most likely nation-state competitor to resent pressures to democratize, and transnational Islamic revivalists, as archetypal nonstate actors who will be encouraged to resist American blandishments. The implication here is not to cease efforts to spread democracy but to recognize that cold war–style openness may have to give way to a subtler form of spreading information about democracy throughout the world.

In terms of strategic foreign policy, a declaratory policy of openness designed to reduce uncertainty, a condition highly prized during the cold war, might actually weaken deterrence and crisis stability in the future. The American style in international interactions remains closely tied to the Wilsonian dictum:

"open agreements, openly arrived at." Most often, this policy means that U.S. reasoning is openly provided to opponents, allowing them to calculate their risks and opportunities quite accurately.[89]

The current Balkan imbroglio provides an example of the manner in which an adversary has been able to maximize its range of maneuver on the basis of information freely and regularly provided by the U.S. government. In the post–cold war world, there may be virtue in creating, and fostering, uncertainty about possible U.S. actions. Certainly, there are times when deterrence will be enhanced if an adversary has to worry about the possibility of an early, credible use of force by the United States or to calculate that the chances for American intervention, at some point, might be high. Interestingly, this is something of a reversal from the cold war, during which uncertainty about the likely U.S. response tended to encourage aggression, a point supported by attacks on South Korea in 1950, South Vietnam in 1965, and Kuwait in 1990 in the wake of ambiguous American signaling.[90]

In the economic arena, the recent creation of a World Trade Organization devoted to the expansion of free trade and the dissemination of intellectual innovation seems a clear indicator that the market principles that served so well during the cold war will be expanded upon, especially given the demise of the former Soviet economic bloc. Upon reflection, however, one may want to consider the need for a more nuanced economic strategy—one not so clearly demarcated between open and closed areas as existed during the cold war, but one flexible enough to allow for the protection of intellectual property and for the use of suasion to obtain a "fair" as well as a "free" market for international trade. The recent, and apparently successful, efforts of the Clinton administration to obtain an agreement to grant greater access to the key automotive sector of the Japanese market are indicative of the manner in which this more nuanced approach might be applied. Indeed, the rapid follow-up of the automotive agreement with a similar U.S. claim on behalf of the photographic film industry suggests that a consistent strategy has been formulated and will be acted on.

The key problem is that, in relative terms, the United States remains far more open than most other states, allowing them to amass wealth through trade while U.S. debts build. This pattern began before the end of the cold war but appears to be accelerating, as the roughly $150 billion U.S. trade deficit in 1994

indicates. It should be noted that the United States initially rose
in prosperity and great power status between the end of the Civil
War and the 1890s while having the most protected economy on
Earth. All this happened during a period in which the British
empire, slavishly devoted to free trade, suffered decreasing
market shares and increasing dependence on foreign financial
support.[91]

On this last point, one sees, even in the writings of Adam
Smith, a sensitivity to the need for nuanced approaches. For
example, in discussing the use of sanctions to force closed markets to open up, Smith argued that "there may be good policy in
retaliations of this kind, when there is a probability that they will
procure the repeal of the high duties or prohibitions complained
of."[92] In the post–cold war world, U.S. policymakers should
heed Smith's admonitions, given the diminution of military
threats in the wake of the Soviet dissolution and the correspond-
ing rise in serious economic challenges. Indeed, the information
age may carry the risk of transforming the international free-
market system into a much more conflictual one, implying a
need to develop the capability to combat neomercantilist networks that are designed to perform well against market-oriented
competitors.[93]

Another questionable aspect of an economic strategy based
on free flows of information concerns intellectual property. The
openness that encouraged the industrial renaissance of postwar
Germany and Japan and allowed the rise of the Asian "tigers"
served the purpose of helping them become viable counter-
weights to the Soviet threat. Today, however, the American gift
of ideas may be contributing to the difficulties of many U.S.
industrial sectors. As Peter Drucker has pointed out in a variety
of forums for years, "knowledge workers" will predominate the
future economic landscape; and their best use will require part-
nership with a new generation of innovative and wily captains
of industry.[94] A world in which ideas may be swift and cheaply
duplicated elsewhere is one in which the U.S. economy may
have difficulty competing when advantages are marginal.

As to the implications for "open" strategies in the military
realm, there is much room for reconsideration, particularly of
such issues as interoperability, forward basing, and the introduction of innovations. During the cold war, there was a distinct tilt
in the direction of openness in these key areas, which tied in
closely with the political demands of U.S. alliance structures. For
example, the North Atlantic Treaty Organization (NATO)

sought out ever better levels of interoperability of weapons systems among coalition partners and required the forward presence in Europe of an entire U.S. field army (more than 300,000 troops) to enhance crisis and deterrence stability. Thus, a great deal of information was conveyed openly to both U.S. allies *and* adversaries. Even the advances in precision-guided munitions were openly touted, to both shore up alliance cohesion and dishearten those Soviets who might still contemplate aggression.

In the post–cold war environment, there are good reasons to question military openness as a predominant grand strategy. Given the quantum shifts in military capabilities inherent in the advances promised by the information revolution, should one still seek to share them with allies or inform potential adversaries of their efficacy? The risk, of course, is that these advantages are "wasting assets," susceptible to diminution as they diffuse. Thus, in a world where allies may lack the constancy they had during the cold war, and where enemies may be both numerous and readily able to adapt to advances, once known, openness may have to give way to a certain degree of guardedness.[95]

With regard to forward basing, which sends a clear signal of commitment to potential aggressors, one must now ask whether such an approach remains optimal. The continuance of a forward defensive strategy has two problems. First, in an information age in which adversaries may all too commonly possess cruise and ballistic missiles capable of bombarding U.S. forces in place, it may become necessary, in the interest of protecting these forces against surprise attack, to keep opponents in the dark as to their whereabouts. As early as the 1960s, Field Marshal Bernard Montgomery raised this issue, arguing that "armies must go to sea." Admiral William A. Owens has taken up this idea with his concept of "mobile sea bases."[96]

The second problem with the amount of information conveyed by forward basing revolves around the fact that the emerging international system may be subject to unruliness in many different regions. Potential aggressors may look at the U.S. force deployment scheme and, if their intended prey is not within some recognizable security complex, may be encouraged to try their luck. Even during the cold war, this problem was considered a possibility and was confirmed, in the eyes of many, when North Korea invaded the South in 1950, not long after Secretary of State Dean Acheson left the latter out of the explicit U.S. "defensive perimeter."[97] In a world with more "Koreas," continued forward basing may condemn those who lack the benefit of U.S. presence to become targets of opportunistic aggression.

Moving toward a more guarded approach could lengthen the period of U.S. military advantage and complicate the calculations of regional aggressors, particularly if U.S. troops might be lurking over the horizon on some "floating fortress." Still, new problems could emerge from this sort of shift. If we do not share information about military advances, we retain our predominance; but this might motivate allies, as well as adversaries, to enter into a new, information-age arms race with the United States. Second, a substantial shift from forward defense to a scheme more reminiscent of "depth defense" (i.e., one that rolls back aggression rather than precluding initial gains) might undermine deterrence substantially, particularly if aggressors engage in limited land grabs or faits accomplis. [98]

These tensions imply the need to think carefully about any move away from the form of military openness employed during the cold war. The price of failing to adjust strategically may be that U.S. advantages are more quickly eroded, undermining deterrence anyway. Perhaps the solution lies in a nuanced approach in which allies and friends are not all treated as equals. In this manner, key military information might flow to some but not others (for example, Britain, but not Gulf War ally Syria), and some regions might eventually have to fend for themselves (for example, Western Europe or South Korea).

The development of a separate informational dimension for post–cold war grand strategy is a task that is yet to be fully addressed. Just what should be the key ends or goals of this dimension? Open access and interconnectivity, from local to global levels, look like good choices, perhaps combined with an international declaration of a "right to communicate." What should be the key means or instruments? The list should probably include the promotion of all manner of advanced telecommunications network infrastructures around the world, as well as the development of new approaches to public diplomacy and to the media. A key consideration for the U.S. government may be learning to work with the new generation of nongovernmental organizations (NGOs), whose growth individually and in vast transnational networks is a major consequence of the information revolution. [99] Indeed, a well-developed information strategy might do more to foster the worldwide spread of democracy than do America's commercial and economic development strategies. Recent research by RAND's Chris Kedzie concludes that "the priority of policies regarding international communication should be at least as high as the priority for foreign economic development and perhaps as high as that of some national security programs."[100] An information strategy designed to spread democracy may even reduce the need to resort to harsh economic or veiled military pressures as part of the grand strategic mix. An informational approach may be more discriminating and less likely to generate either domestic or international political criticism of the means employed, unlike the situation faced when blunter instruments of suasion are utilized. U.S. policy toward Castro's Cuba looks like a case ripe for new thinking along these lines.[101]

Yet, here again, a strategy of openness involves substantial risks as well as opportunities. A key risk inherent in fostering greater interconnectivity is that the United States may expose itself to attacks on its own information infrastructure, which could in turn lead to serious economic and even societal damage. How can this risk be mitigated? Should the United States try to shield its "infosphere" by strictly controlling access, internally and externally? Or can careful mapping of the information infrastructure lead to a more guarded approach that protects critical nodes while allowing the vast majority of the traffic in commerce and ideas to pass uninterrupted? The latter strategy allows ample room for working to spread democracy abroad, while the former might constrain such efforts.

Conclusion: In Favor of Guarded Openness

While the development of information and communications as a distinct, new, fourth dimension of grand strategy is a major recommendation, our concluding admonition is that U.S. strategic choices be reviewed across the spectrum of alternative approaches to openness. That spectrum might be framed by complete openness at one end and preclusive security at the other. Something that might be called "guarded openness" would define the middle range of the openness spectrum.

Guarded openness was, in many respects, the strategy that the United States pursued during the cold war, if not before. It is not a static strategy; moreover, it has not even been discussed much as a strategy. A review might help reveal that, for dealing with the present and future world, the overall profile of where to be open or closed should be based on principles different from those during the cold war. A review might also help ascertain what contextual factors are most important in determining the advisability of moving in open, guarded, or sometimes preclusive directions in specific issue areas. A review could further help identify the mechanisms that should be emphasized for purposes of enhancing and protecting U.S. openness.

Given the strong commercial flavor of so much of the U.S. infosphere, part of the answer may lie in allowing market forces to work out security arrangements. For example, with regard to telecommunications, consumers would presumably flock to companies that dealt best with security requirements, leaving the less adept competitors to founder for lack of customers. Eventually, only the informationally "fit" would survive. Could this pattern be pursued in other, or even most, sectors?

On the other hand, policies should hedge against the following kinds of problems: the potential damage that might be done in some vague "short run" before market forces provide a secure environment, and the possibility of "market failure," that is, the chance that the market might not be able to control risks adequately. Finally, the potential for more efficient alternatives to the market solution should be considered. These points call to mind similarities to the situation that the newly independent United States faced in the late eighteenth century. Many leaders thought that the individual states should form their own industrial policies and take responsibility for protecting their own commerce. Alexander Hamilton, in his famous *Report on Manufactures*, took an opposing view, arguing that these separate approaches would prove both inefficient and likely to fail. His best-known illustration concerned maritime security, wherein he described the foolishness of creating 13 separate state navies when one would be cheaper and better. We urge careful consideration of such Hamiltonian arguments, which should spark, for the emerging era, a *Report on Information*.

Overall, then, our analysis suggests that, in the political and economic spheres, as circumstances require it may prove useful to modify the cold war strategy of maximizing openness or, at least, to develop a nuanced strategy that weaves skillfully between openness and more proprietary approaches. In the military aspects of national power, we urge the elucidation of a similarly flexible approach. The trend toward higher information content in weapons systems and greater decentralization of military organizations should be continued, if not accelerated. At the same time, the emergence of an increasingly fluid, polycentric international system should make us wary of fostering the diffusion of military technological, organizational, and doctrinal innovations—because yesterday's allies may not be tomorrow's.

Our notion here is that, while information has always "mattered," today's information revolution is creating overarching effects that raise "knowing" to a level of importance never before seen. As Richard Barnet once noted of this sea change, "[t]he world now taking shape is not only new, but new in entirely new ways."[102] Indeed, contrary to the popular view that military power may mean less in the information age, we think that it may become more important because of the revolutionary shifts in strategy, doctrine, and organization implied by advances in information technology. The oft-touted political and economic dimensions of national power[103] may carry less weight, or have less utility, than often thought. Meanwhile, developing information as an autonomous element of national power affords the possibility of a more efficient, effective statecraft, especially with regard to the strategic aim of spreading democracy. In sum, while the political and economic tools of power may prove less widely applicable than in the past, both the military and informational aspects of grand strategy appear to be moving in the direction of relatively greater utility.

If all this is sensible and achievable, then Athena will truly have assumed the mantle of Mars, and we shall be the better for it.

Notes

1. Sun Tzu, *The Art of War*, ed. and trans. Samuel B. Griffith (New York: Oxford University Press, 1971), p. 129; Francis Bacon, "Of Vicissitude of Things," in M. A. Scott, ed., *The Essays of Francis Bacon* (New York: Charles Scribner's Sons, 1908), p. 270; Carl von Clausewitz, *On War*, ed. and trans. Michael Howard and Peter Paret (Princeton: Princeton University Press, 1976), p. 147; and Michel Foucault, *Power/Knowledge*, ed. and trans. Colin Gordon (New York: Pantheon, 1980), p. 69.

2. A thoughtful analysis of the continuing, perhaps growing importance of the state, is John Garnett's, "Why Have States Survived for so Long?" in J. Baylis and N. Rengger, eds., *Dilemmas of World Politics* (Oxford: Clarendon Press, 1992), particularly p. 63, where he concludes that "states enjoy decisive advantages over all other organizations in domestic and international affairs." See also Robert Jackson and Alan James, "The Character of Independent Statehood," in their edited volume, *States in a Changing*

World (Oxford: Clarendon Press, 1993). Of the effects of the information revolution on states, they contend that "a major effect has been to enhance [state] significance: the State has been a major supporter and beneficiary of economic, scientific, and technological advance" (p. 6).

3. A similar conclusion is reached by Eugene Skolnikoff in his recent assessment of how today's scientific and technological revolutions may affect international politics. In his view, these revolutions will require the realist and interdependence schools of international political theory to rethink some propositions, but he finds little reason to doubt that "states remain the dominant structural element in the international system." Indeed, "it would not be difficult to construct a scenario in which the emergence of major challenges to the planet or to a large part of human society led to much greater centralization of authority in the hands of a few states in the international system." Eugene B. Skolnikoff, *The Elusive Transformation: Science, Technology, and the Evolution of International Politics* (Princeton: Princeton University Press, 1993), especially pp. 241–246; quotes taken from p. 243 and p. 245, respectively.

4. Indeed, it is not so much the state but rather the empire that dominated the international system after feudalism ended 500 years ago. Empires, because of their size and resources, often survived even gross blunders; witness the resilience evident during the long periods of imperial decline suffered by Rome, Byzantine, Spain, France, Britain, and Russia.

5. Peter F. Drucker, *Post-Capitalist Society* (New York: Harper Collins Publishers, 1993), especially chap. 6.

6. For example, Kenichi Ohmae, in *The End of the Nation-State: The Rise of Regional Economies* (New York, The Free Press, 1995), proposes that transborder "region-states" are on the rise.

7. Our threefold treatment of both information and power is deliberately sketchy and cannot do full justice to the view of any single thinker. Rather, we seek to show that there has been an evolution in how people view these concepts. This evolution has implications that might be missed if one were to focus more on the details of specific views.

8. A classification suggested in Robert Wright, *Three Scientists and Their Gods: Looking for Meaning in an Age of Information* (New York: Harper & Row, 1989), p. 110.

9. Notably, Harlan Cleveland, *The Knowledge Executive: Leadership in an Information Society* (New York: E.P. Dutton, 1985); and Robert Lucky, *Silicon Dreams: Information, Man, and Machine* (New York: St. Martin's, 1989).

10. The cognitive version is used in Jeffrey R. Cooper, "Another View of the Revolution in Military Affairs" (Carlisle, Penn.: Strategic Studies Institute, 1994); and John Rothrock, "Information Warfare: Time for Some Constructive Skepticism" (Stanford: Stanford Research International, 1994, draft). A short version of Rothrock's paper was published under the same title in the *American Intelligence Journal*, Spring-Summer 1994, pp. 71–76.

11. See, for example, Theodore Roszak, *The Cult of Information: The Folklore of Computers and the True Art of Thinking* (New York: Pantheon Books, 1986).

12. Richard Dawkins, *The Selfish Gene* (New York: Oxford University Press, 1989), p. 94.

13. Ibid., p. 329.

14. Ibid., p. 192.

15. Elaborations appear in Steve J. Heims, *The Cybernetics Group* (Cambridge: MIT Press, 1991); in Kevin Kelly, *Out of Control: The Rise of Neo-Biological Civilization* (New York: Addison-Wesley, 1994); in Lucky, *Silicon Dreams;* and in Roszak, *Cult of Information.*

16. See Norbert Wiener, *Cybernetics: or Control and Communication in the Animal and the Machine* (Cambridge: MIT Press, 1948), and Wiener, *The Human Use of Human Beings* (Boston: Houghton Mifflin, 1950); and Marshall McLuhan, *Understanding Media: The Extensions of Man* (Boston: MIT Press, 1964/1994). Also see Heims, *Cybernetics Group.* Shannon's writings are highly technical; but his basic points are presented in books cited above by Heims, Kelly, Lucky, and Wright, among others.

17. Notably, Karl W. Deutch, *The Nerves of Government: Models of Political Communication and Control* (New York: The Free Press, 1963); and John D. Steinbruner, *The Cybernetic Theory of Decision* (Princeton: Princeton University Press, 1974).

18. Wiener, *Cybernetics,* p. 11.

19. Gregory Bateson, *Steps to an Ecology of Mind* (New York: Ballantine, 1972), p. 381.

20. See especially Heims, *Cybernetics Group,* and Wright, *Three Scientists and Their Gods.*

21. A thoughtful exposition is by M. Mitchell Waldrop, *Complexity: The Emerging Science at the Edge of Order and Chaos* (New York: Simon & Schuster, 1992). John Horgan, "From Complexity to Perplexity," *Scientific American,* June 1995, pp. 104–109, voices the prospect that "complexity" studies may turn out to be another academic fad—as tenuous a basis for interdisciplinary theory as "cybernetics" was in earlier decades.

22. Thus, tribes, hierarchies, markets, and networks all exhibit different patterns of control and coordination.

23. James Beniger, *The Control Revolution* (Cambridge: Harvard University Press, 1986).

24. Wright, *Three Scientists and Their Gods,* p. 5.

25. Tom Stonier, *Information and the Internal Structure of the Universe: An Exploration into Information Physics* (London: Springer Verlag, 1990), p. 107.

26. Cited in Wright, *Three Scientists and Their Gods,* pp. 10–11.

27. Ibid., p. 288.

28. Efforts to define power remain risky, for they often verge on tautology. Herbert Simon, in "Notes on the Observation and Measurement of Political Power," *Journal of Politics* 15, no. 4 (1953): 500–516, admonishes his fellow scholars to avoid considering power tautologically, as if it simply amounted to the ability to influence others. His admonition has been difficult to heed. For example, a classic article by Robert Dahl, "The Concept of Power," *Behavioral Science,* 2(1957): 201–215 treated power as essentially the ability to influence others. Formal quantitative studies of power sometimes reflect this emphasis. A. F. K. Organski and Jacek Kugler, in *The War Ledger* (Chicago: University of Chicago Press, 1980), focus on the identification and measurement of "power transitions" and argue that national power "can be defined simply as the ability of one nation to control the behavior of another for its own ends" (p. 5).

29. Kenneth E. Boulding, *Three Faces of Power* (London: Sage, 1989) provides one of the most systematic efforts to classify the dimensions of power. Other attempts, often resulting in fewer dimensions, include P. Bachrach and M.S. Baratz, "Two Faces of Power," *American Political Science Review* 56 (1962): 947–952. Joseph S. Nye, Jr., in *Bound to Lead: The Changing Nature of American Power* (New York: Basic Books, 1990), especially pp. 173–201, makes a pertinent distinction between "hard" (tangible) and "soft" (intangible) components of power.

30. Inis Claude, *Power and International Relations* (New York: Random House, 1962), p. 6.

31. Bruce Bueno de Mesquita's, *The War Trap* (New Haven: Yale University Press, 1981), pp. 102–109, gives an outstanding exposition of this view of power, while also noting the vitiating effects of distance on the projection of material power. He enriches the basic capabilities index by incorporating his variant of the "loss of strength gradient" introduced by Kenneth Boulding, *Conflict and Defense* (New York: Harper & Row, 1962), especially pp. 245–247. The composite capabilities index became one of the foundations of the Correlates of War data set maintained by the Interuniversity Consortium for Political and Social Research.

32. Thomas Hobbes's *Leviathan* calls for using centralized organization to maximize state power. Karl Marx's *Communist Manifesto* heralds an altogether differing view of political organization, in which the greatest gains will come from the "withering" of predatory states.

33. This is a central theme of Herbert Simon, *Administrative Behavior* (New York: The Free Press, 1957). Another example is Philip Selznick, *TVA and the Grass Roots; a Study in the Sociology of Formal Organization* (Berkeley: University of California Press, 1949). Klaus Knorr, *The War Potential of Nations* (Princeton: Princeton University Press, 1956), especially chap. 6–8, notes the overarching importance of administrative efficiency. Tibor Scitovsky, Edward Shaw, and Lorie Tarshis, in *Mobilizing Resources for War* (New York: McGraw-Hill, 1951), provide a policy-oriented (for its day) blueprint for developing a national-level degree of organization to maximize state power.

34. Jack Nagel, "Some Questions about the Concept of Power," *Behavioral Science* 13(1968): 129. This view was thoroughly analyzed in Harold Lasswell and Abraham Kaplan, *Power and Society* (New Haven: Yale University Press, 1950).

35. R. E. Smith, in *The Failure of the Roman Republic* (London: Cambridge University Press, 1955), pp. 47–56, argues that Rome could not realize its power potential until it engaged in a fundamental reorganization, jettisoning its vestigial tribal structures in favor of administrative structures that could effectively command and control its ever-increasing resources and subjects. Of this period of institutional redesign, and the sometimes unpredictable behavior that accompanied it, Smith concluded that "it is a phase through which all States pass during their growth and development" (p. 53).

36. Background appears in David Ronfeldt, "Institutions, Markets, and Networks: A Framework about the Evolution of Societies" (Santa Monica: RAND, DRU–590–FF, December 1993). Sources on the evolution from tribes to early states include: Elman R. Service, *Primitive Social Organization, An Evolutionary Perspective*, 2nd ed. (New York: Random House, 1971); Service, *Origins of the State and Civilization: The Process of Cultural Evolution* (New York: W.W. Norton and Company, 1975); and Joseph A. Tainter, *The Collapse of Complex Societies* (New York: Cambridge University Press, 1988).

37. For a recent example, see David A. Lake, "Powerful Pacifists: Democratic States and War," *American Political Science Review* 86, no. 1 (1992): 24–37, for an argument that less hierarchical systems must respond to constituent demands and thus become inherently stronger than those polities whose rulers may extract surplus from a people without their permission or support.

38. Hans Morgenthau, *Politics Among Nations* (New York: Alfred A. Knopf, 1948), pp. 91–100. On balance, Morgenthau's view of power is dual, for he mixes intangibles like nationalism and militarism with tangible geopolitical factors (pp. 116–120).

39. Nye, *Bound to Lead*, p. 195.

40. See Antonio Gramsci, "Intellectuals and Hegemony," in David McLellan, *Marxism: Essential Writings* (London: Oxford University Press, 1988). It should also be noted that writers identified with the realist approach to international relations have sometimes argued that even such matters as international trading regimes rely heavily on the "hegemonic stability" afforded by the presence and participation of a preponderant state. See Stephen D. Krasner, "State Power and the Structure of International Trade," in Jeffry A. Frieden and David A. Lake, *International Political Economy* (New York: St. Martin's Press, 1987).

41. See Friedrich Nietzsche, *The Will to Power* (New York: Vintage Books, 1964 ed.) and *The Genealogy of Morals* (New York: Carlton House, 1887).

42. On the importance of ideas, see G. W. F. Hegel, *Reason in History*, trans. Robert S. Hartman (Indianapolis: Bobbs-Merrill, 1951). A modern affirmation of the Hegelian view of ideas and power appears in Francis Fukuyama, *The End of History and the Last Man* (New York: Free Press, 1992).

43. Alvin and Heidi Toffler, in *War and Anti-War: Survival at the Dawn of the 21st Century* (Boston: Little, Brown, 1993), emphasize the increasingly immaterial nature of power.

44. Martin Van Creveld, *Technology and War: From 2000 B.C. to the Present* (New York: The Free Press, 1989).

45. Writings in this camp include C. Kenneth Allard, "The Future of Command and Control: Toward a Paradigm of Information Warfare," in L. Benjamin Ederington and Michael J. Mazarr, eds., *Turning Point: The Gulf*

War and U.S. Military Strategy (Boulder, Colo.: Westview Press, 1995); Cooper, "Another View of the Revolution"; Brian Nichiporuk and Carl Builder, *Information Technologies and the Future of Land Warfare* (Santa Monica, Calif.: RAND, 1995); Martin C. Libicki, *The Mesh and the Net: Speculations on Armed Conflict in a Time of Free Silicon* (Washington, D.C.: Institute for National Strategic Studies, National Defense University, McNair Paper #26, 1994); George Stein, "Information Warfare," *Airpower Journal,* Spring 1995, pp. 30–39; Richard Szafranski, "Neo-Cortical Warfare? The Acme of Skill," *Military Review,* November 1994, pp. 41–55; and Szafranski, "A Theory of Information Warfare: Preparing for 2020," *Airpower Journal,* Spring 1995, pp. 56–65. Pertinent but more reserved views are expressed by Steven Metz and James Kievit, "The Revolution in Military Affairs and Conflict Short of War" (Carlisle Barracks, Penn.: Strategic Studies Institute, 1994); and by Rothrock, "Information Warfare" (1994). Two journalists have provided particularly good coverage of key ideas and issues: Peter Grier, "Information Warfare," *Air Force Magazine,* March 1995, pp. 34–37; and Oliver Morton, "A Survey of Defence Technology: The Softwar Revolution," *Economist* 335, no. 7918 (June 10, 1995): 5–20 (special insert after p. 50). For additional discussion, see Arquilla and Ronfeldt, "Welcome to the Revolution . . . in Military Affairs," *Comparative Strategy* 14, no. 3 (Summer 1995).

46. Rothrock, "Information Warfare" (1994), p. 7. Is there a risk of an information-age iteration of industrial-age fascism? If so, no term exists for it yet. The closest is "friendly fascism"—a term coined by socialist sociologist Bertram Gross, *Friendly Fascism: The New Face of Power in America* (Boston: South End Press, 1980), to warn that the new information technologies may be used by government and business to centralize surveillance and control over society. In some places (Singapore?), the information revolution may foster hybrid political systems and practices that purport to be democratic but are not. See David Ronfeldt, "Cyberocracy Is Coming," *The Information Society* 8, no. 4 (1992): 243–296.

47. Colin Powell, "Information-Age Warriors," *Byte,* July 1992, p. 370.

48. Clausewitz, *On War,* p. 147.

49. This perspective is developed at some length in John Arquilla and David Ronfeldt, "Cyberwar is Coming!" *Comparative Strategy* 12, no. 2 (Summer 1993): 141–165.

50. Clausewitz, *On War,* p. 120.

51. Lt. Gen. (USAF) Carl O'Berry, as reported in *Defense News,* September 12–18, 1994, p. 54.

52. Sun Tzu, *Art of War,* pp. 100–101.

53. See, for example, Jeffrey Ethell and Alfred Price, *Air War South Atlantic* (New York: Macmillan, 1983); and, from the Argentine point of view, B.H. Andrada, *Guerra Aérea en las Malvinas* (Buenos Aires: Emecé Editores, 1983), pp. 38–40. Wayne Hughes, Jr. and Jeffrey Larson's, *The Falklands Wargame* (Bethesda, MD: Concepts Analysis Agency, 1986) is an interesting official report that explores the possibilities opened up by alternate targeting. But the most severe critique of Argentine errors is rendered in Air Marshal R. G. Funnell, "It was a Bit of a Close Call: Some Thoughts on the South

Atlantic War," in Alan Stephens, ed., *The War in the Air, 1914–1994* (Fairbairn, Australia: Air Power Studies Center, 1994). Funnell's conclusion is that "properly used, air power could have achieved the Argentine national aim" (p. 229).

54. See David A. Andelman, "The Drug Money Maze," *Foreign Affairs,* July/August 1994, pp. 94–108.

55. McLuhan, *Understanding Media,* quote from p. 346, emphasis added.

56. Psychological operations from an information warfare and special forces perspective is discussed by Col. Jeffrey B. Jones, "Psychological Operations in Desert Shield, Desert Storm and Urban Freedom, *Special Warfare,* July 1994, pp. 22–29.

57. See Jarol B. Manheim, *Strategic Public Diplomacy & American Foreign Policy: The Evolution of Influence* (New York: Oxford University Press, 1994).

58. The term "knowledge strategy" is from Toffler and Toffler, *War.*

59. Szafranski, "Neo-Cortical Warfare."

60. Statements of this notion include: Eric H. Arnett, "Welcome to Hyperwar," *The Bulletin of the Atomic Scientists* 48, no. 7 (September 1992): 14–21; Manuel De Landa, *War in the Age of Intelligent Machines* (Cambridge: MIT Press, 1991); and Les Levidow and Kevin Robins, eds., *Cyborg Worlds: The Military Information Society* (London: Free Association Books, 1989).

61. See Dawkins, *Selfish Gene,* pp. 330–331, where he writes: "What a weapon! Religious faith deserves a chapter to itself in the annals of war technology, on an even footing with the longbow, the warhorse, the tank, and the hydrogen bomb." Eric Hoffer, *The True Believer* (New York: Harper & Row, 1951) pointed out that an all-consuming faith need not be religious.

62. An information quotient, once operationalized, would reflect the informational content of a weapon system relative to its mass and energy. The quotient reflects both the natural and man-made content of that system, in the context of its intended use. Many high-tech weapons systems would probably have high information quotients, but a high-tech system like the strategic nuclear missiles of the Soviet Union during the cold war might have a low information quotient even if it has very high mass or energy quotients.

63. Ronfeldt, "Cyberocracy" proposed the field of "cyberology." Thoughts of moving in this direction should be tempered by reading Heims's *Cybernetics Group,* which recounts an unsuccessful effort in the 1940s and 1950s to create interdisciplinary studies around the concept of cybernetics.

64. A 1962 piece by Arthur C. Clarke, "I Remember Babylon," reprinted with comment in Arthur C. Clarke, *How the World Was One: Beyond the Global Village* (New York: Bantam Books, 1992), pp. 181–193, tells of his encounter with a shady fellow who was purportedly planning to orbit satellites to broadcast television programs that would perversely charm and then undermine U.S. society.

65. Szafranski, "Neo-Cortical Warfare."

66. The concepts of cyberwar and netwar were fielded in Arquilla and Ronfeldt, "Cyberwar."

67. See David Gelernter, *Mirror Worlds, or the Day Software Puts the Universe in a Shoebox . . . How It Will Happen and What It Will Mean* (New York: Oxford University Press, 1991).

68. The extension of single pieces into a line of pieces (a chain network?) might be considered a form of maneuver over time, however.

69. Arthur Smith's *The Game of Go* (New York: Moffat, Yard and Company, 1908), which has gone through many reprintings, remains an unsurpassed, lucid study of the game. Sociologist Scott Boorman, in *The Protracted Game: A Weich'i Interpretation of Maoist Revolutionary Strategy* (New York: Oxford University Press, 1969) assesses the Vietnam War in terms of Go-like principles of strategy. Deconstructionists Gilles Deleuze and Félix Guattari, in *Nomadology: The War Machine*, trans. Brian Massumi (New York: Semiotext[e], Foreign Agents Series, 1986), pp. 10–11, compare war to chess ("a game of State, or of the court") and to *Go* (whose pieces are "anonymous, collective").

70. Smith, *Game of Go*, p. 27, notes that this phrase (*Ji dori go*) is a "contemptuous epithet" for the uninspired conventionality of such strategies.

71. Paul Kennedy, ed., *Grand Strategies in War and Peace* (New Haven: Yale University Press, 1991) adopts this definition in the study of grand strategies from ancient Rome to the present-day United States.

72. An example is provided by the Protestant Reformation in which, despite efforts to restrict the dissemination of the Bible into the various vernaculars, the word did get out. This resulted in a movement which held, first, that the individual could enjoy a direct experience with God, as opposed to one filtered through a religious hierarchy. Second, the liberation of the individual from centralized control encouraged a number of emerging states to seek their own political independence from Rome. Thus, Lutheranism in Germany and Anglicanism in England were movements that ended up fostering national political sovereignty as well as individual freedom of worship.

The classic studies are by Elizabeth L. Eisenstein, "Some Conjectures about the Impact of Printing on Western Society and Thought: A Preliminary Report," *Journal of Modern History*, March 1968, pp. 1–56, and the book version, Eisenstein, *The Printing Press as an Agent of Change*, 2 vols. (Cambridge: Cambridge University Press, 1979). Although the literature on the Reformation era is mountainous, a few studies key on the informational bases of political power. In regard to the German case, the work of German historian-strategist Leopold Ranke, *History of the Reformation in Germany* (London: Oxford University Press, 1905) stands out. Hilaire Belloc's *How the Reformation Happened* (London: Longmans, 1950) provides a similar approach, with keen insight into the Reformation in England.

73. Edward Gibbon's *The Decline and Fall of the Roman Empire*, 7 vols. (London: J.B. Bury, 1900) provides a classic analysis of this crucial difference between the eastern and western empires. He notes that the former's interest in protecting seagoing commerce remained constant, resulting in a first-rate navy that saved the eastern empire's lines of communication time and again during the hard centuries following the collapse of Rome. Joseph A.

Schumpeter, *History of Economic Analysis* (New York: Oxford University Press, 1954), pp. 68–73, addresses this point in some detail, noting that the staying power of the eastern empire was directly tied to its continuing embrace of Hellenistic notions of the power of ideas, markets, and secure lines and means of communication.

74. On this point, Van Creveld, *Technology and War*, as well as his *Command in War* (Cambridge: Harvard University Press, 1985), takes long historical views of these issues.

75. See Manheim, *Strategic Public Diplomacy*, for the view that information may be evolving toward an ever more autonomous role as a tool of statecraft in many settings.

76. See William J. Clinton, *A National Security Strategy of Engagement and Enlargement* (Washington, D.C.: Government Printing Office, 1994).

77. The notion of information as existing autonomously has received some support. See particularly Anthony Smith, *The Geopolitics of Information: How Western Culture Dominates the World* (New York: Oxford University Press, 1980); Hans N. Tuch, *Communicating with the World: U.S. Public Diplomacy Overseas* (New York: St. Martin's, 1990); and Howard H. Frederick, *Global Communications & International Relations* (Belmont, Calif.: Wadsworth Publishing, 1993). With regard to the means by which information strategies may be pursued, attention has long been given to the role of the media. Two early studies whose insights remain very useful are Bernard Cohen, *The Press and Foreign Policy* (Princeton: Princeton University Press, 1963); and David M. Abshire, *International Broadcasting: A New Dimension of Western Diplomacy* (Beverly Hills: Sage Publications, 1976). Chris Kedzie's "Democracy and Network Interconnectivity" (Proceeding of INET '95, Honolulu, June 1995) attends to the important implications of connectivity to the Internet for U.S. interests in fostering democracy worldwide.

78. Rome fell to barbarians whose economies might best be described as "subsistence plundering." The nomadic Mongols had only the most rudimentary notions of markets and trading, yet they conquered the leading Sinic, Muslim, and Orthodox Christian civilizations of their day. Revolutionary France arose from economic collapse to overthrow virtually all of its wealthy neighbors. Finally, Vietnam's peasant economy withstood and defeated the United States while the latter was at the height of its cold war-era power. Thus, one can see that the connections between the three primary elements of power are often quite attenuated.

79. Kennan articulated his vision of containment in a series of lectures during 1946–47 at the National War College, the texts of which can be found in Giles D. Harlow and George C. Maerz, *Measures Short of War* (Washington, D.C.: National Defense University Press, 1991). Walter Lippmann's *The Cold War* (Boston: Little, Brown, 1947) is the compendium of his articles critiquing Kennan. Both were sensitive to the strategic implications of the societal structures of the adversaries, especially Kennan, who noted that "the greatest danger that can befall us in coping with this problem of Soviet Communism is that we shall allow ourselves to become like those with whom we are coping." Cited in Louis Halle, *The Cold War as History* (New York: Harper & Row, 1967), p. 106.

80. Nathan Leites, in *Soviet Style in War* (New York: Crane Russak, 1969), made this case convincingly. The most significant Soviet effort to understand and adapt to the implications of the information-driven revolution in military affairs came from Marshal N. Ogarkov, *Istoriya uchit bditel'nosti* (History teaches vigilance) (Moscow: Voenizdat, 1985). Nevertheless, as noted in E. B. Atkeson, "Soviet Theater Forces on a Descending Path," in Derek Leebaert and Timothy Dickinson, eds., *Soviet Strategy and New Military Thinking* (Cambridge: Cambridge University Press, 1992), p 94· "the Marshal's view of future warfare, incorporating high technology, may have carried with it the seeds of its own frustration. The devices envisioned are enormously costly and some may be beyond the capabilities of the Soviet Union to produce in the foreseeable future." Thus, a shift away from its traditional attritional approach, leavened with some elements of maneuver, may not have been possible.

81. Although formalized in 1979 in Jimmy Carter's Presidential Directive #59, this view had been gaining currency since the 1960s.

82. See David Holloway, *The Soviet Union and the Arms Race* (New Haven: Yale University Press, 1984), especially chap. 3.

83. George Shultz, "New Realities and New Ways of Thinking," *Foreign Affairs*, Spring 1985, p. 716.

84. Tom Stonier, "The Microelectronic Revolution, Soviet Political Structure, and The Future of East/West Relations," *Political Quarterly*, April-June 1983, pp. 137 151.

85. On this point, see Scott Shane's *Dismantling Utopia: How Information Ended the Soviet Union* (Chicago: Ivan R. Dee, 1994), which provides a journalistic post mortem. Readers in search of more scholarly analysis by policymakers and futurists who anticipated the effects of the information revolution on closed societies should be aware of: Peter Drucker, *The New Realities: In Government and Politics, In Economics and Business, In Society and World View* (New York: Harper and Row, 1989); George Shultz, "New Realities"; and Walter B. Wriston, *The Twilight of Sovereignty: How The Information Revolution Is Transforming Our World* (New York: Charles Scribner's Sons, 1992). As secretary of state during the Reagan administration, George Shultz made a number of prescient speeches, notably in 1986, about the extreme difficulties that closed systems like the Soviet Union would have in coping with increased, freer flows of information.

86. George Soros, "Toward Open Societies," *Foreign Policy* 98 (Spring 1995): 72–73. He would have U.S. policy oppose all closed systems, including authoritarian dictatorships friendly toward the United States.

87. · Clinton, *National Security Strategy*.

88. George Kennan, *The Cloud of Danger: Current Realities of U.S. Foreign Policy* (Boston: Atlantic Monthly Press, 1978) voiced this concern long before the current round of interest in spreading democracy. Christopher Layne in "The Unipolar Illusion," *International Security* 17, no. 4 (Spring

1993): 5–51, picks up on this and other points to argue that a U.S. drive for primacy will inevitably provoke a powerful response to curtail it.

89. See especially Michael H. Hunt, *Ideology and U.S. Foreign Policy* (New Haven: Yale University Press, 1987); and Robert Dallek, *The American Style of Foreign Policy* (New York: Oxford University Press, 1983).

90. The connection between ambiguous communications and conventional deterrence failure is examined in detail in John Arquilla, "Louder than Words: Tacit Communication in International Crises," *Political Communication* 9 (Winter 1992): 155–172.

91. Paul Kennedy, *The Rise and Fall of the Great Powers* (New York: Random House, 1987), p. 149, notes that, during the Victorian heyday, Britain's share of world manufacturing output fell from 23 percent to 18 percent. This drop was severe, in that global economic product grew explosively during this period (1880–1900). He also points out two dangerous long-term consequences of an economic strategy of unswerving openness: "[Britain] was contributing to the long-term expansion of other nations . . . [and] weakness lay in the increasing dependence of the British economy on international trade and, more important, international finance" (p. 157). Aaron Friedberg's *The Weary Titan: Britain and the Experience of Relative Decline, 1895–1905* (Princeton: Princeton University Press, 1988) examines these trends, and their consequences, in detail.

92. Adam Smith, *An Inquiry into the Nature and Causes of the Wealth of Nations* (New York: Modern Library, 1937 edition), Book 4, chap. 2, p. 445. Edward Mead Earle, in "Adam Smith, Alexander Hamilton, Friedrich List: The Economic Foundations of Military Power," in Peter Paret, ed., *Makers of Modern Strategy* (Princeton: Princeton University Press, 1986), pp. 217–261, provides a view of Smith as being far less bound by his ideas than those who succeeded him: "His followers were more doctrinaire free traders than Smith was himself" (p. 222). The key point, according to Earle, was that Smith understood that "when necessary, the economic power of the nation should be cultivated and used as an instrument of statecraft" (p. 225).

93. The possible return of mercantilism has been a concern for some time. See especially Robert Gilpin, "Three Models of the Future," in C.F. Bergsten and L.B. Krause, eds., *World Politics and International Economics* (Washington, D.C.: The Brookings Institution, 1975), pp. 37–60. Gilpin shows particular concern about the possibility that a kind of "malignant mercantilism" will emerge.

94. Peter F. Drucker's "The Age of Social Transformation," *Atlantic Monthly* 274, no. 5 (November 1994): 53–80, puts the matter starkly: "Knowledge has become the key resource, for a nation's military strength as well as for its economic strength" (p. 76).

95. Bernard Brodie, in *Sea Power in the Machine Age* (Princeton: Princeton University Press, 1944), explores in depth the dilemma of introducing innovations, in the context of nineteenth century British naval policy. The prevailing view at the Admiralty was of the need to monitor others' progress without revealing their own advances, thus stretching out the Royal Navy's advantages over its nearest competitors.

96. Field Marshal Viscount Montgomery of Alamein, *A History of Warfare* (New York: World Publishing, 1969), p. 564; and Admiral W. A. Owens, *High Seas: The Naval Passage to an Uncharted World* (Annapolis: Naval Institute Press, 1995), especially pp. 162–166. The idea of garrisoning large ground forces at sea was advanced in P. Dadant, W. Mooz, and J. Walker, "A Comparison of Methods for Improving U.S. Capability to Project Ground Forces to Southwest Asia in the 1990s" (Santa Monica: RAND, 1984) which elucidated a concept of "mobile large islands" (MOLIs). See especially Appendix E.

97. Dean Acheson's *Present at the Creation* (New York: Norton, 1969), p. 357 notes the problem and observes that only the "critical Russian error" of walking out of the Security Council, in a dispute over China, allowed the United Nations to respond at all to North Korean aggression without facing a certain Soviet veto.

98. Alexander George and Richard Smoke, in *Deterrence in American Foreign Policy* (New York: Columbia University Press, 1974), consider these forms of aggression among the most difficult to deter, as does John Mearsheimer, in *Conventional Deterrence* (Ithaca: Cornell University Press, 1984), who argues for the need to be able to prevent initial overruns in order to make deterrence work. Paul Huth, in *Extended Deterrence and the Prevention of War* (New Haven: Yale University Press, 1988), argues that maintaining a robust local balance of forces is also a key element of a healthy environment for deterrence.

99. On the rise of new networks of activist NGOs in civil society, see Howard Frederick, "Computer Networks and the Emergence of Global Civil Society," in Linda M. Harasim (ed.), *Global Networks: Computers and International Communication* (Cambridge: MIT Press, 1993), pp. 283–295; James N. Rosenau, *Turbulence in World Politics: A Theory of Change and Continuity* (Princeton: Princeton University Press, 1990); Lester M. Salamon, "The Rise of the Nonprofit Sector," *Foreign Affairs* 73, no. 4, (July/August 1994): 109–122; David Ronfeldt and Cathryn Thorup, "Redefining Governance in North America: State, Society, and Security" (Santa Monica: RAND, DRU–459, August 1993); and Peter J. Spiro, "New Global Communities: Nongovernmental Organizations in International Decision-Making Institutions," *Washington Quarterly* 18, no.1 (Winter 1995): 45–56.

100. Chris Kedzie, "Democracy and Network Interconnectivity," finds, based on quantitative indicator analysis, that democracy correlates more strongly with Internet connectivity than with other touted social and economic factors. His research may raise interesting new questions about Seymour Martin Lipset's famous "optimistic equation," that democracy goes hand-in-hand with prosperity. See Seymour Martin Lipset, *Political Man* (Baltimore: The Johns Hopkins University Press, expanded edition, 1981). Kedzie recognizes that causality may operate in more than one direction, particularly because both democracy and connectivity link to wealth. Whether the point should be about correlation or causality, however, Kedzie's analytic and anecdotal evidence suggest that the positive effects for U.S. interests from the prevalence of communication technologies are too strong to discount if the United States wants to advance its international influence.

However, inasmuch as connectivity is linked with wealth, it is not yet clear whether Kedzie and others have demonstrated only a correlation, or found evidence of a causal relationship.

101. The concluding section of Edward Gonzalez and David Ronfeldt, *Cuba Adrift in a Postcommunist World* (Santa Monica: RAND, R–4231, 1992) recommended the development of a new information and communications policy to open Cuba up and strengthen civil society actors.

102. Richard J. Barnet, "Defining the Moment," *New Yorker*, July 16, 1990, 48.

103. See the discussion of "soft power" in Nye, *Bound to Lead*, especially pp. 187–195.

14

Global Swarming, Virtual Security, and Bosnia

James Der Derian

This paper has its origins in a fax that I received while in England. Would I be willing to give a "Wired-cyber-anarcho-futuristic" perspective on the impact of the information revolution on national security? Judging from the reputation that seemed to have preceded me, I was supposed to lend some futureshock value to the proceedings. That very night I turned on the television to the BBC news to find a video clip of Speaker of the House Newt Gingrich doing his Toffler two-step on MTV, declaiming that we must move from brute force to brain force in Bosnia. If this was the scene from inside, I wondered how I could possibly top that from outside the Beltway.

Luckily I had just come back from the future, or as close as U.S. Armed Forces in Europe can simulate it in Hohenfels, Germany, where the First Armored Division was preparing to intervene in Bosnia. At first scan, Bosnia would appear to have little to do with the information revolution. This is not infowar, cyberwar, antiwar, postwar, or anything else remotely connected to the future. It barely makes it into the present. This is a dirty, atavistic war with static trench lines, wetware-to-wetware combat, and very intense—even if highly imaginary—ethno-confessional hatreds going back to centuries-old holy wars between Christendom and the "Antichrist" Ottoman Turks. Many commentators have bemoaned the resistance of the Balkans to "civilized" reason and modern technologies:

> The abstract humanitarian-moralistic way of looking at the process of history is the most barren of all. I know this very well. But the chaotic mass of material acquisitions, habits, customs and prejudices that we call civilization hypnotizes us all, inspiring the false confidence that the main thing in human progress has already been achieved—and then war comes, and reveals that we have not yet crept out on all fours from the barbaric period of our history. We have learned how

to wear suspenders, to write clever leading articles, and to
make milk chocolate, but when we need to reach a serious
decision about how a few different tribes are to live together
on a well-endowed European peninsula, we are incapable of
finding any other method than mutual extermination on a
mass scale.

So wrote the exiled, out-of-work revolutionary Leon Trotsky in
1912, killing time during the Balkan Wars as foreign correspon-
dent for the *Kievan Thought*, seeking answers to the so-called
Eastern Question of what next after the decline and fall of the
Ottoman Empire.

History never repeats itself. Yet, with the information revolution it does seem at critical times to get caught in a feedback
loop. Now, with the technical reproducibility of war (a.k.a. television), we are witnessing a kind of global swarming, where
workers (world leaders) and drones (voyeuristic viewers) chase
after the queen bees of TV ("This is Christiane Amanpour reporting for Cable News Network from yet another war-torn region of
the world"). Individually, they might be in search of a New
World Order, a Global Village, or only an ephemeral fix of Virtual Community, but together, as the exceptional moment is rendered by real-time TV into permanent movement, they forgo the
security of the hive for the free terror of the global swarm. States
still matter and wars are still fought, but a new border has been
built by the information revolution between those who get stung
(the real-life victims) and those who get the buzz (the viewers).

Clearly the information revolution has given the Bosnia
Question a political urgency and extraterritorial proximity that
the first and second Balkan Wars never had. What Western
leader would now be willing to say, as did Bismarck, that "the
whole Balkan Peninsula is not worth the bones of a single Pome-
ranian grenadier"? Or at least be willing to say it on TV, before
an election, or with a major military budget to pass? These are
the modern imperatives of states working for that elusive "democratic peace," of which Kant wrote and contemporary leaders
now speak. With a new post–cold war transparency, transnational, nonideological television was supposed to spread the
democratic word and to preempt the totalitarian urge.

Technology always cuts both ways, however. Indeed, in the
case of television, the technological edge is multifaceted and
fractal in effect. And Bosnia is not the first war to prove resistant
to the televisual fix. Instead, the ubiquity of the image seems to

have produced a simulation of war, dirtier than the Persian Gulf War, yet just as simulated for the viewer as it is deadly real for the victims. "It is only television!" said French agent provocateur Jean Baudrillard of the Gulf War in a notorious series of articles in *Libération*:

> The United Nations has given the green light to a diluted kind of war—the right of war. It is a green light for all kinds of precautions and concessions, making a kind of extended contraceptive against the act of war. First safe sex, now safe war.

Ever hyperbolic to capture the diabolic nature of the image, what he said then informs us now about Bosnia:

> In our fear of the real, of anything that is too real, we have created a gigantic simulator. We prefer the virtual to the catastrophe of the real, of which television is the universal mirror. Indeed it is more than a mirror: Today television and news have become the ground itself, television plays the same role as the card which is substituted for territory in the Borges fable.

Baudrillard's allusion to *The Book of Sand*, by Jorge Luis Borges, is instructive. An emperor sends out his royal cartographers to make the perfect map of his empire, only to have them return years later with a map that dwarfs the now-shrunken empire; the emperor naturally prefers the model to reality. Like all Borges, not an entirely fabulous tale: Consider the initial reaction of Western leaders when the Berlin Wall took its first hits from the sledgehammers. U.S. President George Bush and Secretary of State James Baker, at a hastily organized press conference, kept pointing to a map on the table in front of them, assuring the public that all frontiers—sovereignty indelibly inscribed on paper—would survive such a historic event. As in the childhood game, paper covers stone taken down by the hammer blows. In contrast, the atlases of Rand McNally (more market oriented than governments to the flux of the times) began to sprout peel-away labels promising replacements should there be any more border changes.

Are we not witnessing in Bosnia the fractal effects of a similar decline of empires, a denial of reality, a retreat into virtuality? A bid for a kind of "virtual security"? Does not television now play the role of the emperor's cartographers, electronically mapping an empire, a state, a history that no longer exists—if it ever did? Now TV adds a human dimension—if not historical depth—to the fable, anthropology to cartography, tales of ancient hatreds that brook no comprehension by the "civilized" viewers. Westerners come to recognize the former Yugoslavia as that region at the edge of the map where the sea monsters lurk: Do Not Go There. The Slovenian social theorist Slovoj Zizek believes this "evocation of the complexity of circumstances serves to deliver us from the responsibility to act . . . that is, to avoid the bitter truth that, far from presenting the case of an eccentric ethnic conflict, the Bosnian War is a direct result of the West's failure to grasp the political dynamic of the disintegration of Yugoslavia, of the West's silent support of 'ethnic cleansing.'" The complexities of Yugoslavia had been lost in the bipolar interstices of the cold war. With its end came an explosion of multipolar truths and multicultural identities.

At the borders of the Bosnia Question, between the military terror inside and diplomatic error outside, truths bitter or otherwise are hard to find. Instead, one finds dissimulations of war and ethnic enmity up hard against simulations of peace and military intervention. On the one hand, the "dissim skills" of Bosnian Serb leader Radovan Karadzic and Serbian president Slobodan Milosevic, honed in the deceit of communism, retooled through the conceit of nationalism, revived—let us call it what it is—a national socialism for the '90s. On the other hand, Western leaders and pundit-cartographers, whether utopian about a new world order of self-determined polities or nostalgic for the lost stability of the cold war, rely once again on the pretense of TV to keep and video-bombs to make what never was peace. At this borderline, mutations of past empires mate with images of perpetual war: Gibbon of *Decline and Fall* meets Gibson the *Neuromancer* in the Balkans; Bosnia as a looped sim/dissim war.

In Germany, the U.S. First Armored Division was simulating a more forceful answer to the Bosnia Question, however. Would it work? In microchip times, is there still a role for the Big Green Machine?

The Bosnia Question took me to the Hohenfels Combat and Maneuver Training Center (CMTC). The U.S. Army owns—or, more precisely, has "maneuver rights" over—a significant piece of real estate in southern Germany, 178 square kilometers in Hohenfels alone. Spread out over the State of Bavaria like an isosceles triangle are the three major sites of the U.S. Seventh

Army Training Command, through which rotate the Europe-based U.S. troops, as well as some units from the British, Spanish, Canadian, and German armies and the Dutch marines, for some laser-simulated warfare as well as for live-fire exercises.

The centers have an interesting heritage. Grafenwoehr, the oldest, was set up by the Royal Bavarian Army in 1907 to "play" some of the earliest *Kriegspiele,* or wargames. It served as the southern tactical arm of the northern Prussian head, most infamously represented by Count von Schlieffen, chief of the General Staff, who in 1905 designed the famous Schlieffen Plan that was supposed to anticipate the next German conflict. Instead, its iron-clad "war by timetable" helped to precipitate World War I, as one mobilization triggered a cascade of others throughout Europe. The two other training centers owe their origins to Hitler's rejection of the Treaty of Versailles, World War I's "peace of the victors," which included the humiliating 100,000 troop limitation for Germany. Rapidly filling up the ranks with new conscripts, the *Wehrmacht* found itself short on training space. Grafenwoehr was expanded and two new sites were created: Wildflecken in 1937 for the IX German Corps, and Hohenfels in 1938 for the VII German Corps.

The morning I drove past the front gate and into the Hohenfels CMTC, I learned a lesser-known part of its history. The tank-crossing sign, resembling World War I lead toys more than the M1 behemoths that skidded up the hill ahead of me, momentarily caught my attention, but it was the more conventional warning sign for "Cobblestones: Slippery When Wet" that seemed out of place. I later asked my handler, the very smart, very affable Colonel Wallace, why the short strip of quaint cobblestone interrupted the finely graded modern asphalt road into the base. He thought it had been left intact as a tribute to the Polish construction workers. I later filled in the blanks: Hohenfels, begun in 1938 and finished in 1940, had evidently been built by Polish *Sklavenarbeiter,* slave laborers. "Slippery when wet" was to become something of a coda for me during my visit to Hohenfels. Wars, when gamed, tend to lose their history of blood and deception.

The reason I was there had taken on a special urgency. Two weeks before my arrival at Hohenfels, North Atlantic Treaty Organization (NATO) air strikes on Bosnian Serb ammunition dumps triggered the Serbs to take more than 300 United Nations (UN) peacekeepers hostage. The cold peace flared hot when French soldiers in Sarejevo fought back after Bosnian Serbs disguised in French uniforms and UN blue helmets tried to take the Vrbanja Bridge. Britain and France announced plans to send a rapid reaction force. It seemed like the right time to come to Hohenfels to observe an "Operation other than War."

Just what that meant was supposed to be the subject of the morning brief, but confusion reigned, not least because some-time between my first fax-barrage requesting a visit to the base and my arrival, a name change had taken place. "Operations other than War" had been replaced by the more anodyne "Stability Operations." Word had not quite gotten through the ranks, however, and people kept shifting back and forth between the two. The confusion mounted as I sat in a darkened theater with my two handlers, Captain Fisher and Colonel Wallace, on either side and listened to the opening of Major Demike's multimedia, name-negating "brief." The major clearly had a take-no-prison-ers attitude toward the English language: "Army units from USAREUR (troops in Europe) rotate through the CMTC (I got that one) at least once a year for 21 days of Force-on-OPFOR training" (good guys versus bad guys), "situational training with MILES in the Box" (dial-a-scenario field exercises using lasers rather than bullets), "BBS training" (not bulletin board systems, but networked computer battle simulations with units based elsewhere), and "after-action reviews" (video presentations of what went right or wrong on the battlefield).

Major Demike got into the technology with vigor: "We have at CMTC the most realistic battlefield. The instrumentation sys-tem is state of the art. It is the best in the world." He skipped through technology like the MILES (Multiple Integrated Laser Engagement System) for firing and recording laser hits, the microwave relays that allowed for near real-time production of the video after-action reviews, and the simulated mortar and artillery capability. To punctuate the point, Colonel Wallace stepped in: "Once a unit goes into the Box, with the exception that they're shooting laser bullets, and that a guy, instead of fall-ing down with a gunshot wound, will read from a card he's car-rying in his pocket how badly hurt he is, virtually everything we do is real. There's nothing simulated in the Box."

After a long slog through computer graphics on the organi-zation and function of the CMTC, we finally got to the geopoliti-cal gist of the next day's "stability operation." Up came a map of "Danubia," trisected into "Sowenia," "Vilslakia," "Juraland," and, looking very much like a small fiefdom among them, the CMTC. The major's pointer started to fly: "Three separate countries have split off from Danubia—Sowenia and Vilslakia are at odds with each other. When we want to transition into high-intensity conflict, we have Juraland, which has heavy forces, come in on the side of one or other of the parties." Prodded to utter the word "Bosnia" just once, he would go no further, except to say that the scenario was based on intelligence sources, CNN reports, and the "threat books." For my benefit he did add, "You don't have to be a rocket scientist to figure out what this is modeled on."

No rocket scientist, I resorted to a kind of semiotics to sort out the countries. The new countries of the disintegrating Danubia bore some obvious similarities to the region of Yugoslavia; to the former republic, now independent state, of Slovenia, or perhaps the western enclave of Slavonia contested by the Croats and Serbs; and, of course, to the Jural mountain range. "Vilslakia" remained a mystery. The countries surrounding Danubia were familiar enough that I sought out my own intelligence source, Microsoft's CD-ROM version of Cinemania '95. It was not needed for the country to the northwest: "Teutonia" referred to the early Germanic tribes. But "Freedonia," to the northeast of Danubia, was clearly taken from the 1933 war satire *Duck Soup,* in which Groucho Marx so effectively played the power-hungry dictator of said country that the real dictator Mussolini banned the film in Italy. Below Danubia was "Ruritania," the country in the clouds that provided the surreal setting for W. C. Fields's 1941 classic, *Never Give a Sucker an Even Break.* What should one make of the Army's strange choice of simulated countries? Probably nothing much, except that some wargamer had a sense of humor as well as history—and, perhaps, also something for Margaret Dumont, who plays in both comedies the great dame (or Great Dane, as Fields might have quipped). Still I wondered whether Bosnians would get the joke.

The briefing ended with a short video of a "stability operation." By way of introduction, Colonel Wallace informed me that "none of this stuff is staged, it's all from live footage taken by the Viper video teams in the Box." Before I could fully enjoy the colonel's knack for paradox, the lights dimmed, the screen flickered, and Graham Nash was singing about "soldiers of peace just playing the game." The first clip was of a confrontation between partisans and soldiers that escalates into heated words; the last was in the same tent, with handshakes and professions of friendship being exchanged. In between, UN convoys are stopped by civilians; soldiers go down, wounded or dead; a body-bagged corpse is spat upon by a partisan; food supplies are hijacked by townspeople; a female member of the media gets shoved around; a bomb explodes and panic ensues in the town streets; a sniper fires on a humvee; dogs sniff for explosives; infiltrators are caught in a nightscope; a UN flag waves defiantly; and an old man drops to his knees in the mud in front of a humvee, begging for food. More in the sentimental aesthetic of an AT&T advertisement than a hyperreal MTV clip, it was strangely moving. I was disarmed by it.

The mood shifted quickly when the major concluded the briefing by handing me a four-inch-thick pile of documents. The rest of the day was a whirlwind of briefs-to-go. First stop was the "Warlord Simulation Center," full of desktop computers and Sun Microsystem computers for planning, preparing, and running simulations in the Box, out of the Box, or through the cyber-Box—that is, simulation networking, "remoting via satellite in and out of the Box to anywhere in the world." Next stop was a cavernous warehouse full of MILES gear under the watchful eye of Sergeant Kraus, who probably gave the best brief of the day. A man who clearly loved his job—or was just eager for some human company—he was as articulate as his lasers ("instead of a bullet, it sends out 120 words on a laser beam; in the center are eight kill words; anything else is a wound or near miss") as he made his way through the various shapes, types, and generations of lasers and sensors, all set up on a variety of weapons and menacing mannequins. He was stumped only once, when I asked what would happen if a Danubian sneaked up and hit one of his dummies on the head. Would any bells and lights go off? "Excuse me?" he said. "ROE?" Colonel Wallace intervened to explain: "Against the rules of engagement. One-meter rule. No physical contact in the Box." It seems that one conveys body-to-body harm with real words, not laser words, e.g., "I am butt-stroking you now, so fall down." I would later find out that in operations other than war, the rules of engagement were there to be broken.

The day ended with an interview with the pugnacious commander of the base, Colonel Lenz, who made a persuasive case for stability operations as essential training for the increasing number of missions in that "gray area between war and peace." He would not, however, be drawn out on the relationship between stability operations and Bosnia, especially when I queried him about the possibility that some might find the notion of stability based on the status quo to be offensive, in both senses of the word, when stabilization is perceived to be an enemy of justice or, simply, just deserts. "That's above my pay grade," was the colonel's reply. At the end of the interview he kindly suggested a debrief after my visit to the Box: "I've got people upstairs who can suck a guy's brain dry."

That was sufficient incentive to stay up that night and wade through the stack of papers that I had been given. The bulk of it was a 400-page document called the "Coordinating Draft of the Seventh Army Training Command White Paper of Mission Training Plan for Military Operations Other Than War." The introduction conveyed the philosophy of operations other than war and—after I waded through all the acronymic muck and bureaucratese ("Traditional MTP crosswalk matrixes for references and collective tasks are also included in this MTP")—the final paragraph emerged as a reasonably clear summary of the purpose of the plan:

> As we continue to maintain our proficiency in traditional wartime operations, our forces must also be ready to operate effectively in non-traditional roles. Units involved in conflicts anywhere within the full spectrum of operations will always face some elements of a complex battlefield. These elements include civilians in the area of operations, the press, local authorities, and private organizations. This White Paper is designed to assist leaders at all levels to more fully understand and prepare for these new challenges.

In postmodern terms, the White Paper was this year's model for the high-tech, post–cold war simulations and training exercises that would prepare U.S. armed forces for pre-peacekeeping noninterventions into those postimperial spaces where once- and wannabe-states were engaged in postwar warring. In terms of past experiences rather than future threats, Somalia, Haiti, Rwanda, and—judging from the many references to the *British Wider Peacekeeping Manual*—Northern Ireland lurked between the lines. Yet, in this simulated shadowland between military combat, police action, and relief aid, other clouds of global swarming could be discerned: Bosnia, yes; but why not as the next operation other than war, a counternarcotics operation in Mexico? Or a quarantine of a paramilitary survivalist camp in Idaho? Or checkpoints and convoy escorts through a persistently riotous Los Angeles? This week, however, the enemy at Hohenfels reflected the headlines.

Very early the next day I headed for the Box, where the warring ethnic groups of a disintegrating "Danubia" were about to make life very hard for the visiting First Armored Division. The morning began with a low fog—confirmed by the weather report at yet another brief, the "Battle Update for Rotation 95–10." The mission: "To provide humanitarian assistance and separate belligerent factions." It was broken down from the level of UNDANFOR (United Nations Danubian Force) commander to squadron tasks and included equipment lists, tactical rules of engagement, task force organization, and maps with vehicle and troop positions that were presented through a series of computer graphics. A schedule of major events followed, some of which required translation from the briefer, like "1100—SCUD Ambush of Convoy" (not the missile, but the "Sowenian Communist Urban Defenders") or "2230—JERK Raid vs. Care Facility in Raversdorf" (again, not Steve Martin, but the "Jurische Ethnic Rights Korps," guerrilla forces operating in the south sector). By the end of the brief I was in bad need of a scorecard.

Finally we were on our way to the Box. During the short ride through a gently sloping open terrain with trees on most of the hilltops, Colonel Wallace did the eco-army routine—"there are more trees and grass growing now than when we got here"— and, as if on cue, a substantial herd of deer dashed across the road in front of us. The valleys and hillsides looked pretty chewed up by all the maneuvers, and portable toilets dotted the landscape; but the fauna seemed to appreciate the fact that the U.S. Army—unlike the Bavarian hunters outside the Box—were shooting blanks.

The first stop was a UN checkpoint, one of many where civilians were stopped and forced to do a kind of self-search for weapons or explosives. Most of the M1 tanks and Bradleys had their turrets reversed, the universal symbol of nonaggression (or surrender). We arrived with a UN food convoy that was supposed to pass through the mock-town of Übingsdorf. The town came complete with the steep-roofed houses of Bavaria, a church with a steeple (no sniper in sight), a cemetery (no names on the gravestones), a mix of Vilslakian and Sowenian townspeople (dressed by a retired psychological-operations sergeant in what he described as "the eastern European 'grunge' look," accessorized with the requisite MILES vest), and a mayor who wore a green felt fedora and insisted that the food be unloaded for his hungry people.

Language differences, a belligerent crowd, and an aggressive reporter with an intrusive cameraman all jacked up the tension level: Lieutenant Colonel Vladimir, commander of the local Vilslakian garrison, was refusing to bring the rabble to order. Chants for food in a kind of pidgin German—*Essen, Essen*—made voice communication difficult. Suddenly the crowd began to move toward the trucks and a few rocks were thrown. The U.S. troops began to retreat, but already some of the townspeople were clambering up onto the trucks. It was then that one of the soldiers broke the first rule of engagement by grabbing a civilian to toss him off. "One-meter rule, one-meter rule!" shouted the observer/controllers on the scene. Some tanks and Bradleys, probably called up by the besieged sergeant in charge of negotiating with the mayor, came roaring up to join the convoy. The situation died down when the townspeople were rounded up and put under guard. Negotiations resumed, resulting in something of a compromise: The army would unload the food at the local UN headquarters. Nonetheless, after the troops pulled out, I watched as some of the townspeople pulled off the most realistic maneuver of the day: They scampered off with some of the large crates of food. Colonel Wallace later told me this was not in the script. I had witnessed some Box Improv.

The script-writers clearly had it in for this convoy. At just about every checkpoint, food had to be traded for safe passage. As we roared ahead in the colonel's humvee for high ground, I noticed an observer/controller crouched in the ruins of a building probably dating back to the *Wehrmacht* days. A bad sign. As the convoy descended the hill, all hell broke loose—machine-gun fire from the hills, smoke bombs marking hits, and the light-and-sound show of MILES sensors going off. The M1 tanks and Bradleys reacted sluggishly to the ambush, not moving, and worse, keeping their turrets reversed in the defensive posture, making it impossible to identify the enemy with thermal sights. Instead, someone from the convoy called in for a Cobra helicopter gunship, breaking another rule of engagement: Only minimum or proportional force should be used in a counterattack, to prevent a needless escalation of violence. From the last two engagements, it seemed apparent that the shift from war/sim to peace/sim was not going to be an easy one.

Other answers to the Bosnia Question come in a deeper shade of gray. When I plugged operations other than war into the new grid of information warfare and national security, I had hoped to gain some new insights into the difficult and often dangerous relationships Bosnia produced—between technology and violence, media and war, us and them—relationships now extant in the post-cold war disorder as well. In spite of the baying of the Western triumphalists, the only empire to emerge victorious from the end of the cold war was what Edmund Burke after an earlier revolution in Europe called the "empire of circumstance." The peace that followed, cold or hot, became an especially bad war for people in the borderlands like the Balkans, people who emerged from the thaw of once-rigid bipolar powers and truths into a traumatized condition of ethnic as well as ethical insecurity. All kinds of politicians, pundits, and soldiers-as-diplomats, feeling what Nietzsche called "the breath of empty space," rushed into this geopolitical flux and moral void with electoral promises (from U.S. president Bill Clinton to French president Jacques Chirac) and nationalist propaganda (from Karadzic's hard cop to Milosevic's soft cop). Others created a parallel universe of computerized simulations (operations other than war) and dissimulations (genocide as ethnic cleansing). The majority, I would say, have hung back and avoided the void. Whether they have maintained their angelic status is another question.

Still, the Bosnia Question, simulated, reported, agonized over, remains unanswered—and the possibility is high that it cannot be answered by traditional geopolitics and statecraft. Capital, information, technology, drug, and refugee flows are supplanting and in some cases subverting the powers not just of the international society but of the sovereign states themselves to manage the deleterious effects of global swarming. Contemporary world politics as a hiveless cloud of angry bees remains at best a metaphorical question, not a conclusive answer.

Nevertheless, I do think that Bosnia has produced a new set of questions about the future of warfare and peacemaking. Have we moved beyond that modernist moment—so aptly expressed by the poet William Butler Yeats—when the center no longer holds, to a kind of permanent postmodern movement of power? Does the West's self-identity—whether it is the sovereign state, the sovereign self, or a suprasovereign European Union—then become dependent upon a non-European Other? In other words, does Europe actually *need* Bosnia, the danger it represents, the otherness it embodies, for its own, on-the-fly, identity formation? After Bosnia, would another balkanized, postimperial parastate become the next dumping ground for the West's violence? In the fickle light of television, the information revolution began to look much less glorious and the future of sim/dissim wars more ominous.

Nevertheless, after my accelerated travels, there was a final speed bump at the National Strategy forum on "The Information Revolution and National Security" that caused some reflection. The setting, the First Division Museum, was eerily apt: It had been founded by the former editor and publisher of the *Chicago Tribune*, Col. Robert McCormick, who had fought at the battle of Cantigny in World War I with the First Division. Propaganda poster art from the period covered the conference room walls. One in dark sepia tones from 1917 stood out from the rest: "Save Serbia, Our Ally."

That evening, the former director of Central Intelligence, James Woolsey, gave the dinner address, "The Impact of New Information and Communications Technologies on National Security." The opening to his talk was pure cyberpunk, drawing from Neal Stephenson's *Snow Crash* to make the point that people were coming to prefer the cyberspatial order of the "metaverse" to the chaos and instability of the real world. He punched the message home with a line that drew the most laughs: "The Internet may be anarchic—but then we look at Bosnia." Woolsey, who probably gave the end of the cold war its best if bleakest sound bite—"The dragon has been slain but the jungle is filled with a bewildering variety of poisonous snakes"—mixed metaphors and captured paradoxes with a kind of blithe power. In Bosnia, the simulated swords of the dragon-slayers and the cartographic pens of the diplomats had failed, abysmally. Four years of war in the gut of Europe were soon to be stopped—but not yet resolved—by air strikes, a truce-conference in Dayton, Ohio, and the compellent power of the First Armored Division. Still, that night, the Net took on a new and appealing light as the metaphor and medium, if not the manager, of the New Chaos.

Note

The author would like to thank the MacArthur Foundation, McCormick Tribune Foundation, and St. Antony's College, Oxford, for their support on this project.

15

Regional Powers and Information Warfare

Ahmed Hashim

It may seem curious to write about the revolution in military affairs generally and, specifically, information warfare in the Third World[1] five years after the devastating defeat of one of its leading military powers, namely Iraq, by a powerful coalition headed by the world's leading military power, the United States. For about a century and a half, a number of nations, mostly Middle Eastern and Asian, have been striving to close, or at least narrow, the military-technological gap that had emerged between them and the industrialized West. It is in this light that we must see the frantic efforts by Third World states to attempt military modernization and reforms: to wit, Mohammed Ali in Egypt in the 1820s, the Ottoman Turks and Qajar Persia in the mid-nineteenth century, the *Tzu-ch'iang yun tung* or Self-Strengthening Movement in China between 1860 and 1895, and, last but not least, those of Meiji Japan. All but the last—which succeeded in the context of an all-encompassing modernization of Japan itself—failed miserably. The rapid evolution of science and technology in Japan from 1870 onward was one of the important factors behind the emergence of that country as a serious military power that defeated China in 1894–1895 and Russia in 1904–1905.[2]

The military-technological gap between European states and most of the rest of the world was best exemplified by the famous ditty by the British poet Hilaire Belloc on nineteenth-century colonial wars: "Whatever happens, Thank God we have got the Maxim Gun and they have not."[3] Now, it seems from the perspective of the last decade of the twentieth century, the military-technological gap has become a "yawning chasm" because of the far-reaching developments taking place in the nature of warfare in the advanced industrial states.[4]

Nonetheless, it would be wrong to believe that it has been only technology that has accounted for the disparity in military power between the West and the rest. The gap has had much to with the differences in organizational capabilities between the Europeans and their non-Western cobelligerents: in other words, in the ability of the European West to marshal effectively a finite number of social and economic resources to create formidable fighting machines. Most important, the organizational and administrative skills that have not been matched in non-European civilizations (save among, perhaps, the Mongols) have provided Western states with a significant advantage. Despite their ability to construct extraordinary monuments such as the Pyramids and the Great Wall of China, non-European civilizations have not equaled the Europeans—and with the emergence of the United States, the West in general—in the creation of national fighting power.[5]

The evolution of warfare has been periodically punctuated by sudden radical changes in the nature of war.[6] More precisely, these so-called revolutions in military affairs (RMAs) take place when a combination of technological, social, organizational, doctrinal, and politicoeconomic changes transform the way wars are waged.[7] Although there have been a number of RMAs throughout history, military historians and strategic thinkers have engaged in a long debate over what constitutes an RMA and how many there have been.[8] In the late twentieth century the phenomenal developments in information technologies are the driving force behind the changes taking place in the current revolution in military affairs. The information technologies in question—microelectronics, sensors, computers, automated control systems, telecommunications systems, and data processing systems—will be the key factors in the transmission of intelligence in real time; rapid location of enemy targets; relaying of information about such targets; continuous 24-hour operations; ability to engage in "deep strikes"; quest to control information and to be "information-dominant" on the battlefield; and enhancement of lethality, range, accuracy, and firepower of conventional weapons.[9] The result of these combined changes is a "dramatic increase—often an order of magnitude or greater—in the combat potential and military effectiveness of armed forces."[10]

This essay constructs a rough typology of military powers in the Third World that will try to contribute to a better understanding of the role of information warfare (IW) in those countries. In particular we want to advance our understanding of information war in advanced Third World military powers, a subset that includes but is not limited to the People's Liberation Army (PLA) of the People's Republic of China (PRC). Although we need to analyze briefly what important regional powers such as Pakistan and India are writing about the dynamic changes occurring in the area of conventional warfare because experts in both countries have written copiously about the phenomenon,[11] the main focus of the essay is the PLA, which has taken the lead in the Third World in writing about the current information-driven RMA.

Typology of Military Power in the Third World

Nonstate, Antistate, and Semistate Warfare

I choose to refer to this type of warfare as "Aideed warfare," after the Somali warlord, Mohammed Farah Aideed; and it will represent a challenge to the United States in the future. Ultimately, the ability of the United States to destroy such "pests" if measured solely by the yardstick of military power is not in doubt. Nonetheless, it will not be easy for the United States to bring to bear its high-tech conventional military superiority in the context of operations conducted in "failed" states where chaos, domestic violence, economic collapse, and nonexistent infrastructure are the order of the day.

John Keegan has done much to qualify the long-established concept that it is only the state that can make war, arguing that it is erroneous to believe that there is one way of warfare in human society.[12] The modern state that emerged in the West is a relatively recent phenomenon that arose from the ashes of feudal Europe consumed by the Thirty Years' War. War made the state, in the sense that it created states where none existed before and helped solidify the requisite institutions for a monarch to wage war more effectively and with greater sustainability. It is also clear that, so far, history has proved the Westphalian state the most efficient and deadly institution for the waging of war in human history, and it is the Western state that has attained a capacity for war-making that continues to be envied by non-Western powers.

The rest of the world has striven mightily and often unsuccessfully to create war machines in the image of those of the West. Yet, there have existed throughout history and there will continue to emerge in the future nonstate, protostate, and even antistate actors that have waged and will wage war differently. These are clearly entities about which one cannot say that the state—assuming there is one—has a monopoly on the instruments of violence, if we follow one of Max Weber's well-known definitional criteria of what a state is: "a human community that successfully claims the monopoly of the legitimate use of physical force within a given territory."[13]

The more technologically backward or the more socially collapsed a society—as, for example, Somalia is—the more culturally alien to us will be elements of their asymmetrical strategy. On the one hand, we may be able to comprehend and applaud the following tactic:

> A Somali warlord or his ilk may not have to gain an ultimate strategic advantage to win. He may indulge in the subtleties of information warfare and global public relations by manipulating the power of satellite news broadcasting to influence an event without recourse to superior weaponry. . . .[14]

On the other hand, we may not find the following example easy to absorb culturally or intellectually:

> A tribal leader, meanwhile, may conduct information warfare with technologies that predate Thomas Edison. Aideed's followers in Somalia reportedly communicated U.S. troop activity to their peers by beating wooden sticks on oil barrels.[15]

Yet, the primitiveness of the method did not make it any less effective in transmitting information about the activity of American troops.

In the future, Aideed warfare will no doubt have its more sophisticated practitioners whose tactics and methods will approach guerrilla warfare but who will also combine the use of information technologies and asymmetrical strategies drawn from their cultural background (and from the political and geographical context of the conflict they are engaged in) to inflict severe losses on their enemies. In particular, it is worth noting the ability of nonstate warriors to manipulate First World public opinion via global satellite television—technology possessed, ironically, by the adversary. This is an extremely effective, inexpensive, and increasingly popular form of information warfare among such groups such as Somali clans, Bosnian Serbs, and Chechen rebels.

In this context one can suggest further avenues for future research by looking at the limitless number of bloody nonstate/

guerrilla wars that have transpired this century. Michael Collins's brilliant war of revolutionary terror against British intelligence capabilities in southern Ireland and the Chechen war against Russia in 1994–1995 are but two illustrative examples.[16] Although I want to concentrate on Michael Collins here because he is less familiar to us, it seems important to point out the fact that the Chechen guerrillas, particularly during the Russian fiasco at Pervomoskaie in early January 1996, were better supplied with communications equipment than the Russian government: it seemed that "every Chechen had a Motorola walkie-talkie."[17] Similarly, the guerrillas fighting the Indian army in the Kashmir conflict are better equipped than the Indians with communications equipment, including frequency-hopping radios. Finally, in southern Lebanon, Hizballah, the Islamist guerrilla group confronting the Israelis, has come a long way from the days when it was a ragtag force. It has received tremendous help from the Iranians, who have supplied it with good communications equipment, better intelligence, and more flexible organizational structure.

Michael Collins—the supreme revolutionary terrorist—presents us with another form of deadly warfare that could become virulent by making use of the revolution in information technology. No so-called revolutionary terrorist in the Third World (or even in the West in the 1970s) in contemporary times measures up to the standards of Michael Collins.[18] His genius lay in a number of interrelated tactical practices:

- First, in his practice of clandestinity—the essential characteristic was the invisibility of the "clandestines" within the environment in which they operated; as one analyst put it, the clandestines "looked exactly like everybody else."[19] Mohammed Farah Aideed would clearly understand and approve of this, as he himself practiced it in one way or another against the foreign forces during the Somalia imbroglio.[20]
- Second, Collins practiced the art of rationalistic terror—in the sense that it was directed at British intelligence and information without seeking to cause deliberate collateral damage to the civilians. He achieved this goal through his creation of a professional force of rapid-reaction assassins who neutralized British information-gathering and intelligence by identifying and "terminating" British intelligence and security officials.[21]

- Finally, Collins showed an acute understanding of the importance of disseminating news of his terrorist activities via rumor and the media. This terror, which was directed at British command and control and instruments of repression, had to reach a mass audience in Ireland, Britain, and the rest of the world.

It is not too difficult to imagine the havoc that could be caused by a ruthless and committed revolutionary terrorist of the Michael Collins model armed with a highly secure and impenetrable clandestine organization and the technologies of the information age.

Nuclear Pretenders: Regional Powers with Weapons of Mass Destruction and Asymmetrical Strategies

This category includes major military powers in the Third World with large conventional armies and weapons of mass destruction capabilities ranging from ballistic missiles through chemical to biological and nuclear weapons. These are powers with serious grand strategic problems and technological, social, and organizational constraints in the creation of effective military power. Their military weaknesses are most obvious in the conventional arena: they are owners of large and obsolescent conventional forces that are increasingly difficult to fund and to reequip with high-tech weapons systems. Their awareness of this fact has led these large conventional powers to seek asymmetrical strategies in nonconventional weapons or weapons of mass destruction (WMD). Weapons of mass destruction are of considerable political-military utility for powers that will be left behind in the race toward a more sophisticated and higher form of conventional warfare—especially that made possible by the new information technologies.

A possible secondary strategy will be for them to attempt to leverage advanced conventional military technology in certain branches or services to create small niches of military excellence. In fact, we may find such powers developing three-legged military structures consisting of conscript, professional, and small specialist niches as displayed in the pyramidal diagram (figure 1).

- The specialist force niche is designed to (1) provide the capability to retaliate and (2) attack high-value targets and

Figure 1.   Regional Power Conventional Force Structure

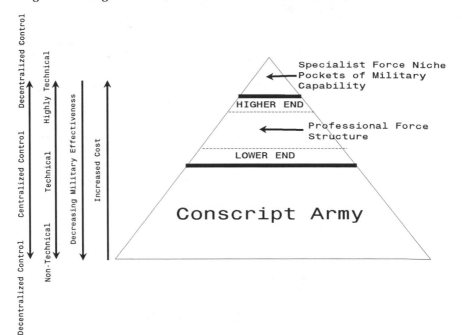

maximize the casualties of advanced industrial states through cruise missile units, mobile ballistic missile units, electronic warfare, special forces, and deception, camouflage, and concealment units.

- The professional force structure staffs the traditional weapons platforms—tanks, airplanes, and ships. It wages war against advanced forces in conjunction with the specialist niche force and can be used in countercoups, internal/regime security, and power projection against regional adversaries.

- The conscript army is virtually useless for combat that involves power projection, but is useful for civic duties, economic activities, and waging a people's war against invaders.

The primary politicostrategic goal of these niches will be to survive the blows of an information-dominant adversary (i.e., a Western power) and to inflict on it the maximum casualties possible, thus creating an adverse political impact in the West. Such a structure would be costly. It is, however, less costly than building a smaller and entirely professional force structure and more combat effective than having a largely conscript force structure.

Ultimately, however, even if the powers in this category were to acquire advanced conventional war capabilities and were suddenly endowed with the required technical talent, it is far from clear that they would be able to wage information warfare. Possession of weapons systems does not automatically endow military forces with the ability to utilize them. Military powers in this category have armed forces that have consistently shown a lack of organizational flexibility in the waging of war. These powers have been unable to achieve *jointness*—which refers to the ability of different services (air, land, and sea) to fight effectively together, creating an effect that is greater than the sum of its parts—or even to fight combined arms operations on a sustained basis. Their wars bring to mind Eliot Cohen's characterization of "distant battles" in the Third World as dominated by land warfare and a systematic inability to integrate into operations using aerial and naval power.[22] Many wars in the Third World have essentially been ground wars with desultory or ineffective participation by the other two services.[23]

There are a number of reasons for the inability of different services to fight effectively together. First, because they were not large arms producers, many of the significant conventional military powers of the Third World found themselves with, or deliberately chose, different suppliers for different services of their military establishments. Thus, services not only had different weapons systems but developed incompatibilities in logistics, doctrine, and modus operandi.

Second, in many large Third World militaries there never arose a culture of interservice cooperation or coordination. Often jealous of one another and fighting for a bigger or the biggest slice of the defense budget, the services in many Third World states exist as autonomous fiefdoms headed by service chiefs more interested in playing national politics or defending their turf (their service).[24]

Third, in many Third World countries, political rulers have specifically discouraged cooperation among the individual services because they have often cooperated to "get rid of" their country's political rulers. The history of Iraqi political evolution is notorious in this respect: many times over the past several decades, armor units and the air force have joined to conduct coups. The regime of Saddam Hussein has gone to great lengths to control the armed forces by waging a form of information warfare against it, including the use of intensive ideological indoctrination and the maintenance of overlapping layers of surveillance. The focus of the regime's surveillance was the air force and armor, where frequent purges, rotations, retirements, and the segmentation of communications, coupled with the rarity of joint exercises, acted to ensure that these two branches were among the worst in the Iraqi armed forces during the Iran-Iraq and Gulf Wars.[25]

Major Third World Nuclear Powers with Niche Potential in IW

Pakistan and India are two advanced Third World military powers whose respective military establishments and voluminous output on military affairs are a source of envy and admiration in other Third World states. Following the Gulf War of 1991, Pakistani policy and defense planners accepted the fact that drastic and far-reaching changes in the nature of war have occurred.[26] Pakistani analysts have noted, among other things, the major asymmetries in technological capabilities between the coalition forces and Iraq during the Gulf War in favor of the former, notably in the areas of electronic warfare; command, control, communications and intelligence (C^3I); airpower; and night-fighting.[27]

While noting some of the areas in which Iraq managed to achieve some measure of success (for example, survivability of political command and control or deception and camouflage), Pakistani analysts recognize that there is not much that Pakistan can do about the technological aspects of high-tech conventional warfare for a variety of reasons. First of all, despite having one of the most formidable military establishments in the Third World and despite being a nuclear power, Pakistan is one of the world's poorest nations, with an abysmally low per capita income level. It has not invested sufficiently in its defense industries or, more pertinent to the topic of our study, in its scientific and technological infrastructure (in which it lags behind its chief rival, India).

For Indian defense planners, the Gulf War has demonstrated the devastating effects of nonnuclear high-technology weapons:

The advent of sophisticated weapon systems and force multipliers have drastically changed the scope and magnitude of modern war. Besides the lethal, long range weapons of pinpoint accuracy, the employment of effective surveillance devices and electronic warfare have so compounded the complexity of warfare that commanders are left with limited reaction time for taking decisions based on large flow of data which can no longer be effectively processed by slow and cumbersome manual procedures. *The ability to use vast operational information and react to fast changing situations may well prove to be one of the most important battle winning factors in future wars.*[28]

The Indian officer quoted above laments the fact that the computer culture has not taken root in the Indian armed forces despite the use of computers in the services since the 1960s. This is a remarkable state of affairs in light of the fact that India is a major force in the global computer software industry.[29] The result is that automation of command, control, and communications within the Indian armed forces has been haphazard and inefficient. He then proceeds to enumerate the reasons why information technology has been approached in a lackadaisical manner.

First, the decision to promote a new technology among personnel who are inadequately prepared for or poorly trained in information technologies will lead to overreliance on technical experts or specialists whose esoteric skills and language few will understand. Moreover, these specialists "try to utilize the new technology to serve their own limited purpose of gaining informal authority and importance rather than enhancing the overall effectiveness of the organization" of which they are a part.[30] It goes without saying that commanders in charge must prevent skilled technicians from losing sight of their main goal, which is to serve the organization. Second, a bigger obstacle is the fact that the senior echelons of the officer corps have not yet recognized the necessity of diffusing the computer culture throughout the armed forces.

In conclusion, an appreciation of the organizational flexibility needed for the adoption of information technologies required by high-tech warfare does not yet exist in the Indian armed forces.[31] There seems to be an inherent bureaucratic resistance to change and organizational innovation.[32] This would seem to include an aversion to domination by the "technical specialists," as opposed to what Eliot Cohen calls the "specialists in direct combat."[33]

Advanced Conventional Military Powers of the Third World

There may emerge in the not-too-distant future an important category of conventionally advanced military powers in the Third World.[34] What would characterize these advanced conventional military powers? First, their high-tech military prowess will be largely a result of "spin-ons" from advanced commercial information technologies such as high-speed computers, sensors, advanced software, semiconductors, and artificial intelligence and from advanced manufacturing technologies such as computer-assisted design and machining (CAD/CAM).[35]

Second, such powers will be able to field militaries that can achieve jointness among their various services and conduct combined arms warfare. Moreover, such countries will be able to field a higher percentage of technical specialists in their armed forces than other regional powers.

Entry into such a category is limited by the very advanced nature of conventional power generated by these states. It includes or will include in the near future the following countries: Israel, Taiwan, South Korea, and much further in the future—and of immense portent for the United States—the People's Republic of China, which is the subject of a brief analysis below. Israel is the only country in the Middle East that fully understands the evolution of information war as a theoretical construct. It is the only Middle Eastern state that has the technological, doctrinal, and organizational capability to wage high-tech warfare.[36] As a result, Arab states may genuinely believe that Israeli conventional forces are capable of conducting a mini–Desert Storm against their conventional power.

The PLA and Information War

Judging by the quantity and quality of literature put out by the PRC on the current revolution in military affairs and information warfare, it is quite clear that Chinese defense analysts and the PLA are giving serious consideration to the dramatic technological, organizational, and doctrinal changes occurring in the realm of conventional warfare in recent years. The Chinese view of information war can best be understood by looking at it from a number of different perspectives.

Global Events and Changes in Chinese Geostrategic Thinking

First, an understanding of a number of global events and changed geostrategic circumstances, coupled with developments in Chinese strategic and military thinking, is a prerequisite to understanding evolving Chinese thinking about the changing nature of war.

The Chinese "defeat" in the Sino-Vietnamese War of 1979. This brief border war showed that the PLA was incapable of waging modern war. Although the characteristics of IW were not widely apparent at that time, the war highlighted the fact that the Chinese military did not have a military remotely capable of constructing a rudimentary information war infrastructure. Its communications systems were pitiful, and its equipment was easily jammed by the forces of the People's Army of Vietnam. Its C^3I system and electronic warfare (EW) capabilities were even worse. Last but not least, it proved incapable of conducting combined arms operations. In short, not only was the PLA a military unready to leap into the information age, it proved that it was barely part of the industrial age.

The PLA and the changing role of nuclear weapons. Although nuclear weapons were important during the cold war both strategically and militarily (although they were never used), their importance will decline in the era of postindustrial, high-tech conventional warfare. Nonetheless, the PRC will not ignore the modernization and enlargement of its nuclear weapons inventory.

The PLA and doctrinal changes. The long-held, elaborate, and well-developed structure of military thought and doctrine in the PLA has undergone considerable change since the mid-1980s. In shifting their focus away from fighting protracted, large-scale wars with adversaries like the USSR to focus on limited local wars, the Chinese have realized that they need to build mobile rapid-reaction forces.[37] They have also come to realize that information technologies will constitute a significant force multiplier for these combat units.

The PRC's assessment of other Asian powers. In recent years the PRC has begun to pay more attention to the emergence of

Japan not only as a major economic and financial power, but also as a potentially serious military power with an advantage in high-technology weaponry. This Chinese assessment is based on the recent expansion of the scope of Japanese defense thinking: namely, the decision to expand and improve an already highly modern self-defense force, increase defense expenditures, and accelerate science and technology research—in which Japan already excels.[38]

The PLA and the lessons of the Persian Gulf War.   Although it is important to recognize that the PLA did not begin to think about or implement military modernization for high-tech war because of the Gulf War, that conflict has nonetheless had a tremendous impact on thinking and planning in the PLA over the past five years.[39] Initially, the PLA believed that the Iraqis might actually perform well and inflict severe reverses on the coalition; but as the conflict unfolded, the stunned PLA witnessed the efficacy of technologically advanced warfare. The PLA emerged with a commitment to rectifying its weaknesses in the areas of EW, C3I, airpower, and night vision equipment.[40]

PLA Evaluation of Social and Technological Changes in Warfare

Second, what are the underlying social, philosophical and technological changes that constitute the driving forces behind the changing nature of warfare in the information age?

War is no longer an industrial but a postindustrial phenomenon. War has already gone through two ages, the agricultural and the industrial, and it is now entering that of information. War is still clearly about victory, but more so than in the past, information will be the critical factor in bringing about victory. The technologies of the late twentieth century that have emerged largely in the civilian field have given information this decisive role. This Chinese formulation is remarkably similar to that advanced by Alvin and Heidi Toffler in their book, *War and Anti-War*. In Chinese eyes, the PLA is still in the early industrial phase of warfare, and yet it might face technologically superior enemies in the future that are well established in the postindustrial information age.[41] These states will have powerful and comprehensive information enhancement and information suppression technologies.

Recognition of this fact has led the Chinese to pay more attention to the state of their science and technology infrastructure.

The PRC and the reevaluation of science and technology.
Between 1948 and the mid-1970s, science and technology (S&T) had a checkered history in the PRC. Despite the Central Committee's issuance of the great call for "marching toward science" and the formulation of the country's first long-term science and technology development program in 1956, S&T policy was hostage to the collapse of Sino-Soviet relations in 1960 (which terminated all technical cooperation between the two Communist states and caused the withdrawal of Soviet technical expertise); political turmoil occasioned by the so-called Great Proletarian Cultural Revolution of 1966–1976; and a general denigration of the role of intellectuals, scientists, and experts in the creation of national power. The long-term adverse impact of the Cultural Revolution on all aspects of the Chinese educational system cannot be underestimated.[42]

Naturally, these events or trends negatively affected the institutionalization of technology in the armed forces, where the Cultural Revolution imposed the ideological value that "redness" was more important than "expertness" with dire consequences for armed forces training, readiness, and modernization.[43]

The PLA emphasis on military modernization and the role of science and technology was given a strong push forward by Chairman Deng Xiaoping, who emerged as leader of China in the 1970s. Chairman Deng was aware not only of the fact that the People's Republic was 25 to 30 years behind the West in civilian and military science and technology, but also that science and technology were the "primary productive forces"—the essential elements necessary for China to emerge as a developed and technologically advanced state. In this context, the adoption by the Chinese Communist Party of a flexible diplomatic approach and of an economic-growth-oriented policy in the early 1980s enabled the PRC to obtain advanced foreign technology to try to improve its weaponry and modernize its weapons designs.

Moreover, the Chinese are also aware that information technology is an increasingly important subunit of science and technology research:

> At present, the information industry is on the eve of a revolution. New technologies characterized by digitalization,

network systems, mobility, intelligence, and comprehensive-
ness will thoroughly change the existing working methods
of design, production, marketing, services, and banking, as
well as people's lifestyles. . . . The revolution in the information industry will be a major catalyst in the development of
computer, microelectronics, photoelectronics, lasers, automation, telecommunications networking. . . . [44]

Like others, the Chinese realize that while the impetus for these
far-reaching changes comes from the civilian sector, they will
affect the development of warfare. Advances in sensors, Global
Positioning System receivers, microelectronic technologies, and
new technologies such as lasers and artificial intelligence constitute the overall information technology base that is having a
crucial impact on warfare and military development. Their diffusion to the military sector will lead to the computerization of
weaponry, combat command automation, combat force digitization, and the instant collection of combat action data. Chinese
analysts have concluded that information technologies have
become an integral aspect of high-tech warfare in the twenty-
first century and those militaries that are in the forefront of
these developments will be at the cutting edge of military
power. [45]

The Military Characteristics of Information Warfare

Third, what do the Chinese see as the military characteristics of
information warfare? Chinese writings refer to precision-
guided munitions, particle beam weapons, microwave weapons, long-range strike munitions, electronic warfare capabilities,
stealth technologies, space-based weapons, robotic vehicles
(vehicles that possess information-acquisition and processing
capabilities) and C3I infrastructures as the key weapons systems of information warfare. Traditional weapons platforms
such as airplanes, ships, tanks, helicopters, and armored personnel carriers will be "information-intensified" (i.e., equipped) on
a major scale with advanced electronic warfare systems, telecommunications systems, and computers. [46]

The Operational Characteristics of Information Warfare

Fourth, what are the operational characteristics of information
warfare as perceived by the Chinese? Control of information

becomes a key goal, as is its denial to the enemy, together adding up to information dominance on the battlefield. In an information-intensified battlefield, everything one does will be transparent—meaning readily observable or easily seen. If there is a significant gap between the information capabilities of adversaries, however, what transpires on the battlefield will be transparent only to one side.

In the information age, what matters is not so much the hardware at one's disposal but the efficiency of that hardware as measured by its ability to achieve its aim; for that, one needs information. As one Chinese analysis concludes:

> Our sights must not be fixed on the firepower warfare of the industrial age, rather they must be trained on the information warfare of the information age.[47]

The decentralization of command will be a key operational characteristic, with command authority being dispersed, command procedures streamlined, and commanders at all levels provided with the capabilities provided by information technologies to see true battlefield conditions at all times and in real time. Consequently, information systems and C^3I nodes become the attack target of choice, in contrast to the past (i.e., the industrial warfare era) when the main objective was the destruction of the enemy's forces and material assets.

In contrast with wars of the industrial era, which were generally wars of attrition or wars of annihilation,[48] wars in the information age will be wars of incapacitation directed at command and control and information nodes. The victim may still have much of its military intact but will not have control over it.

The PLA's View on Building an Integrated High-Tech IW Capability

The open literature on PLA military developments indicates that there are at least four aspects to the creation of armed forces able to wage war effectively in the information age and under high-tech conditions.

First, there is a renewed emphasis on continuing and deepening the process of modernization of the PLA. As Vice Chairman of the Central Military Commission Liu Huaqing put it in 1993, "While the state makes economic construction its central task, the Army makes modernization its central task."[49] It is now even more imperative to hurry the modernization process within the armed forces because the multipolar world that is unfolding will be characterized by the emergence of many types of conflicts and by a sharpening of conflicts.

Second, there are also considerable exhortations to intensify high-tech training of the PLA.[50] In 1993 the armed forces intensified high-tech training with the beginnings of reforms in operational tactics, training methods, and PLA logistics. In 1994 the armed forces began the process of analyzing and devising ways to deal with the problems that had cropped up during the training reform period of 1993. Training reforms will institute new operational concepts that will suit the needs of operations under high-tech conditions. The PLA will intensify efforts to master high-technology weapons systems, with a focus on analyzing the special strengths of "formidable enemies." These efforts will lead to the institutionalization of new training methods that will simulate actual warfare as much as possible and that will include an opposition force (OPFOR) made up of "Blue Army" (Western?) units that combine flexible tactics, innovative thinking, and unconventional methods pitted against a low-tech and somewhat "plodding" industrial-era "Red Army" (PLA?) that does things by the book.

Third, Chinese officers, officials, and defense analysts have called for making use of China's tradition of flexible fighting methods and combining them with high-technology capabilities.[51] Chinese writings on the changing nature of warfare differentiate between waging an information war against enemies with superior information technologies and superior weapons and enemies with capabilities inferior to those of the PLA. China will remain inferior to serious potential enemies in the realm of information warfare for a long time. Its best hope is to adopt its traditional warfare method of "you fight your way, I'll fight my way," using its strengths to attack the enemy's weaknesses. In order to reduce the enemy's advantage, however, China's traditional way must be married to its emerging information warfare capability.

The Chinese have not fallen into the trap of thinking that a revolution in military affairs is only, or even primarily, a technology-driven phenomenon. Their very strategic culture and military history act as a break against falling into the trap of technological determinism. Yet, at the same time, they have clearly recognized the falsehood of stressing "redness" at the expense of "expertise," human spirit and fervor at the expense of

material excellence. These variables work in tandem with one
another.

Fourth, Chinese analysts have called for cultivation of technical talent to maximize the potential of information warfare.
Chinese defense analysts have argued that specialist technical
knowledge or technical talent must be cultivated in the research
laboratories and research institutions. There must be close coordination among the universities, research centers, and the military establishment.

Technical talent must be cultivated among the commanders:
"they must have the ability to conduct comprehensive analysis
and policy-information processing and to understand themselves and the enemy, the battlefield, and have a capacity for
strategic thinking and an open mind."[52] Technical talent must be
diffused among the combat and support personnel. The role of
this latter group in information warfare is critical because a large
number of personnel will be engaged mainly in information collection, transmission, and assessment in order to provide commanders with real-time data. Thus, the Chinese are also aware of
the fact that warfare of the future will require the emergence of
technical experts who are not warriors in the traditional sense.[53]

PLA Weaknesses in Information Warfare:
In Lieu of a Conclusion

There will be few countries in the Third World in the short and
medium terms that will be able to understand the full nature of
the changes taking place in warfare, and fewer still will be able
to wage information warfare. Writing about and dissecting the
RMA theoretically and conceptually and actually being able to
conduct high-tech information-intensive warfare are two totally
different things. Whether the PLA succeeds in the latter is
another matter altogether.

The Chinese are aware that they lag considerably behind the
West in terms of science and technology. While numerically
impressive, the PLA is still in many ways an immobile and
antiquated behemoth that cannot project military power over
long distances. Its command, communications, control, and
intelligence network is still relatively rudimentary; it lacks precision-guided munitions; and it has a backward electronic warfare
system.[54]

It is not clear that this will remain the case in the future, particularly in light of China's recent phenomenal economic growth

and the Chinese leadership's determination to modernize the country, including its armed forces.[55] As one recent study pointed out: "China's very rapid economic growth, if sustained, will not only improve its capacity to pay for selected high-technology imports, but will also advance China's industrial, technological and scientific base such that it will be able to make quite significant technological leaps. . . ."[56] Although the author of these remarks points out the possible limitations that the Chinese military is likely to continue to labor under 15 to 20 years from now, the belief that technologically backward nations cannot succeed in innovation in the realm of strategy and doctrine is erroneous. Moreover, the PRC is behaving in ways that are beginning to alarm its regional neighbors and the United States: claims to islands in the South China Sea and its threats to the "renegade" province of Taiwan are among the most worrisome trends.[57]

It is true that the United States, despite severe problems with its educational system, continues to be the knowledge society par excellence, which gives it a commanding "information edge," as two analysts put it.[58] U.S. defense planners and policy-makers, to whom these observations are addressed—because any revolutionary changes in key foreign militaries do have an impact on our national security—rest on their Gulf War laurels and succumb to the belief that other powers, particularly potential "peer" contenders, will not devise ways to deal with U.S. superiority in IW or devise methods to neutralize U.S. superiority. The study of the current RMA and its impact on the future of war is an expanding field, judging by the quantity of literature appearing. So far, however, little has been written about the information-based RMA and the Third World. Undoubtedly, the PRC and other Third World powers will continue to devote further analyses to the field of information warfare. It is hoped that this essay will help provoke further research into this area.

Notes

1. The term "Third World" is used generically to refer to a very large and nonhomogeneous part of the globe. The author does not ignore the very pronounced differences within this body of states. Some parts are not even in the Third World anymore but because of their abject poverty or failure as states could be called the Fourth World. Others are close in economic and military power to the lower level or midlevel of the category known as

advanced industrial states that includes the West and the former states of the Eastern bloc. The fact that the more advanced states of the West are no longer industrial but postindustrial information societies merely highlights the gap.

2. See John Marks, *Science and the Making of the Modern World* (London: Heinemann, 1983) pp. 408–417; for an excellent and detailed analysis of the evolution of military technology in Japan see the book by Richard Samuels, *"Rich Nation, Strong Army": National Security and the Technological Transformation of Japan* (Ithaca: Cornell University Press, 1994).

3. Quoted in Barry Buzan, *An Introduction to Strategic Studies. Military Technology and International Relations* (London: Macmillan, 1987), p. 37

4. This was described in "We have the high tech, they have not," in Survey: Defence in the 21st Century, *Economist*, September 5, 1992, pp. 12–14.

5. For a somewhat similar but differently formulated idea, see Geoffrey Parker, "What is the Western Way of War?" *Military History Quarterly* 8, no. 2 (Winter 1996): 86–95. Despite the West's superiority in material, organizational, social, and administrative aspects of war against the non-Western world, it is not true that it has uniformly been superior to its non-Western cobelligerents in matters of strategic thought, doctrine, and ways of war.

6. On the issue of radical change see the recent essay by Eliot Cohen, "A Revolution in Warfare," *Foreign Affairs* 75, no. 2 (March-April 1996): 37–39.

7. I will not engage in unnecessary debates about definitions about what the RMA is and what is the relationship between it and information technologies. I think, however, that the term RMA is more all-encompassing and accurate than the original term, military-technical revolution, which overly stresses the technological at the expense of the doctrinal and organizational, for example, and is too close to its Soviet origins. Nor is the term information warfare (IW) encompassing enough. Within the framework of this paper IW or information technology is considered the key characteristic or component of the current RMA. This definition and subsequent brief discussion are based on those found in Michael Mazarr, *The Revolution in Military Affairs: A Framework for Defense Planning*, Strategic Studies Institute, U.S. Army War College, 1994, pp. 1–26; General Gordon Sullivan and Colonel James Dubik, *War in the Information Age*, Strategic Studies Institute, U.S. Army War College, 1994, pp. 1–11; Thomas Ricks, "How Wars Are Fought Will Change Radically, Pentagon Planner Says," *Wall Street Journal*, July 15, 1994, p. 1, 3; Andrew Krepinevich, "Cavalry to Computer: The Pattern of Military Revolutions," *National Interest*, Fall 1994, pp. 30–42.

8. For concise assessments of military revolutions in the past see, inter alia, Michael Howard, *War in European History* (Oxford: Oxford University Press, 1976); Jeremy Black, *A Military Revolution: Military Change and European Society 1550–1800* (London: Macmillan, 1991). For a recent evaluation of these debates see Clifford Rogers, ed., *The Military Revolution Debate:*

Readings on the Military Transformation of Early Modern Europe (Boulder: Westview Press, 1995).

9. Andrew Krepinevich, "Keeping Pace with the Military-Technological Revolution," *Issues in Science and Technology* X, no. 4 (Summer 1994): 23–29.

10. Krepinevich, "Cavalry to Computer," p. 30.

11. To cite but a few, see for example, Maj.-Gen. Yashwant Deva, "Electronic Weapons: The Shape of Things To Come," *Indian Defence Review*, October 1993, pp. 77–83; S. Paranjpe, "India's Defence Policy: New Perspectives," *Indian Journal of Strategic Studies* XVII (1992): 32–43; Major M. Kumar, "Electromagnetic Compatibility for the Armed Forces," *Combat Journal*, December 1991, pp. 68–72; Group Captain M. K. Rana, "The Operating of Software Controlled Weapons," *Indian Defence Review*, July 1992, pp. 102–104; Wing Commander Ashraf ul-Haq, "New Concepts in Warfare," *Shaheen: Journal of the Pakistan Air Force*, XXXVIII (December 1992): 47–50; Col. E. A. S. Bokhari, "Satellite Warfare Potentials," *Pakistan Defence Review* 5, no. 1 (June 1993): 122–135.

12. John Keegan, *A History of Warfare* (London: Pimlico, 1993).

13. H. H. Gerth and C. Wright Mills, eds., *From Max Weber: Essays in Sociology* (New York: Oxford University Press, 1947), p. 78.

14. Gary Stix, "Fighting Future Wars," *Scientific American*, December 1995, p. 98.

15. Stix, "Fighting Future Wars," p. 98.

16. I am collecting research data on these two wars to write an analysis of them in my more extensive paper on the Third World and information warfare.

17. Private conversation with an expert on the Former Soviet Union and Russia, January 1996.

18. It is also my hunch that most revolutionary terrorists of contemporary times either have not heard of or ignore Michael Collins, so wrapped up are they in the mystique of Che Guevara, Carlos Marighela, Mao Zedong, or Ho Chi Minh, revolutionary guerrillas waging true guerrilla conflicts in different contexts.

19. M. R. D. Foot, "Revolt, rebellion, revolution, civil war: the Irish experience," in Michael Eliot-Bateman et al., *Revolt to revolution: Studies in the 19th and 20th century European experience* (Manchester: Manchester University Press, 1974), p. 182.

20. T. E. Lawrence had a similar approach, but in a different context, when he led the Arab revolt against the Ottomans. As he put it when comparing conventional armies and guerrilla units, suppose that the latter were to see themselves as ". . . an influence . . . an idea, a thing invulnerable, intangible, without front or back, drifting about like gas? (Conventional) Armies were like plants, immobile as a whole, firm-rooted, nourished through long stems to the head. We might be a vapour, blowing where we listed. . . . " See Col. T. E. Lawrence, "The Evolution of a Revolt," *Army Quarterly* 1, no. 2 (October 1920).

21. See Tom Bowden, "Ireland: background to violence," in Michael Eliot-Bateman et al., *Revolt to revolution*, pp. 209–210.

22. For more details see Eliot Cohen, "Distant Battles: War in the Third World," *International Security* 16, no. 4 (Spring 1986): 143–171.

23. See Michael Carver, "Conventional War in the Nuclear Age," in Peter Paret, ed., *Makers of Modern Strategy: from Machiavelli to the Nuclear Age* (Princeton: Princeton University Press, 1986), pp. 779–814.

24. A classic example of such a situation was to be found in the Argentinean armed forces (and other Latin American militaries). See Robert Scheina, "Argentine Jointness and the Malvinas," *Joint Forces Quarterly*, Summer 1994, pp. 95–101.

25. This has been examined in some detail by Stephen Biddle and Robert Zirkle, "Technology, Civil-Military Relations, and Warfare in the Developing World," unpublished paper, August 18, 1994.

26. See Ross Masood Hussain, "Military Technology in South Asia: A View From Pakistan," mimeo., 1995, p. 1.

27. See Lt. Col. S. A. N. Durrani, "Lessons from the Gulf War," *Pakistan Defence Review* 4, no. 1 (June 1992): 85–105.

28. Maj.-Gen. A. N. Sinha, "Computerisation in the Army," *Defence Management* 21 (Indian College of Defence Management, Secunderabad) no. 1 (October 1993): 5.

29. For more details see "India's Software Industry," *Financial Times*, December 6, 1995, pp. I–VI.

30. Ibid., p. 6.

31. The weaknesses of the Pakistani and Indian armed forces with respect to information warfare are extensively analyzed in my research paper.

32. Sinha, "Computerisation in the Army," p. 9.

33. Cohen, "Revolution in Warfare," p. 49.

34. In my opinion it is currently limited to Israel only, but not for long. A subset that constitutes a unit of one does not make a category, however. Japan is an advanced high-tech military power, but it is not part of the Third World. The same goes for Australia, an advanced Western state that is actually conducting serious research into twenty-first-century war.

35. For extensive details see Richard Bitzinger and Steven Kosiak, *Windows of Opportunity: The Potential Military Application of Japanese Advanced Commercial Technology Transfers to East Asia*, Defense Budget Project, September 1995, pp. 1–10.

36. For excellent analyses of what accounts for Israel's prowess in advanced conventional warfare see Hirsh Goodman and Seth Carus, *The Future Battlefield and the Arab-Israeli Conflict* (New Brunswick: Transaction Publishers, 1990); and Anthony Cordesman, *The Arab-Israeli Military Balance and the Peace Process* (Boulder: Westview Press, 1996), especially chap. IX, "The Impact of Qualitative Factors and the 'Revolution in Military Affairs,'" pp. 101–132.

37. On these changes see, for example, Shulong Chu, "The PRC Girds for Limited, High-Tech War," *Orbis* 38, no. 2 (Spring 1994): 177–191; Paul Godwin and John Schulz, "Arming the Dragon for the 21st Century:

China's Defense Modernization Program," *Arms Control Today*, December 1993, pp. 3–8.

38. See *Joint Publications Research Service, China*, April 10, 1989, pp. 6–12; *Joint Publications Research Service, China*, May 14, 1990, pp. 10–14; *Joint Publications Research Service, China*, March 12, 1991, pp. 16–19; Robert Deifs, "A two-front threat," *Far Eastern Economic Review*, December 13, 1990, pp. 29–30.

39. The information here comes largely from conversations with Gerrit Gong at CSIS; Harlan Jencks, "Chinese Evaluations of 'Desert Storm': Implications for PRC Security," *Journal of East Asian Affairs* VI, no. 2 (Summer/Fall 1992): 447–477; and Patrick Garrity, *Does the Gulf War (Still) Matter? Foreign Perspectives on the War and the Future of International Security*, Center for National Security Studies, Los Alamos National Laboratory, Report no. 16, 1993, pp. 77–80.

40. See Garrity, *Why the Gulf War Still Matters: Foreign Perspectives on the War and the Future of International Security*; Jencks, "Chinese Evaluations"; and You Ji, "High-Tech Shift for China's Military," *Asian Defence Journal*, September 1995, pp. 5–10.

41. See *Foreign Broadcasting Information Service, China* (henceforth *FBIS-CHI*), July 6, 1995, p. 29.

42. Marshall Goldman, *China's Intellectuals: Advise and Dissent* (Cambridge: Harvard University Press, 1981), p. 137.

43. This ideological view was vigorously but unsuccessfully challenged by Marshal P'eng De-Huai at the turn of the 1960s.

44. *FBIS-CHI*, December 1, 1995, p. 26.

45. *FBIS-CHI*, June 14, 1995, pp. 26–32, and October 6, 1995, p. 37.

46. See *FBIS-CHI*, June 14, 1995, p. 27.

47. *FBIS-CHI*, July 6, 1995, p. 30.

48. The famous German military historian Hans Delbruck was responsible for developing the idea of two distinct strategies: *niederwerfungstrategie* (annihilation) and *ermattungstrategie* (exhaustion/attrition). See Gordon Craig, "Delbruck: The Military Historian," in Paret, ed., *Makers of Modern Strategy*, pp. 342–343.

49. *FBIS-CHI*, August 18, 1993, p. 17.

50. See *FBIS-CHI*, February 27, 1995, p. 32; July 31, 1995, pp. 42–43; September 20, 1995, pp. 22–23; September 22, 1995, pp. 28–30.

51. For a more extensive analysis see *FBIS-CHI*, July 6, 1995, pp. 32–36.

52. *FBIS-CHI Daily Report*, July 6, 1995, p. 36.

53. For a Western formulation see Cohen, "Revolution in Warfare," pp. 48–50.

54. For an excellent analysis of the PLA's weaknesses see David Shambaugh, "China's Military: Real or Paper Tiger?" *Washington Quarterly* 19, no. 2 (Spring 1996): pp. 19–36.

55. Michael Swaine, "China," in Zalmay Khalilzad, ed., *Strategic Appraisal 1996*, Project Air Force (Santa Monica: RAND, 1996), pp. 204–205.

56. Paul Dibb, *Towards a New Balance of Power in Asia*, Adelphi Paper No. 295, International Institute for Strategic Studies (Oxford: Oxford University Press, 1995), p. 85.

57. Much has been written on the PRC's new "muscular diplomacy" and arms buildup. For more topical views see "Les revendications de Pekin sur la mer de Chine du Sud inquietent les pays voisins," *Le Monde*, December 27, 1995, p. 2; Jean-Claude Pomonti, "L'Asie du Sud-Est le theatre d'une impressionante course aux armements," *Le Monde*, December 27, 1995, p. 2; Francis Deron, "La tension avec Taiwan revele le poids politique de l'armée en Chine," *Le Monde*, February 8, 1996, p. 2; Peter Montagnon and Laura Tyson, "Beijing plays to weaken Lee's hold," *Financial Times*, March 8, 1996, p. 6; Bill Gertz, "Missile tests raise fear of Chinese aggression in Asia," *Washington Times*, August 15, 1995, pp. A1, A6; Nayan Chanda, "Fear of the Dragon," *Far Eastern Economic Review*, April 13, 1995, pp. 24–28; Edward Luce and Ted Bardacke, "Fear of Beijing fuels Asean arms spending," *Financial Times*, February 28, 1996, p. 6; William Branigin, "As China Builds Arsenal and Bases, Asians Fear a 'Rogue in the Region,'" *Washington Post*, March 31, 1993, pp. A21, A27.

58. See Joseph Nye, Jr. and William A. Owens, "America's Information Edge," *Foreign Affairs* 75, no. 2 (March-April 1996): 20–36.

16

The Impact of the Information Revolution on Strategy and Doctrine

Daniel Gouré

Information and communications, what is termed in modern military construction C^{4}I (command, control, communications, computers, and intelligence), have always been the centerpiece of successful warfare. History is full of stories of battles won or lost because of the fate of a single piece of information. As warfare has become more complex, so have the information requirements.

It is always tempting to see a universal truth in any major economic, technological, or social change that can be applied with equal validity and utility to any other area. Changes in information and computing technologies have had dramatic effects in diverse areas, from industry and commerce, to media and entertainment, to government and politics. It is currently held that a parallelism exists between the changes taking place in the civil world and the changes taking place in military affairs. There is also talk of the "revolution in military affairs," the "military technological revolution," and "information warfare," all of which argue for a revolutionary change at least in the means and methods of warfare and, in some cases, in national security, military strategy, and military doctrine. The deans of futurology, Alvin and Heidi Toffler, have translated their revolutionary views on Third Wave economics and social organization into an equally revolutionary view of warfare in their most recent publication, *War and Anti-War*.[1] In it, the Tofflers argue that information-based societies must create information-based armies that can fight wars in ways fundamentally different from, and inherently superior to, their First and Second Wave adversaries.

This view of a new age of warfare has also been argued by two very distinguished people, Adm. William A. Owens, recently retired vice chairman of the Joint Chiefs of Staff, and Dr. Joseph Nye, former assistant secretary of defense. In a recent article for *Foreign Affairs* they unveiled a vision of the future, one in which emerging capabilities in battlefield awareness, communications, precision strike, and assessment would provide not just strategic and battlefield dominance, but political controls over potential adversaries.[2] As described by Admiral Owens elsewhere, this capability would be built on a "system of systems," an architecture that would provide not only enhanced war-fighting capability but new capabilities for conflict prevention, peacekeeping, and arms control.[3]

There is no doubt that the new technologies will enhance military capabilities and, if properly exploited, should provide substantial improvements in U.S. military potential. Beyond the obvious uses of these improved means for gathering data, transmitting it, and refining it into information, there remains a central question: does the revolution in information and computational technologies presage an equally profound revolution in military affairs? Some observers believe that the information revolution will mean an end to modern warfare.[4] The argument goes as follows: if preparations for war—increased production of weapons, mobilization of forces, and movement to frontiers—can be readily viewed both by the prospective victim of aggression and by the international community, then the aggressor is less likely to act.

The "info war" culture also tends to make two dangerous assumptions regarding the future. The first is that the U.S./Western lead in these technologies can be converted into dominant military capabilities that opponents will not be able to find ways to circumvent, thus denying the utility of these new capabilities. The second is that we will never face an equally capable adversary, one who possesses equivalent technology as well as industrial resources, manpower, territory, and a desire to fight. In this regard, we are perhaps ill served by the too-easy victory of the war in the Persian Gulf. The lessons of the Gulf War with respect to information and targeting systems may apply only to environments such as that of Iraq and Kuwait. And even here, we should remember enormous efforts were expended in a failed effort to destroy Iraqi mobile missile (SCUD) launchers.

The place to look for revolutionary effects may not be the information/computational systems themselves but the opportunities they provide for better exploiting portions of the combat environment. For example, these new information-related technologies may give rise to an explosion in the use of space for civil and military purposes.

It is important to recognize that no revolution occurs in isolation: that is, an information revolution alone will not transform either industry or the military. Revolutions tend to come in clusters.[5] Technologies in a number of different areas undergo transformative experiences almost simultaneously. Therefore, prior to forming a judgment regarding the impact of information technologies on strategy and doctrine, we need to understand what has changed in other military and dual-use technologies. For example, what is the relationship that might develop as new information capabilities are married to stealth, high-intensity explosive technologies, or nonlethal weapons? Warfare consists of much more than merely information. It must consider all the elements to make up the deployment and use of force.

The Impact of Information on the Battlefield

The most important effect of the information revolution on strategy and doctrine is that for first time, the possibility exists of turning C4I from a coordination function to a function for the management of all aspects of military power. Military leaders have never had the C^4I to manage forces to the limit of their effective capability. They have always relied on mass, firepower, surprise, and so forth to make up for inadequacies in C^4I. In addition, mass was employed to make up for problems with the management of forces. The Soviet military, for example, echeloned its forces at all levels so that it did not matter that the plan could not stand the first encounter with the enemy. They put forces in to overwhelm or encircle.

The purpose of battle in war is to place organized force against an opponent in order to defeat it. There are four key elements to successful battle: mass, mobility, reach, and firepower. Historically these have been used in different ways and combinations to achieve battlefield success, whether with archers at Crécy, Mongol horseman at Samarkand, or Panzers at Sedan.

All military forces attempt to achieve coherence—defined as the placement of overwhelming force at the point of maximum leverage within time to do decisive damage. In doing so they are limited by the character of their forces, the maneuverability of the mass, the mobility of the force, the range of its firepower, and so on. They are also limited by the state of their intelligence, their knowledge of the location of the decisive point, their ability to communicate that knowledge to their subordinates, their mobilizing and moving forces, and their assessment of the effects of their actions and those of the opponents. Historically, it has often been preengagement maneuvers that determined victory. Generals had to guess or use intuition to decide where the decisive point would be, predeploy forces, and trust in luck.

It is in organizing forces and the four elements of combat capability, within the limits of their command and control, that great generals shine. They attempt to achieve coherence by managing not only their own forces but those of their enemies as well. Classically, the ways one managed both one's own forces and enemy forces were fairly limited:

1. *Set-piece battle with forces massed at a specific point to achieve a breakthrough.* This was the approach from the Greek phalanx through Alexander's army, up to Marlborough at Blenheim and Napoleon at Borodino and Waterloo.

2. *Prebattle maneuver.* This places the opponent in a position that exposes a vulnerable side, reduces the opponent's mass at the decisive point or allows one's own predeployed mass full access. Clear examples would include the Greek victory at Marathon, Hannibal at Cannae, and Napoleon at Austerlitz.

3. *Echeloned operations or the attempt to pile-drive through an opponent's line.* The Soviets were masters at echelonment.

4. *Surprise.* Whatever form of combat organization one attempted, surprise generally offered the opportunity to organize and mass forces, define targets, set fire plans, and maneuver before the enemy could respond. In a sense, surprise permits control over information requirements on the attacker's side and information availability on the defender's side.

Even for the great generals, the problem on the battlefield was that the capacity to kill was constrained by the limits on coordination. Thus, at Austerlitz, Napoleon's most famous victory, more than 60 percent of the opposing army escaped. Similarly, even in the great encirclement battles of the Russo-German War in July, August, and September, 1941, sufficient Russian forces remained—or, conversely, the Germans were sufficiently slowed in their advance—that the Germans could not obtain a decisive victory. Only when opposing forces were trapped or forced to hold position, and the adversary had overwhelming force plus the advantage of determining the time and place of attack, could a truly annihilating battle take place.

This limit on the capability to conduct decisive battle remained even as the means of warfare continued to mature. Mass became more important as soldiers were armed with muskets and, then, repeating rifles and, later still, armored vehicles. Mobility increased tremendously with the advent of the gasoline-powered vehicle. Reach increased through the development of air power, vertical envelopment, and the steamship; and firepower has obviously increased greatly since ancient times.

At the strategic level, the reasons for continued difficulty in conducting decisive warfare came from the increasing scale and scope of combat. As military capability increased, so too did the territory over which wars were fought. The strategic rear of the army became a target in its own right. In a sense, the capability for destruction was constantly outpaced by increases in the demand for coverage.

At the tactical or battlefield level, the problem of limits on effectiveness has come from four sources: (1) limits on the ability to practically integrate and synchronize operations of different forces with different mobility, firepower, reach, and mass; (2) the need to alter organization and deployment patterns in the face of changes in firepower and reach on the other side (for example, in the Civil War it became impossible to conduct battles in line and column because of firepower. Once one dispersed forces for survivability, one lost coordination and reduced coherence); (3) inadequate intelligence, particularly once a battle was joined; and (4) limits on the ability to give orders, assess the status of forces, and redirect forces and fire because of the limits on communications.

Additionally, battle created a "fog of war." In a previous era, dust, powder, smoke, and so on caused problems. In modern warfare the fog is just as real but caused by different factors. Now fog is created by electronic warfare, by camouflage, cover, and deception, and by the intermixing of combatants and non-combatants. Limiting the fog of war or maintaining the ability to coordinate forces meant accepting compromises on the mass, mobility, reach, and firepower that one would employ on the battlefield, thus limiting the ability to achieve a decisive result.

As a result, we compromised on force structures, deployments, equipment, and even employment because of C^3I (command, control, communications, and intelligence) limitations. Now we do not have to do that. That is the essence of the emerging revolution in military affairs. It is not that information technologies have outstripped conventional military capabilities, but quite the opposite: the capabilities of C^3I have finally caught up to where the rest of warfare has been for decades. We have been able to move force at jet speeds—or warheads on ballistic missiles at orbital velocities—for many years. The problem was where to place that firepower and when.

We can now exploit, both technologically and organizationally, the full-spectrum potential of military elements, jointly or singly, unrestricted by C³I limits. In essence, we have moved from commanded, to coordinated, to coherent battle. To exploit this new found capability, however, we need to know what kind of military strategy we will pursue and what complementary capabilities exist in the domains of mass, maneuver, and firepower to accompany and reinforce the influence of information technologies.

The New Revolution: The Information Technologies Battlefield

The role of information in warfare has been in subtle transition since the late 1700s. Emerging in this period were democratic revolutions, the popular press, the mature nation-state, and mass armies. The scope of warfare and battles expanded greatly. Entire nations were called to arms, and armies grew into the hundreds of thousands. In this environment, the role of information changed radically.

In the time of Napoleon and Clausewitz, the battlefield expanded to the point at which the commander could no longer see or control the entire engaged force. The great commanders were those who could make intuitive decisions and act decisively on the available fragments of information to win the battle. The leading theorists of war of the time could only explain the outcome of these immense battles as products of chance, the moral courage of individual soldiers, and the genius of the great commanders. Information, thus, was assigned a limited role. The commander's demand for more and better information remained, however, and conspired with technology to provide solutions for the new battlefield's challenge. The telegraph, radio, and hot air balloon are examples of early solutions to the information problem; satellite imagery and communications, sophisticated command centers, and battlefield computers are their modern counterparts.

If the role of information on the Napoleonic battlefield was limited, information's role at the strategic level had become more important. Governments realized that the ability to rally a nation to arms depended on a national information system that could regularly and quickly reach the masses, and thus emerged public propaganda—largely facilitated by the technology of the printing press. Ironically, the American and French Revolutions are the earliest examples of the power of the press to aid in the overthrow of outmoded governments—governments, it should be added, that failed to recognize the power of the new technologies.

Beginning in the nineteenth century, governments' influence over national information systems became paramount in their ability to wage war. Since their inception, democracies have struggled with the balance between government control and media autonomy during war or in the pursuit of national interests. Different balances have been used by various governments during the American Civil War, World War I, World War II, and all the wars in between and since. The Soviet Union and Fascist states took government control of the media to the extreme, creating state propaganda machines that kept their populations on a constant wartime footing.

For many observers, particularly in the military, the Gulf War signaled the dawn of a new era in war-waging. Commanders, soldiers, and news people returned from the Persian Gulf with the singular impression that information technologies had won the war. Satellite imagery, airborne surveillance, space-based navigation systems, electronic eavesdropping capabilities, and precision targeting appeared to provide the coalition forces with an overwhelming advantage. One had only to look at the films of F-117 bombing runs over Baghdad in which bombs were steered to the precise point on the target marked by a set of crosshairs to be convinced. Electronic warfare suites confused and blinded enemy radars; radar-homing missiles defeated Iraqi air defenses. Thermal and infrared imagers allowed U.S. forces to turn night into day and operate around the clock. Unmanned air vehicles saw their first use in combat, as did systems such as the Joint Surveillance and Tracking System and the Tomahawk cruise missile.

From this experience, a consensus emerged among those in the military and their civilian counterparts in the defense community that the future of conflict would be in what was loosely described as information-based warfare. Information-based warfare consisted of a number of interrelated parts: near-time surveillance and targeting of both fixed and mobile targets, rapid dissemination of information, and precision attacks on targets based on so-called smart munitions. In one way or another these parts came to dominate the operational planning, organizational reforms, and acquisition plans of the services under various guises or names (e.g., the U.S. Army's Force XXI initiative;

Expeditionary Power Projection; Global Power, Global Reach; and the U.S. Marine Corps' Sea Dragon).

Even before the end of the cold war, the military was focusing on the use of new information technologies to improve capabilities and expand their operational flexibility. The Gulf War demonstrated the extent to which the military had successfully adapted information to the needs of warfare. Based on the successes of the Gulf War, it was argued that a new revolution in warfare had taken place, one that would transform strategy, doctrine, operational art, and force structure.

Others took the Gulf War experience even further, creating what might be described as the cult of information. Not satisfied with exploiting the potential of new information technologies for command and control, surveillance, and targeting, many in the military embraced a theory of "information-only war." Advocates of this view expand the idea of an information revolution to a revolution in the very nature of society. They assert that the ability to access the totality of information and to communicate with others outside the controls of national governments constitutes a fundamental political change. Information technology (coupled to robotics) offers a prospect for a radical change in industrial processes and economic activity. The proponents of this view even suggest the information networks will create alternative organizational options for societies and individuals, creating virtual political movements and the prospects for virtual governments.

The advocates of this view of the future argue that information technology is leaping ahead at an exponential rate, thereby creating potential for a new form of warfare. These observers also assert that the technology that is weaving together society and becoming the "spinal cord" of economic vitality is rapidly creating conditions for a more modern form of conflict, "information warfare," which is no longer limited to the battlefield or the simple use of propaganda targeted at combatants or their respective publics. Information war would be a form of conflict that attacks the central nervous system of a state, undermining governments and economies with the press of a button. The very integrity of information—whether financial records, government proclamations, or news reports—could be put in jeopardy, sending quakes through the foundations of financial markets, economic systems, and societies.

The theory of information warfare has opened the minds of war fighters and national security strategists to the immense power and potential future uses of information. Leading thinkers in the field were quick to point out that the commercial world is leading the information revolution, reshaping the civilian world faster than the battlefield. As a result, the broader role information dominance might play in U.S. national security strategy came under consideration.

The explosion of computers, networks, and databases would create a new field of battle. "Cyber soldiers" would tap into and target a foreign government's entire information system or individuals operating within it. The impact of such tampering could be profound. The balance of international financial markets could be affected. The perceptions of an entire population might be changed. Leaders could find themselves stripped of their legitimacy and means of survival. The possible repercussions of such information war measures, however, are subject to open speculation.

As in economics and the environment, altering one variable in the global information networks can have far-reaching, unintended, and undesirable effects. In an international system increasingly linked together, events and conditions in one part of the globe are instantly reported in others. The emerging linkages of markets, systems, and communities are not entirely transparent. Ripples can flow through the international system in entirely unexpected ways.

The Revolution Critiqued

There is a certain plausibility to the scenarios painted by those who see an "information revolution" when one looks at the explosion of media and media tools in the civil sector: computers, cellular telephones, the Internet, digital broadcast satellites, and shortly, Iridium and the like. Access to information is viewed as crucial to modern economies. Indeed, the growth of the service sector of advanced industrial nations and the creation of postindustrial economies are cited as evidence of a revolution in commercial-social relations with implications for military affairs. In particular, advocates of information-based warfare point to the alleged "delayering" of industry because of information as portending a similar shift for the military.

In some respects, this so-called revolution is even older than its advocates suggest. Many of its elements date to the Second World War. One can argue that the British invented basic information warfare. The Battle of Britain was won as a result of

Britain's superior information (radar) and control (fighter command). Deception and information management were part of Allied efforts. Remember Ultra and the "bodyguard of lies"? Modern means of information warfare (for example, computer viruses, false data, or jamming) may represent a significant qualitative advance over techniques employed by the Allies and the Axis powers from 1939 to 1945, but conceptually, the operations themselves have changed very little.

World War II also illustrates some of the limits of information dominance in at least some respects, however. Stalin was fully apprised of Hitler's invasion plans but chose to ignore them. The U.S. military in the Pacific was forewarned by Washington of potential Japanese aggression but misunderstood or misinterpreted the warnings. Yet, there is a presumption that more data mean more knowledge, more knowledge leads to better understanding, and understanding will serve as the basis for better decision-making. In a perfect world, that is true. Reality, however, often gets in the way. The process of combat dominates the flow of information, not the other way around.

It is important to remember that information is only one component of a war-fighting or combat capability. Even with precise information, it is necessary to strike and destroy the target. When targets number in the thousands, the cost of striking them becomes high. The effort expended in attacking thousands of precisely located and tracked targets is compounded by that of supporting and sustaining both the information and strike systems employed.

There is something highly mechanistic about the current approach to revolutions in military affairs. There is no sense of the dynamic—of warfare as politics or art with highly changeable features. There is a tendency to view potential adversaries as caricatures of either ourselves or the former Soviet Union (so-called peer competitors) or of Iraq (the major regional contingency [MRC] threat). It is assumed that opponents do not learn or exploit technological or strategic opportunities; at best they may engage in "niche warfare" via terrorism or nuclear blackmail.

Similarly, the concept of war under the banner of information-based warfare resembles a shooting gallery, a set-piece battle in which superior U.S. firepower is concentrated on a relatively defenseless opponent. The objective, similar to that in the Gulf, is simply to win the firefight, to break the enemy force, leading to a return, more or less, to the status quo ante. What is significant in this conception is the ability of the United States to solve the problem of insufficient destructive power (the capacity to kill the adversary in sufficient numbers to destroy its army)—thereby obviating the need for operational art, maneuver, and even strategy. This is accomplished by relentless air strikes against a supposedly defenseless and relatively immobile opponent. Under these conditions, given adequate intelligence and targeting, the problem of modern war is reduced to one of logistics: the ability to maintain adequate flows of weapons and fuel.

In short, the precision/information/C3 construct of a revolution based on new information capabilities must be approached very cautiously for a number of reasons:

- Adding information systems to ships, tanks, and aircraft wrings the last measure of utility from the military revolution of the 1920s and 1930s. While enhancing the performance of tanks, aircraft, and ships, information-based warfare will not change the way the United States (and other advanced countries) conducts war in any fundamental way. We still envision war to be a process, perhaps swifter than in the past but still dominated by large-scale combined arms conflict. As Desert Storm showed, such wars are dominated not by information, precision strike, or stealth but, in the end, by numbers and by logistics. In logistics and support we are still subject to the old problems of lift tonnage/miles. Information-based warfare also does not address the problems of the growing cost and operational inflexibility of a large, heavy, and complex force posture designed for continental war against the Soviet Union.

- A revolution based on new information capabilities does not change the important factors related to the erosion of the defense industrial base, which is critical to the production of the platforms that will house and employ the new information systems.

- The construct of such a revolution does not adequately address the revolution in military affairs occurring among potential adversaries, specifically their access not only to weapons of mass destruction and ballistic missiles but also to a broad range of capabilities including space-based surveillance and communications, modern cruise missiles, advanced diesel submarines, and modern combat aircraft.

- This construct does not recognize the risks involved in reliance on expensive precision systems to perform traditional missions. Such systems are cost-effective only if the conflict can be won swiftly. We cannot afford to conduct large-scale protracted conflicts relying solely on precision weapons. Yet, every campaign scenario for future MRCs necessitates the expenditure of thousands of precision mu nitions. Thus, if an MRC is not won in 100 hours, costs begin to escalate dramatically.

- There is no reason to believe that information warfare alters the balance against equals, so-called peer competitors. A peer competitor will possess the resources, material, and technology to counter an MRC-based strategy and force posture. It will have the advantage of interior lines of communication and proximity to the battlefield, whereas the United States will have to project its power. In particular, a peer competitor will not be defeatable in the kind of temporally and geographically limited campaign that is currently the focus of force planning. Unless the United States has taken the necessary actions in peacetime, a peer competitor can be expected to contest the United States for control of space, the air and ocean approaches to its territory, and the beaches and airheads. Finally, the focus on information technologies, particularly at the theater level, creates vulnerabilities that can be exploited by a talented foe.

A revolution in information technologies by itself will not cause a change in strategy or doctrine. As the above discussion indicates, the revolution envisioned by the advocates of so-called information warfare requires the combination of information capabilities with long-range strike and rapid mobility of forces. Although we have already experienced the revolution in information, long-range strike and force mobility capabilities are lagging. In 2010, U.S. airpower will still depend almost entirely on F-15s, -16s, and -18s, all of which were designed in either the 1960s or the 1970s, and on a bomber force dominated by some number of aging B-52 and B-1 bombers. According to current plans, the total number of advanced strike platforms in the inventory will be about 500: some 460 F-22s and 20 to 40 B-2 bombers. In the area of mobility, the only bright spot is the decision to buy some 120 C-17s. The rest of U.S. air transport will be deteriorating rapidly because of age and use. Sealift will have improved only slightly. More important, the forces themselves, air and ground units, are so heavy and require so much logistical support that moving them is a lengthy and cumbersome process. It should be noted that moving a single division from Germany to Bosnia, a distance of some 400 miles, took nearly two months. Old strike capabilities and antiquated ground forces that are ponderous to move will not be able to exploit the newfound advantages of battle space awareness and information dominance, nor will the new information technologies themselves address critical needs in war-fighting.

Finally, if there are reasons to approach with caution the idea of information-based warfare, then there is even greater reason to withhold judgment on the idea of information-only warfare.

The advocates of this view generally assert that the new revolution can make up for all the side effects and potential negative consequences of conventional warfare. Many suggest that with the new information-orientated revolution, nations can have real-time, ultraprecise, theaterwide, deep-ranging, nuclear-equivalent, rapid-fire, near-bloodless victories by relying on sensors, communications, and computers. The idea is often openly stated that with information-only warfare armies can have what amounts to rapid, bloodless wars. This may be a form of backlash to the effort over more than 40 years to think the unthinkable and make plans for a massive, global conventional war.

The "unconscious" wish is evident in the title of Alvin and Heidi Toffler's book *War and Anti-War*. This book is relatively popular in the military, including with Gen. Gordon Sullivan (former army chief of staff) and the Air Staff. *War and Anti-War* argues that we are moving from an era of so-called Second Wave warfare with its emphasis on mass, attrition, and bombardment to one based on Third Wave information technologies, which will be inherently more precise and less damaging. Perhaps this argument reflects the belief/wish of society and planners that the cold war be the war to end all wars. Because we cannot envision an enemy of equivalent character, we can choose to pursue those capabilities that will enable us to fight lesser engagements swiftly, decisively, and "bloodlessly."

Information is really ancillary or supportive of basic human, societal, and economic functions. It allows a wider view, greater access to distant places, and the ability to manipulate things that are inanimate (electrons, bank accounts, and so forth). It does not fundamentally change the basic features of life and human activity, however. Although some information is good, it is not clear that more is better. Also unclear is the extent to which modern society has been shaped by or is dependent on information, as the proponents of this view would have us believe.

Information warfare in all its forms (command and control, communications, reconnaissance surveillance target acquisition (RSTA), battle damage assessment (BDA), deception, jamming, and so on) is a necessary support function of modern warfare. It may be more like military medical services, however: one cannot fight without it, but it will not be decisive in winning the war. Certainly, no one organizes a military establishment and a concept of operations around medical services.

Will better information, in near real time, enable an army to create the decisive engagement that would win the war? The most plausible answer is no, for two reasons. First, even if we can see the battlefield clearly and understand it completely, we cannot affect it decisively in the time available. This is a function of "destructive capacity." We simply cannot "kill" the adversary in sufficient numbers to destroy its army. In modern warfare we can do great damage, but in almost any conceivable case, we cannot do sufficient damage to affect the war itself. Historically, few battle were so decisive (Cannae being the example generals have tried to emulate for 2,000 years).

The second reason is that winning a battle and winning the war are two very different things. Even Cannae did not produce a strategic victory for Carthage. Napoleon often achieved operational success with only one or two battles in a campaigning season. Yet he fought three wars against Austria and two against Prussia, and he was continually at war with Russia and England. Repeated defeats on the battlefield were insufficient to bring down large nations with enormous population reserves and the industrial capacity to equip new armies almost from scratch.

One additional point on the limits to the so-called information revolution: There is a tendency for information advocates to erroneously extend the experience of the civil world to that of the military. There are endless discussions of how information technology and real-time communications will allow organizations to flatten their structures, remove middle managers, and more closely marry the different functions of the organization. The problems with this view are twofold. First, flattened structures work only in highly predictable and structured environments. When the problems are marketing, producing, selling, and delivering products and services, one can flatten structures. Military operations are more complex than any civilian enterprise. The fog of war alone dictates that one cannot routinize military activities. One can flatten logistics and support hierarchies, but the argument for extensive flattening of combat command functions does not fit. The second reason is that even in the civilian world, the general experience has been that more communications technology means a greater need for face-to-face interaction, given increasing scope of operations and the rise of new issues. As a result, more managers may be needed, not fewer.

Notes

1. Alvin Toffler and Heidi Toffler, *War and Anti-War* (New York: Little Brown, 1993).

2. William A. Owens and Joseph Nye, "America's Information Edge," *Foreign Affairs* 75, no. 2 (March-April 1996): 20–36.

3. William A. Owens, "The Emerging System of Systems," unpublished paper.

4. See Martin C. Libicki and James A. Hazlett, "Do We Need an Information Corps?" *Joint Forces Quarterly*, no. 2, September 1993.

5. William H. McNeill, *The Pursuit of Power* (Chicago: University of Chicago Press, 1982).

17

Information Warfare: The Burden of History and the Risk of Hubris

C. Kenneth Allard

My topic concerns both the burden of history and the risk of hubris for those of us—in uniform and out—who are trying to make sense of rapid changes in information technology and what they suggest for warfare in the information age. Human beings have histories; so do their organizations and institutions. If that history matters at all, then it should certainly discipline our expectations about just how far and how fast these institutions and organizations can adapt to fundamental change. History and the risk of hubris should caution us as well about the fallacy of assuming that the information revolution will necessarily convey distinct military advantages to the United States.

Indeed, were he alive today, Hilaire Belloc might well be tempted to view today's cheerleaders for the revolution in military affairs (RMA) in much the same way that he satirized his own century's celebration of the Maxim gun: "Whatever happens,/ We have got/ The RMA,/ And they have not." In fact, this revolution may well turn out to be more notable for equalizing power between the have and have-not countries than for concentrating it still further in the First World.

But there should be no doubt that the information revolution will require fundamental changes in the U.S. defense establishment, changes that will be both more *painful* and more *urgent* than many observers currently suspect:

- *painful* because of the need to upset familiar ways of doing business, including the present authority of the military services to procure their own command and control systems; and

- *urgent* because of the need to move quickly, not only to avoid building a new set of expensive, redundant twenty-first century "information stovepipes" but also to prevent the predictable information pathologies that any future opponent is certain to use against us.

The techno-hype surrounding these issues makes it especially important to make some key distinctions, particularly the difference between the current military-technical revolution and the future revolution in military affairs. The principal difference between these two concepts is that today's military-technical revolution involves the application of the microchip to existing ways of doing business.[1] As impressive as these efforts often appear, they usually represent only marginal improvements in our preferred patterns of warfare—and especially in the perpetuation of the dominant weapons systems in each service. To borrow an admittedly overworked but apt simile, this is like paving over the existing set of cow paths rather than building entirely new and more efficient road networks. A revolution in military affairs, however, is what happens when institutions and organizations go through a Gestalt-switch resulting in a truly revolutionary set of developments.[2] Obvious examples in this century include the advent of airpower, the blitzkrieg, the adoption of the carrier-centered naval task force, and, most profoundly, the development of nuclear weapons.

These revolutionary developments are largely unpredictable, usually as to their real causes but always in their ultimate effects. For example, the development of naval aviation was an ongoing military-technical revolution that took place throughout the interwar years. Despite those evolutionary developments, the real mother of invention was the sudden loss of our battleships at Pearl Harbor. At the Battles of the Coral Sea and Midway over the next several months, a series of truly revolutionary innovations transformed the carrier from a mere reconnaissance platform to the dominant weapon system of U.S. naval power that it has remained ever since.

It is worth remembering that the carrier revolution—like many others in military history—was produced by a combination of shock, serendipity, and sheer desperation; similarly, its larger implications became apparent only through the 20/20 hindsight of the historian. Thus, one can see the need to avoid overconfidence in predicting the ultimate effects of a future revolution in military affairs. In fact, those Pentagon leaders, think tankers, and associated contractors confidently touting U.S. "mastery of the RMA" at the start of this latest information revolution suggest nothing so much as fifteenth-century Roman cardinals. Vatican councils of that era must surely have heard similarly optimistic predictions concerning the utility to the church of Herr Gutenberg's recently invented printing press.

Questions of infallibility aside, the ability of the Vatican to predict such unintended consequences as the Reformation or the
Thirty Years" War was probably no better or worse than ours to
define the "end state" of the RMA.

A Cautionary Tale about Change

This admittedly depressing thought unfortunately prompts
another: that revolutions in military affairs are perennially held
hostage to the narrow, demeaning, and gritty bureaucratic agendas of military organizations that, like the poor, are seemingly
with us always. Like most other organizations, the American
army, navy, and air force present a constantly mixed bag of
advances and retreats, of progress and retrenchment. Although
the services in their separate identities have generally served
the nation well, their most consistent challenge in the twentieth
century has been the quest for greater teamwork. The tightly
networked "information operations" of twenty-first-century
warfare will require an exponential increase in the functional
integration of the nation's military forces—just as systems integration has paced the business process improvements of cutting-
edge commercial firms. Because the military services possess
both a venerated tradition of functional autonomy and the legislative authority to procure their own separate command, control, and information systems, it is worth asking if they are up
to the challenge of producing this higher level of information-
age joint combat power.

The question of technological innovation in highly traditional organizations is as old as it is interesting, so it is especially
instructive to consider the record of a previous revolution in military affairs as bequeathed to us by one of the most perceptive
observers of these things, Elting Morison. In his classic study
"Gunfire At Sea," Morison recounted the unlikely process that
brought about the late-nineteenth-century revolution in naval
gunfire. Prior to this revolution, cannon fire at sea was much the
inaccurate craft it had been for 500 years, despite recent improvements in range with the development of 12-to-14-inch rifled
naval guns. In 1899, for example, five ships blazed away for 25
minutes at targets 1,600 yards away, achieving just two marginal
hits. By 1906, however, the revolution was complete: a single
gunner on a single ship fired for one minute at a target 1,600
yards distant and hit the target 15 times—half in the bull's-eye.
These and similar results amounted to what was literally an

order-of-magnitude improvement of 3,000 percent in just six years.[3]

The key technological improvements that brought about this revolution were the increased range of the guns, sighting tele- scopes, and improved elevating mechanisms. The real innova- tion consisted of combining these elements into the new principle of continuous aim firing. Here

Morison identified three constituencies that displayed para- doxically great strengths and great limitations in playing out their respective roles:

The Insurgents.   Admiral Sir Percy Scott of the Royal Navy and Lieutenant William Sims of the U.S. Navy were the main protagonists of this case, bringing together the technical ele- ments that made the revolution possible and forcing the estab- lishment to take notice. Their burden was an occupational hazard common enough among innovators even in our own times: an abiding sense of their own rectitude usually expressed as outraged indignation against all who opposed them. Morison describes this quality as "permanent insurgency" and notes that it made acceptance of the new ideas all the more difficult.

The Technicians.   The guns, the gears, and the telescopes on which the revolution of continuous aim firing rested would not have been possible had it not been for the inventors and techni- cians who conceived these instruments in the first place. The inhibition of these talented people was their fixation with their particular instrument (or part of the process) at the expense of the larger objective of improving naval gunfire. Interestingly enough, all the elements that Scott and Sims brought together had been in place for at least eight years, while the most impor- tant element—the rifled cannon—had been present for more than 40 years. Morison attributed the slow pace of progress to

> the pain with which the human being accommodates himself to changing conditions. The tendency is apparently involun- tary and immediate to protect oneself against the shock of change by continuing in the presence of altered situations the familiar habits, however, incongruous, of the past.[4]

The Establishment.   It is always easy to deride naval and mil- itary establishments—past and present—as the living embodi- ments of the "familiar habits . . . of the past." Nonetheless, they should also be given credit for two significant contributions: serving as the institutional repositories for the transfer of warfighting skills from one generation to the next; and acting as the winnowing mechanisms that continuously filter the many good ideas from the few that actually work in the ultimate test of combat. Within this capability, however, lies an important contradiction that persists to the present day: military and naval establishments are built around dominant weapons systems. That fact, together with the accumulated weight of personal and institutional agendas, produces an instinctive form of behavior that will always give great weight to the status quo and its perpetuation.

Morison's summation of this case is sufficiently succinct and hard-hitting to warrant recitation here:

> the men involved were *victims of severely limited identification.* They were presumably all part of a society devoted to the process of national defense, *yet they persisted in aligning themselves with existing parts of that process.* . . . So these limited identifications brought these men into conflict with each other, and the conflict prevented them from arriving at a common acceptance of a change that presumably . . . they would all find desirable.[5] (emphasis added)

Probably the most remarkable thing about this passage is that it was originally delivered in 1950, long before the disciplines of total quality management and corporate reengineering underscored the importance of process. If anything, these insights reinforce the impact of Morison's warning that those who contribute to a process (military, industrial, sociological, academic, or political) cross the line from benefit to cost at the moment they become fixated with narrow concepts, attitudes, or conventions. Having crossed that line, they quickly move from being essential "stakeholders" to assuming the more familiar role of barriers on the road to progress.

Although Morison mentions it only briefly, a major part of the U.S. Navy's reluctance to explore the potential revolution in naval gunnery was its fixation with the recent victory in the Spanish-American War. Basically, this was the nineteenth-century equivalent of "If it ain't broke, don't fix it." Because they confirm the always powerful tendency toward conventional wisdom, few more powerful inhibitors to military progress exist than victories, especially overwhelming victories against a lesser opponent. So what are the lessons that Morison may still have to teach us as we wrestle with the implications of history and the risk of hubris in next-generation warfare?

Current Perspectives on the Military-Technical Revolution

Amid all the uncertainty surrounding this field, there is little question about two things: that information is transforming warfare as profoundly as it is altering most other aspects of our civilization; and that the end of this process is nowhere in sight. John Arquilla and David Ronfeldt are certainly correct in their assertion that the information content of our weaponry has gone up even as the raw numbers of those weapons have gone down.[6] The Gulf War represents another way station in the evolution of that 50-year trend, especially with its demonstration of the critical linkages between electronic warfare; intelligence, surveillance, and target acquisition; and the precision-guided munitions (PGM) fired from many different air, land, and sea platforms. Those developments demonstrated as well the validity of a principle adopted by the U.S. Army following an exhaustive analysis of the 1973 Middle East War, the first real PGM conflict: What can be seen can be hit; what can be hit can be killed.[7]

Almost 20 years later, the most visible symbols of this new form of warfare became the televised images of Tomahawk missiles cruising over downtown Baghdad or laser-guided bombs slamming dead center into their targets. Equally important were those information-rich engagements that took place well beyond the reach of television cameras: tanks making first-round hits at 3,000-meter ranges, coalition fighters being guided to both air and ground targets by AWACS (airborne warning and control system) and JSTARS (Joint Surveillance Target Attack Radar System) reconnaissance aircraft, and ground forces navigating with pinpoint precision through the electronic wizardry of Global Positioning System receivers. If there is increased information content in a diminishing number of weapons, there is also a quantum increase in the information routinely sought, provided, and used at progressively lower echelons. This development is already well understood in every information-age business, but the same fundamental tensions between rapid information flows and hierarchical control that punctuate modern corporate life are now fully present in most military structures as well.

But the capabilities demonstrated during the Gulf War must be balanced against a number of key vulnerabilities[8]:

Time. The coalition forces in the Gulf War had the priceless advantage of time, six months from the Iraqi invasion of Kuwait to the launching of the campaign that eventually expelled them. Not only was this gift of time from a quiescent adversary required to move military forces and their equipment to the Gulf, but it was also needed to perfect the information infrastructure needed to prosecute the war on U.S. terms.

Opposition. One of the basic vulnerabilities of the "extended weapon systems" (the phrase originates with Dr. Thomas Rona, one of the pioneers in this field) wielded by information-age military forces is that they are susceptible to countermeasures by a determined adversary. In Saddam Hussein, we had the distinct advantage of an opponent who not only gave us time to get our act together but did nothing that seriously opposed our extended weapon systems. Worse yet, Saddam adopted all the worst features (centralization, hierarchy, rigidity) of a Soviet-style command and control system yet failed to exploit the classically aggressive qualities of Soviet radioelectronic combat. The coalition forces took full advantage of both failings.

Interoperability. Although the larger question of U.S. institutional underpinnings is considered below, the problem of interoperable information systems is sufficiently important to warrant attention as a separate issue. This uniquely American problem springs from a long historical tradition in which service rather than joint perspectives have driven the development of command and control systems. In the Gulf War, time and a lack of opposition permitted the "work-arounds" and "band-aid" solutions that permitted these "stovepipe" data systems to function. Similarly, when 28,000 U.S. troops were deployed to Somalia in late 1992, a series of vexing interoperability problems plagued the force until various "work-arounds" were found. In one celebrated example reminiscent of the Grenada invasion a decade earlier, the U.S. Army hospital in Mogadishu could not communicate with U.S. Navy hospital ships operating offshore, nor were army helicopter pilots cleared to land on them.[9]

Because both the capabilities and shortcomings demonstrated by the Gulf War have become increasingly well understood, Pentagon planners have sought to exploit the former while trying to correct the latter. Each of the military services has announced comprehensive modernization plans that feature information technology as the centerpiece of efforts to improve the "situational awareness" of commanders on the land, at sea, and in the air. The idea here is to use those data to answer the three basic questions of combat commanders: *where are my forces? where is the enemy?* and *how do I get at him?* Answering these questions more rapidly and accurately than the opposing commander conveys "information dominance," an advantage that is rapidly becoming the sine qua non of next-generation warfare.

Elting Morison would have been the first to understand that these modernization efforts (and especially the founding of separate information warfare centers in the army, navy, and air force) have all taken place within the cultures of the dominant weapon systems wielded by each service: armor and artillery for the army, carriers for the navy, and manned piloted aircraft for the air force. Given their cultures and histories, this situation could hardly be otherwise, despite the usual rhetoric about "thinking outside the box."

Therefore, there has been great interest in "dominant battlespace awareness," a bold technological vision advanced by Admiral William Owens, former vice chairman of the Joint Chiefs of Staff (JCS). His concept envisages the melding of current and next-generation sensors, C^4I systems, and shooters to provide an integrated picture of a 200-nautical mile, three-dimensional battlespace. The idea is to provide 90 percent coverage of all forces in this area, in any weather, day or night, with a level of knowledge about the enemy so profound that his actions could be predicted.[10]

Two numbers are particularly significant here: the concept envisages, first, a 10,000-fold increase in the amount of information flowing through a typical joint force and, second, doing so within 10 years. To achieve these goals, this approach emphasizes the aggressive use of commercial developments in digitization, processing power, bandwidth, direct broadcasting, and global positioning. The effect on future warfare? Try imagining a vast game of three-dimensional electronic chess played out in real time throughout this large and very lethal battlespace. The coin of this realm would be the instantaneous exchange of information—what I refer to as "the war of the databases."

There is no question that Admiral Owens's vision is as bold as it is flawed. For one thing, it makes no allowances for the differences in the operational environments of land, sea, and aerospace or for the widely differing numbers or characteristics of the forces deployed there. Land forces, for example, typically contain 20,000–30,000 targets to be pinpointed. Many of these potential targets resist that characterization by becoming extremely adept at using terrain, vegetation, and similar features of an environment that is far more "cluttered" and "dirty" than either the sea or aerospace—and therefore much less susceptible to electronic or other forms of penetration. Combat or peace-keeping in any urban environment, for example, is a severe operational challenge for which technology at best provides only incomplete answers.

It is also questionable if the 90 percent efficiency in information coverage that Admiral Owens advocates is a realistic goal. Although a 90 percent advantage over any adversary is always preferable, marginal advantages in the real world are usually much less. It is even more doubtful that these marginal advantages can be achieved without significant advances in software, especially those relating to automatic target recognition. We also need to make quantum improvements in our ability to merge many different military databases if we are to keep up with the fire hose of information contemplated in the next generation of sensors. This problem is the military version of "data warehousing," to use the current term of art; but the ability to rationalize the current Babel of different databases and standards is a precondition to achieving either "dominant battlespace awareness" or anything resembling it.

Despite these flaws, the real worth of the Owens vision is that it may well be a potential investment strategy for the future. As always, however, the real question is how to weld separate service-specific capabilities into a single coherent system. As the admiral tactfully noted in comparing the respective modernization plans of the services,

> The visions they sketch are remarkably similar. . . . Each recognizes that its efforts are part of a larger undertaking. I believe this undertaking is the U.S. revolution in joint military affairs.[11]

In an equally shrewd way, the Owens vision attempts to sidestep the usual bureaucratic food fights over roles, missions, and force structures:

It is not the kind of conceptual framework that leads immediately into discussions of numbers of Army divisions, or
aircraft carriers, or air wings. . . . The system of systems is
fundamentally a joint military entity. No single service can
build it alone—only coordinated interactions of all the services can produce it. When it is constructed fully, each of the
services will be far stronger.[12]

Therefore, even if seen solely as an exercise in institutional
goal-setting, dominant battlespace awareness—or the "system of
systems"—has complemented narrower service perspectives
with a startling vision of the near-term technological possibilities
during a time in defense planning when all other realities are
considerably less promising.

Although those possibilities may be the carrot, the need for a
big stick has hardly vanished. Because the Goldwater-Nichols
Act gives the JCS vice chairman considerable powers in defining
and rationalizing the often competing requirements of the military services, Admiral Owens was able to establish the first of
the so-called Joint Warfare Capability Assessments (JWCA) to
compare service requirements across nine critical functions such
as strategic mobility, strike, air superiority, command and control, and information warfare. Although still very much an
experiment, the JWCA process provides a potential means to
assess programs coming before the Defense Acquisition Board
by ensuring that service-driven program requirements match
joint military judgments. In the same way, judgments aided by
the JWCA process are intended to assist the chairman of the Joint
Chiefs in providing his statutorily mandated assessment of the
programs and budgetary submissions of the military services.
Seen in this way, the JWCA process can provide an empirical
means to convey joint military judgments, long recognized as
one of the weaker aspects of the planning, programming, and
budgeting system. As Admiral Owens pointed out in defending
the JWCA initiatives, "Changing times require changes to planning processes that were built for an era that has passed."[13]

The Permanently Operating Factors: Institutional Constraints

Such revived disciplines and improved methods of analysis will
surely be required in coming to grips with the ongoing military-
technical revolution, let alone the vaunted RMA. Many of the

institutional constraints outlined above are so basic to the U.S. military context that they approximate the "permanently operating factors" that Soviet military science once used in describing the basic boundaries of warfare. Although many constraints might be listed, my focus on history and the risk of hubris suggests four: budget; institutional overhead; technology insertion; and acquisition reform.

Budget.   The grim realities of the defense budget have rapidly progressed from byword to cliché. Oddly enough, however, the prospect of reduced defense spending has not noticeably changed the basic terms of reference for a military establishment nourished on considerably higher resource levels throughout the cold war. A number of studies have demonstrated that there is a zero-sum game of historic proportions coming as current force structures, expanded peacekeeping commitments, more expansive readiness requirements, and elaborate modernization plans compete for declining defense dollars.[14] Ironically, at the very moment in which technology holds the brightest promise, its affordability has seldom been more in question.

Institutional overhead.   The institutional overhead referred to here reflects not only current force structures but equipment levels—especially those relating to information technology. Assistant Secretary of Defense for Command, Control, Communications, and Intelligence (C^3I) Emmett Paige, Jr. has estimated that there are between 5,000 and 9,000 command and control systems currently operated by the Department of Defense (DOD), many of them redundant "legacy systems" left over from the cold war. Not only are these systems expensive, they get in the way every time we conduct joint operations. In Somalia, for example, U.S. forces deployed with 10 different service-specific data systems to handle a host of common administrative functions.[15]

Thus, there has been a well-recognized requirement to pare these systems down to more reasonable levels. Although the Defense Information Systems Agency (DISA) has been charged with the unenviable task of helping to identify and retire redundant "legacy" systems, each of these systems is deeply embedded into existing service infrastructures that include extended families of administrators, experts, contractors, subsystems, and logistical support networks. Underlining the difficulty of the problem, Assistant Secretary Paige candidly noted in July 1995 that "our progress (has been) far less than anticipated."[16] Although the real number of C^3I systems remains in dispute, the only major system that DISA has clearly been able to "turn off" has been the seventies-era "Worldwide Military Command and Control System."[17]

Technology insertion.   The same legislative authority that empowers the military services to preserve redundant C^3 systems also complicates the modernization process. Because Title 10 of the United States Code gives the services the power to "organize, train and equip" their respective forces, they pursue separate paths in modernizing their C^3 systems—despite the invariable obeisance to "jointness" and the fact that C^3 problems rarely stop at service boundaries. This is again an old problem, but one that is at the heart of the perennial difficulty that U.S. forces have had in fielding interoperable command and control systems.

The latest effort to reconcile service differences without altering their present responsibilities is a JCS/DISA-sponsored technological construct called the "Global Command and Control System" (or GCCS, not coincidentally pronounced "Geeks"). This concept envisions the gradual consensual evolution of agreements by the services on the "common operating environments" featured by their future systems. Although the goal of interoperability by consensus is laudable, GCCS is very much "business as usual." It is really a building code, not a top-down architecture requiring unambiguous choices between winning and losing systems. Its approach does not feature a grand design but rather a forlorn hope that by selecting "best of breed" components, the overall system will evolve "through incremental improvement."[18] It may be so; but unless that future evolutionary path is a more Darwinian "survival of the fittest," GCCS seems unlikely to eliminate the problems of interoperability it purports to solve.

A decade after the Goldwater-Nichols reforms, joint teamwork is still secondary to the all-important quest by the military services to field the next generation of command and control systems in order to perpetuate the existing set of dominant weapons systems. A particularly galling example of the problem could be seen during a 1995 field demonstration in which Admiral Owens and the members of the Joint Requirements Oversight Council (JROC) participated. Although the exercise was supposedly devoted to solving interoperability issues, technological duplication of the worst sort could be seen in the separate army and air force operations centers set up for theater missile defense. Despite the importance of this mission and the heavy pressure on limited development funds, these two separate systems with identical functions were united only by their respective target sets.[19]

Although such practices are usually defended as an internal competition to demonstrate the vaunted "best of breed" system, the fact is that such approaches are little more than thinly disguised fights over future roles and missions. More profoundly, however, this problem reflects the fact that the military services instinctively tend to see any problem—including any new set of technological possibilities—primarily in terms of themselves. Precisely as Elting Morison suggested, this self-referential pattern means that new technological possibilities are primarily calculated to preserve and extend the dominant weapons system and the existing operational culture within the service. The idea that other services may have encountered similar technological problems and possibilities is not normally considered at the critical early stages in the development process. Far from instinctively asking "Who else has this problem?" hard-charging program managers normally view the "joint" part of the systems acquisition process as a contest to obtain JCS ratification of established service preferences. Not surprisingly, technology insertion is often handicapped by such less than optimal approaches, with interoperability often the accidental by-product of bureaucratic compromises or "quick fixes" under the pressure of impending combat.

Acquisition reform.   No factor is seemingly more permanent or more ponderous than the interlocking legal and regulatory regime by which the U.S. government procures goods and services. If there is good news here, it is attributable to the success of the Clinton administration (led by Vice President Al Gore and Defense Secretary William Perry) in promoting the far-reaching Defense Acquisition Streamlining Act of 1994 under the rubric of "reinventing government." This legislative record has been augmented more recently by the 104th Congress, which enacted a second set of reforms with the 1996 Defense Authorization Act.

Some of the most significant reforms have centered on commercial-military integration, in part because of a new understanding that such streamlining will be the price of continued technological innovation. That understanding rests in turn on three things:

- The growing importance of information technology in a wide range of products and systems required by the defense establishment;

- The rapid pace of change in technological generations. By some estimates, this turnover occurs every 12 to 18 months, a sharp contrast with defense acquisition programs that typically run 3 to 5 years;

- The substitution of commercial innovation as the prime mover of technology. With reduced defense funding, declining leadership in the marketplace, and more rapid technological cycle times, DOD clearly needs to accommodate itself to prevailing business standards, not vice versa.

Despite the progress represented by these recent reforms, implementation through the regulatory process will take time. Even more problematic is the issue of transforming the defense acquisition workforce into entrepreneurial risk-takers skilled in sophisticated surveillance of the commercial marketplace—something that they are not now and are not likely to be any time in the foreseeable future.

An Agenda for the Next Secretary of Defense

The next secretary of defense will preside over a series of technological innovations that will have a lasting effect on the U.S. defense establishment. He or she will do so, moreover, through a process in which each of Morison's three great constituencies—technicians, insurgents, and the establishment—can be expected to play their respective roles. The leadership challenge will be to keep these players from succumbing to the ever-present tendency toward the "limited identifications" that inevitably lead to internal conflicts, expensive failures, or even military disasters.

So how might the next secretary of defense set the technological terms of reference to increase the opportunities for success? Four basic policy choices are critical:

1. *Rationalize and reduce DOD's overhead in outdated C³I systems.* It is clear that DOD simply has too many command and control systems, many of them redundant or technically obsolete. It is also clear that sheer inertia will keep these systems functioning in the absence of a draconian mandate by the civilian leadership of the department. To halt the present practice of mortgaging the future by indefinitely postponing the day of reckoning, the overriding policy objective should be prompt and large-scale reductions in the numbers of these systems. The appropriate model for such an effort might well be the Base Realignment and Closure Commissions, which demonstrated that the equitable distribution of pain was best accomplished through clarity of mandates, schedules, and expectations. Given a similar charge, a specially convened panel of the Defense Science Board could produce similar results.

2. *First by directive, and then by the required legislative changes, remove from the military services their current authority to procure separate command and control systems.* The military services provide a superb means of transferring critical war-fighting skills from one generation to the next. Within the confines of existing missions, they are similarly great engines of innovative thought and development. They are not particularly good, however, at asking the question, "Who else has this problem?" before developing separate C³I systems. In the U.S. system, the most logical choice for redirecting the present service-based C⁴I approach is to give this authority to the chairman of the Joint Chiefs and to have him exercise it through the Joint Staff. Although it currently lacks budgetary authority, the Joint Staff does the day-to-day integration of the command and control systems actually used by the combatant forces; it is consequently in the best position to appreciate the potential tradeoffs in the command and control systems actually needed to achieve the most effective integration of joint combat power.

3. *Make commercial-military integration the basis for reducing and rationalizing DOD institutional overhead.* Thanks to recent reforms, federal procurement law now mandates a preference for commercial products, especially those that can be purchased "off the shelf" for military use. DOD's development of C⁴I systems consequently needs to be guided to take full advantage of cutting-edge commercial possibilities even before they are available "off the shelf." For example, DOD databases, both for business as well as for operations and intelligence, are as proverbially "stand-alone" as are their parent C⁴I systems. Nonetheless, commercial vendors are now offering a whole new class of "data warehousing" products that use advanced software not only to reconcile different databases but also to allow their information to be shared and enhanced through various "data mining" techniques. DOD is likely to benefit from these and similar commercial applications—but only if it is carefully prepared for those opportunities well before they become generally available.

It will be considerably more difficult but equally essential to use the emerging commercial capabilities to reduce redundant support structures in each of the services. For example, the advent of secure, reliable global satellite communications—Motorola's Iridium, for example—has the clear potential to replace some communications channels that the military was previously forced to provide for itself. These commercial sources are also in the best position to keep abreast of the latest technologies and to provide these capabilities at the lowest cost. It remains to be seen, however, if the military systems that they can replace will be quickly removed from service. If they are, it will be increasingly difficult for the existing signal establishments in each of the military services to justify their current force structures, much less their budgetary and administrative clout.

4. *Inculcate in the next generation of the DOD acquisition corps the bedrock principles of "jointness" and "commercial-military integration."* The recent progress in procurement reform is unlikely to be sustained without considerably more attention to the problem of selecting, training, and advancing the next generation of acquisition professionals. Without a significant degree of further education, no one raised in the current climate of procedure-laden, risk-averse defense systems management is likely to be successful in the highly opportunistic, entrepreneurial exploitation of commercial technology that will be the sine qua non of the future. The task of the newly created Defense Acquisition University can therefore be nothing less than orchestrating the constant reinvention of a futures-oriented curriculum featuring the procurement of joint, commercially based information systems. In those tasks, it will be well advised to seek out firsthand the insights of cutting-edge commercial information and technology companies, both to get a firm grip on the future and to provide continuing insights on changing technological approaches.

The agenda outlined here is at best an approximation of the major tasks confronting a Defense Department that must not automatically assume that the information revolution necessarily conveys U.S. superiority. Furthermore, although there is a lively and timely debate about whether high tech or low tech is the likelier form of future wars, the issues discussed here must be resolved if the United States is to be prepared for future conflict at any point on the spectrum of violence.

Nor should we assume in addressing ourselves to these problems that the presently benign geopolitical circumstances the United States enjoys will endure forever. Perhaps the most effective way to convey this thought is suggested by an anecdote that President John F. Kennedy was fond of recounting. The great French statesman Clemenceau one day noticed a bare spot in his landscape. Calling the gardener, Clemenceau suggested planting an oak tree on that very spot. "But Excellency," said the gardener, "an oak tree takes 50 years to grow to maturity." "In that case," replied Clemenceau, "plant it this afternoon."

Notes

1. I am indebted for this key point to my colleague Martin Libicki. See pp. 27–58 in his monograph, *Dominant Battlespace Knowledge* (Washington, D.C.: National Defense University Press, 1995).

2. This is the military equivalent of what Thomas Kuhn describes in his classic work *The Structure of Scientific Revolutions* (Chicago: University of Chicago Press, 1970).

3. Elting E. Morison, "Gunfire at Sea: A Case Study in Innovation," in *Men, Machines and Modern Times* (Cambridge: MIT Press, 1966), pp. 17–44.

4. Ibid., p. 18.

5. Ibid., p. 41.

6. See chapter 13, John Arquilla and David Ronfeldt, "Information, Power, and Grand Strategy: In Athena's Camp."

7. U.S. Army, *Field Manual 100–5, Operations* (Washington, D.C.: Headquarters, Dept. of the Army, July 1, 1976), p. 2–6.

8. See the author's chapter, "The Future of Command and Control: Toward a Paradigm of Information War," in Benjamin Ederington and Michael Mazarr, eds., *Turning Point: The Gulf War and U.S. Military Strategy* (Boulder, Colo.: Westview Press, 1995), especially pp. 170–175.

9. Ibid. For an analysis of the historical, organizational, and technological dimensions of the interoperability problem, see the author's *Command, Control and the Common Defense* (New Haven: Yale University Press, 1990) and *Somalia Operations: Lessons Learned* (Washington, D.C.: National Defense University Press, 1995).

10. See Adm. William A. Owens, "The Emerging System of Systems," *Proceedings* 212, no. 5, (May 1995): 35–39. See also Admiral Owens's introduction to *Dominant Battlespace Knowledge*, ed. Martin C. Libicki (Washing-

ton, D.C.: National Defense University Press, 1995) and Martin C. Libicki, *What is Information Warfare?* (Washington, D.C.: National Defense University Press, 1995).

11. Owens, "The Emerging System of Systems," p. 36.

12. Ibid., p. 38.

13. Ibid. p. 36. See also Admiral Owens's explanation of the role of the JWCA process in strengthening the Joint Requirements Oversight Council, or JROC, in his article "JROC: Harnessing the Revolution in Military Affairs," *Joint Forces Quarterly*, no. 5 (Summer 1994): 55–57.

14. For a cogent analysis of this problem, see Don M. Snider, Daniel Gouré, and Stephen Cambone, *Defense in the Late 1990s: Avoiding the Train Wreck* (Washington, D.C.: Center for Strategic and International Studies, 1995).

15. The exact number of C^3I systems operative in DOD seems very much in the eye of the beholder. Assistant Secretary of Defense (C^3I) Emmett Paige, Jr. used the 9,000 figure in an address, "Re-engineering DOD's Operations: Information Management Impact," Vienna, Va., September 14, 1993. Other estimates have suggested that the number might be as low as 5,000. The more troubling question, however, is why no one seems to know for sure. On the number of administrative C^3I systems in Somalia, see the author's *Somalia Operations: Lessons Learned*.

16. Memorandum by Assistant Secretary of Defense (C^3I) Emmett Paige, Jr. to Secretaries of Military Departments, et al., Subject: "Selection of Migration Systems/Applications," Washington, D.C., July 10, 1995.

17. Interview with Maj. Gen. David J. Kelley, vice director, Defense Information Systems Agency (DISA), Arlington, Va., February 22, 1996.

18. Written briefing by Rear Adm. J. A. Gauss, deputy director, Defense Information Systems Agency (DISA), January 29, 1996.

19. The cited demonstration took place in the author's presence at Hanscom Air Force Base, Massachusetts, during the Joint Warrior Interoperability Demonstration, September 1995. For a discussion of this demonstration (which omits any critical mention of this problem), see the November 1995 edition of *Signal* magazine.

Selected Bibliography

C. Edward Peartree

Implications of the Information Revolution

Benedikt, Michael, ed. *Cyberspace: The First Steps*. Cambridge, Mass.: MIT Press, 1991.

Burstein, Daniel, and David Kline. *Road Warriors: Dreams and Nightmares Along the Information Highway*. New York: Dutton, 1995.

Computer Science and Telecommunications Board, National Research Council. *Realizing the Information Future: The Internet and Beyond*, Washington, D.C.: National Academy Press, 1994.

"Cyberspace: The Software that will take you there." *Business Week*, February 27, 1995. (Special report: overview of coming innovations and challenges in banking, finance, and business in information age.)

Department of Commerce. *Global Information Infrastructure: Agenda for Cooperation*. Washington, D.C.: Government Printing Office, 1995.

Gates, Bill. *The Road Ahead*. New York: Penguin, 1995.

"The Information Revolution." Special Issue, *Business Week*, 1994. (General overview, mainly on business aspects of information revolution: issues include, Information economy, how technology is changing business and workplace, information security, telecommuting, e-mail, encryption and the future digital society.)

Negroponte, Nicholas. *Being Digital*. New York: Knopf, 1995. (A sanguine view of the digital, information-driven future. Good introduction to some technological changes, although not for everyone stylistically.)

Rheingold, Howard. *Virtual Reality*. New York: Touchstone, 1993.

Roszak, Theodore. *The Cult of Information*, 2d ed. Berkeley: University of California Press, 1994. (A technological "nay-sayer" disputes the utopian aspects of the information revolution. Recommended.)

Sikorovsky, Elizabeth. "U.S. to help build Global Info Infrastructure." *Federal Computer Week*, March 6, 1995, p. 8. (G7 to lead the way to digitized future.)

Sterling, Bruce. *Islands in the Net*. New York: Ace Books, 1988. (Seminal sci-fi take on information war that originated concepts of "cyberwar" and "netwar.")

Stoll, Clifford. *Silicon Valley Snake Oil*. New York: Random House, 1995.(A less sanguine view of the digital future.)

Swisher, Kara. "Internet's Reach Grows, Survey Says." *Washington Post*, October 31, 1995, p. 1. (37 million surfers in North America and growing according to CommerceNet/Nielsen survey.)

Weiser, Mark. "The Computer for the 21st Century." *Scientific American*, September 1991. (Special Issue: Communications, Computers, and Networks. A seminal and highly recommended piece.)

Wouters, Jorgen. "We Are What We Speak." *Washington Technology*, 9, no. 20, January 26, 1995, p. 13. (Is computer techno-jargon transforming language?)

Information Security and CyberCrime

"Bankers, Other Groups Warn of NII Sabotage, Theft, Fraud." *Telecom Data Report*, vol. 3, August 1, 1994. (American Bankers Association dialogue with Clinton administration over security on new digital networks.)

Carney, Dan. "Cybercop wages War on Crime." *Federal Computer Week* 9, no. 3, February 6, 1995, p. 1. (Profile of Scott Charney, Chief, Computer Crimes Division, Department of Justice.)

Cheswick, William and Steven Bellovin. *Firewalls and Internet Security: Repelling the Wily Hacker*. Springfield: Mass.: Addison-Wesley, 1994.

Computer Science and Technology Board, National Research Council. *Computers at Risk*. Washington, D.C.: National Academy Press, 1991. (Serious treatment of problems of hacker attacks and computer crime.)

"DataCop 2001: The Integrated Officer." *Washington Technology* 9, no. 18, December 22, 1994, p. 16. (The digitization of modern law enforcement.)

Hafner, Katie, and John Markoff. *Cyberpunk: Outlaws and Hackers on the Computer Frontier*. New York: Touchstone, 1991.

"Information Security Losses Increasing at U.S. Corporations Says new Ernst & Young LLP and Information Week Survey." *Business Wire*, November 18, 1994.

Kabay, M. E. "Prepare Yourself for Information Warfare." *Computerworld*, March 20, 1995. (A discussion of the threat posed to the corporate world by information warfare.)

Kehoe, Louise. "Crime on the line." *Financial Times*, March 3, 1994. (On security, encryption, and U.S. export controls.)

Leslie, Jacques. "Digital Photopros and Photoshop Realism." *Wired*, May 1995. (Digital manipulation of photographic and video imagery and potential for abuse.)

Mason, John. "Russian in $2.8 million Citibank computer fraud." *Financial Times*, August 18, 1994, p. 1.

Meyer, Michael, and Daniel Glick. "Keeping the Cybercops Out of Cyberspace." *Newsweek*, March 14, 1994. (Discussion of why computer users have a "Big Brother" complex.)

Mulqueen, John T. "Bankers See Internet as Risky Business." *Communications Week*, April 10, 1995, p. 1.

Neumann, Peter G. *Computer Related Risks*. Springfield, Mass.: ACM/Addison-Wesley, 1994. (Excellent work, with a refreshing lack of polemic. Covers gamut of risks to computer and information systems, both accidental and intentional, from technical perspective. Greatest emphasis on commercial/private threats, not military.)

Office of Technology Assessment, U.S. Congress. *Issue Update on Information Security and Privacy in Network Environments*. Washington, D.C.: Government Printing Office, June 1995.

Organization for Economic Co-operation and Development. *Information Computer Communications Policy: Guidelines for the Security of Information Systems*. Paris: OECD, 1992.

Panettieri, Joseph C. "Are Your Computers Safe?" *Information Week*, March 13, 1995, p. 14. (Corporate leaders express concern for computer vulnerabilities.)

Raine, Linnea P., and Frank J. Cilluffo, eds. *Global Organized Crime: The New Empire of Evil*. Washington, D.C.: Center for Strategic and International Studies, 1994. See chap. 3, "Hacking through the Cyberspace Jungle."

Ramo, Joshua. "A SWAT Team in Cyberspace." *Newsweek*, February 21, 1994. (Discusses the mission of the Computer Emergency Response Team—CERT.)

Rendleman, John. "CommerceNet Launches Pilot Internet-Security Program." *Communications Week*, April 17, 1995, p. 8.

(Consortium promoting commerce on Internet tests security system.)

Schwartau, Winn. *Information Warfare: Chaos on the Electronic Superhighway.* New York: Thunder's Mouth Press, 1994. (Popular journalistic treatment of broad array of "hacker" crime and information security issues.)

Schwartz, John. "Chipping in to Curb Computer Crime." *Washington Post*, February 19, 1995, p. A1. (Federal law enforcement cooperation in cracking Kevin Mitnick case.)

Slata, Michelle, and Joshua Quittner. *Masters of Deception: The Gang that Ruled Cyberspace.* New York: HarperCollins, 1995.

Stoll, Clifford. *The Cuckoo's Egg: Tracking a Spy through the Maze of Computer Espionage.* New York: Random House, 1992.

Sussman, Vic. "Policing Cyberspace." *U.S. News and World Report*, January 23, 1995, p. 55. (Law enforcement, security, and privacy in the information age.)

Wilder, Clifton. "How Safe is the Internet?" *Information Week*, December 12, 1994, p. 13. (Corporations report hacker break-ins; CommerceNet consortium seeks to promote business security on 'net; clash of hacker and corporate cultures feared.)

Information Revolution and the Military

Alexander, David. "Information Warfare and the Digitized Battlefield." *Military Technology,* September 1995. (Defining information war and deciding how it should be integrated into new military doctrines.)

Allard, C. Kenneth. *Command, Control, and the Common Defense.* New Haven: Yale University Press, 1991. (Deals with challenges of C^2 in joint warfare, with particular emphasis on information age challenges.)

Anselmo, Joseph. "Information Needs Grow as Budgets Shrink." *Aviation Week & Space Technology*, November 7, 1994. (The military's demand for more information systems is in conflict with defense budget reductions.)

"Army Intelligence Melds New Doctrine, Technologies." *Signal,* December 1995.

Arquilla, John. "The Strategic Implications of Information Dominance." *Strategic Review*, Summer 1994.

Arquilla, John, and David Ronfeldt. "Cyberwar is Coming!" *Comparative Strategy* 12, no. 2 (April-June 1993): 141–165. (Important and widely cited work that perceptively analyzes the strategic implications of information warfare; compares future "cyberwarriors" to the Mongol horde.)

Baumard, Philippe. "From InfoWar to Knowledge Warfare: Preparing for the Paradigm Shift." Available: http://www. indigo-net . . . nnexes/289/baumard.htm.

Berkowitz, Bruce D. "Warfare in the Information Age." *Issues in Science and Technology,* Fall 1995. (Offers solid overview of basic defense issues and the need for resolution of current conflicts between democracy and national security, defense and commerce, etc.)

Bigelow, Bruce. "Cyberwarriors—Pentagon's new priority: Train troops to cripple computers and enemy forces they control." *San Diego Union-Tribune,* August 13, 1995. (National Defense University's School of Information Warfare and the DOD's new campaign to heighten awareness of the threats of information war and computer security.)

Black, Peter. "Soft Kill: Fighting Infrastructure Wars in the 21st Century." *Wired,* July-August 1993.

Brewin, Bob. "DoD releases strategy for global network." *Federal Computer Week* 9, no. 5, March 6, 1995, p.1. (DISA plan for secure DOD network instead of marketplace-provided network.)

"Budget Plan Leaves Military Computers Vulnerable to Intrusion." *Defense Daily,* September 16, 1994, p. 423. (Top information systems officials concerned about lack of funding to deal with hacker attacks; C^3I capabilities are at stake.)

Campen, Alan D., ed. *The First Information War: The Story of Communications, Computers, and Intelligence Systems.* Fairfax, Va.: AFCEA International Press, 1992. (Perspectives on information-based warfare during the Gulf War. Influential text.)

Campen, Alan D., and R. Thomas Gooden, ed. *Cyberwar: Security, Strategy, and Conflict in the Information Age.* Fairfax, Va.: AFCEA International Press, 1996.

Canavan, Gregory, "Simulation, Computing, Information, and Future Warfare." Los Alamos National Laboratory LA-12490-MS.

Chang Menxiong. "Information Intensified—A Mark of 21st Century Weapons and Military Units." *FBIS-CHI,* June 14, 1995. (Article on Chinese perspectives on information warfare.)

Constance, Paul. "G.I.s demand complete field gear: boots, rifle, e-mail—Army memos find yesterday's luxuries—comm resources—are today's basic battlefield requirement." *Government Computer News,* April 29, 1996.

Cooper, Pat. "DSB: Arm Soldiers With Instant Data—Pentagon Digital Map Plan Would Take Battle Images to Front Lines." *Defense News,* January 15–21, 1996.

————. "Information Warfare Sparks Security Affairs Revolution." *Defense News,* July 12–18, 1995. (Director of C^4, Admiral Cebrowski, talks about the cyber-revolution in the DOD and the vulnerability of the United States to computer attack.)

————. "Internet link to defense data may be too easy." *Army Times,* January 22, 1996.

Cooper, Pat, and Robert Holzer. "America Lacks Reaction Plan for InfoWar." *Defense News,* October 2–8, 1995. (Fears of unpreparedness of DOD to respond to infowar threats provoke review.)

Der Derian, James. "Cyber-deterrence." *Wired,* September 1994. (U.S. Army digital battlefield and AWE—Advanced Warfighting Experiment.)

"EW Expands into Information Warfare." *Aviation Week & Space Technology,* October 10, 1994.

Fialka, John J. "Pentagon Studies Art of 'Information Warfare' to Reduce Its Systems' Vulnerability to Hackers." *Wall Street Journal,* July 3, 1995.

Fitzgerald, Mary C. "Russian Views on Information Warfare." *Army,* May 1995. (Russian emphasis on importance of EW and C^3I as force multipliers—warfare of future as duel of information systems.)

Garigue, R. "Information Warfare: Developing a Conceptual Framework." Available: http://www.cse.dnd.ca/~formis/overview/iw.

Gillian, Andrew. "Army to swap battlefields for computers." *Sunday Telegraph,* May 5, 1996.

"Government Will Fund Research Study of Future 'Information War.'" *Washington Telecom News,* November 8, 1993.

Greczyn, Mary. "Army Raises Info Warfare Risks From Off-The-Shelf Buys." *Defense Week,* January 16, 1996.

Grier, Peter. "Information Warfare." *Air Force Magazine,* March 1995. (Information will be the most crucial aspect of the future battlefield.)

Information Security Program Regulation: U.S. Department of Defense. Upland, Pa.: Diane Publishing, March 1994.

"Information Warfare—Not a Paper War." *Journal of Electronic Defense* 17, no. 8 (August 1994): 55. (Information dominance as goal of future commanders in wartime; role of new Air Force Information Warfare Center.).

"Information Warriors Raze Vital Data Chains." *Defense News*, March 1995. (Concern that DOD is lagging in real-time communications across services; cites Defense Science Board study on "Information Architecture for the Battlefield"; need for coherent information warfare strategy and national policy.)

"Infowar Disputes Stall Defense Policy." *Washington Technology*, May 25, 1995. (CIA director John Deutch and top intelligence officials call nation's electronic infrastructure vulnerable to attack; privacy, encryption, and national security needs debate stalls policy.)

Joint Security Commission. *Redefining Security: A Report to the Secretary of Defense and the Director of Central Intelligence.* Washington D.C.: Government Printing Office, 1994.

Joint Staff, C^4 Systems Directorate. "C^{4}I for the Warrior." Publication of the Joint Staff, June 12, 1993.

Kraus, George F. "Information Warfare in 2015." *Proceedings*, August 1995.

Kurzweil, Raymond. "May the Smartest Machine Win: Warfare in the 21st Century." *Library Journal*, October 1, 1993. (Discusses the importance of computer technology in future military success.)

Levis, Alexander, and Ilze Levis, eds. *Science of Command and Control: Coping with Change.* Washington, D.C.: AIP Information Systems, December 1994.

Libicki, Martin C. *The Mesh and the Net: Speculations on Armed Conflict in the Time of Free Silicon.* Washington, D.C.: National Defense University Press, March 1994. (Overview of implications for modern warfare of rapid change in information technology; information as force multiplier.)

————. *What is Information Warfare?* Washington, D.C.: National Defense University Press, 1996. (Systematically attempts to define information war [and what it is not]; outlines seven forms of information warfare and speculates about their impact on future conflict; also makes distinctions about what infowar will *not* do—information warfare seen as a support function, not as a true medium of war.)

Libicki, Martin, and James Hazlett. "Do We Need an Information Corps?" *Joint Forces Quarterly*, Autumn 1993.

Masaud, Sam. "Soldiers take their offices to the battlefield." *Government Computer News*, April 15, 1996.

Massari, Chester A. "The Dynamics of Information Security." *Defense Electronics* 26, no. 8 (August 1994): 16. (Department of Defense technology being transferred to commercial sector.)

McCarthy, Shawn P. "Overseas Hackers Force DoD to Revise System Security." *Government Computer News*, vol. 13, July 14, 1994.

──────. "Who's in charge of computer security? The feud goes on . . ." *Government Computer News*, vol. 14, April 3, 1995. (DOD and civilian agencies battle over government information security.)

Minihan, Tim. "Intelligence Agencies Build Their Own Internet with Security a Major Goal" *Government Computer News*, vol. 14, January 9, 1995, p. 8. ('Intelink' to function as DOD, NSA, CIA secure internet.)

──────. "U.S. can win with best IT, Gingrich says." *Government Computer News*, vol. 14, February 20, 1995, p. 1.

Molander, Roger, Peter Wilson, and Andrew Riddile. *Strategic Information Warfare*. Santa Monica: RAND, 1996.

Morton, Oliver. "The Information Advantage." *Economist*, Special Survey: "The Software Revolution," June 10, 1995. (Thorough and provocative overview of the ways in which information technology is driving a revolution in military affairs.)

Munro, Neil. "The Pentagon's New Nightmare: An Electronic Pearl Harbor." *Washington Post*, July 16, 1995, p. C1.

──────. *The Quick and the Dead: Electronic Combat and Modern Warfare*. New York: St. Martin's Press, 1991.

Nye, Joseph S. Jr., and William A. Owens. "America's Information Edge." *Foreign Affairs* 10, no. 2 (May-April 1996). (How the information revolution is changing the world to U.S. national security advantage.)

Oder, Brig. Gen. Joseph. "Battlefield Digitization." *Army*, May 1995. (How advances in digital technology will allow real-time force synchronization—Army strategy of HTI (Horizontal Technology Insertion) to improve warfighting capabilities; role of TRADOC Battle Labs in defining operation needs and experimentation.)

Paige, Emmett. "Retaining the Edge on Current and Future Battlefields." *Defense Issues* 10, no. 85. (Remarks by Assistant Secretary of Defense for C³I).

Rapaport, Richard. "World War 3.1 The Shape of Things to Come?" *Forbes*, October 7, 1996, p. 125. (How information technology revolutionized the IFOR deployment in Bosnia.)

Rothrock, John. "Information Warfare: Time for Some Constructive Skepticism." *American Intelligence Journal*, Spring-Summer 1994.

Ryan, Lt. Col. Donald E. "Implications of Information-Based Warfare." *Joint Forces Quarterly*, Autumn/Winter 1994–1995). (Overview and speculations about how IBW [information based warfare] might change the shape of conflict and U.S. operations/strategy.)

Scott, William B. "Information Warfare Demands New Approach." *Aviation Week and Space Technology*, March 13, 1995. (Pentagon will rely on commercially developed space and ground-based networks to conduct cost-effective information warfare over next decade.)

"Services Gear Up for Information War." *Defense Daily*, September 8, 1994, p. 377. (Navy, Air Force, Army designate information warfare commands and Joint Staff Electronic Warfare Center; Defense Science Board study "Information Architecture for the Battlefield" recommends increased DOD emphasis on information war.)

Sikorovsky, Elizabeth. "Hackers escalate hits on Defense networks." *Federal Computer Week*, June 12, 1995.

Stein, George J. "Information Warfare." *Airpower Journal* 9, no. 1 (Spring 1995). (Calls for visionary information warfare doctrine and strategy in order to produce technology that will ensure dominance on revolutionized information-age battlefield.)

"Study Backs Improving Information Systems for Commanders; Defense Science Board's study 'Information Architecture for the Battlefield.'" *Defense Daily*, December 22, 1994. (Comments on recommendations made by study to enhance ability of commanders and forces in combat operations.)

Sullivan, Gen. Gordon. "A New Force for a New Century." *Army*, May 1995. (Comments on future of Army; role of ADO [Army Digitization Office] to determine needs of future.)

Sullivan, Gen. Gordon, and Col. James Dubik. "War in the Information Age." *Military Review*, April 1994.

Szafranski, Richard. "A Theory of Information Warfare: Preparing for 2020." *Airpower Journal* 9, no. 1 (Spring 1995).

Todd, David. "Gird for Information War; U.S. Must Control Combat on Cyberspace Front." *Defense News*, March 14, 1995.

Toffler, Alvin, and Heidi Toffler. *War and Anti-War: Survival at the Dawn of the 21st Century.* New York: Little, Brown, 1993. (Highly influential text with section on information war and technology change.)

"The 21st Century Land Warrior—The Army Becomes Dominant Gene in Soldier Evolution." *Armed Forces Journal,* February 1995.

Urban, Ellison C. "The Information Warrior." *IEEE Spectrum,* November 1995.

Waller, Douglas. "Onward Cyber Soldiers." *Time,* August 21, 1995. (Cover story, "CyberWar," with supplementary articles.)

Wang Pufeng. "Meeting the Challenge of Information Warfare." *FBIS-CHI,* July 6, 1995. (Chinese general views importance of information warfare.)

You Ji. "High Tech Shift for China's Military." *Asian Defense Journal,* September 1995. (The Chinese PLA changes doctrine to adapt to modern high-tech war, including advanced C⁴I systems.)

Law, Civil Society, and the National Interest: Conflict in the Computer Age

Barlow, John Perry. "Decrypting the Puzzle Palace." *Communications of the ACM* 35, no. 7 (July 1992). (A critique of government motives regarding cryptography.)

Berghel, Hal. "U.S. Technology Policy in the Information Age." *Communications of the ACM* 39, no. 6 (June 1996): 15.

Branscomb, Anne Wells, *Who Owns Information?: From Privacy to Public Access.* New York: BasicBooks, 1994.

Cavazos, Edward, and Gavino Morin. *Cyberspace and the Law: Your Rights and Duties in the On-Line World.* Cambridge, Mass.: MIT Press, 1994.

Denning, Dorothy E. "To Tap or Not to Tap." *Communications of the ACM* 36, no. 3 (March 1993). (An argument in favor of the Clipper chip by someone outside of government.)

Drake, William J., ed. *The New Information Infrastructure: Strategies for U.S. Policy.* New York: Twentieth Century Fund Press, 1995.

"EU Promotes Infobahn—IT Superhighways." *Computing,* October 13, 1994. (European Union gives top priority to developing info superhighway to promote European commerce.)

Fallows, James. "Open Secrets." *Atlantic Monthly*, June 1994. (Offers a pro-Clipper chip argument, downplaying the perceived controversy.)

Garfinkle, Simson. *Pretty Good Privacy.* Sebastopol, Calif.: O'Reilly & Associates, 1995. (History and background of encryption debate an d development of PGP—public key cryptography. Manual for use of PGP and applicable laws).

"Government as Facilitator and Catalyst: Annenberg Panelists Call for Consensus on Telecommunications Privacy, Security." *Communications Daily*, March 6, 1995. (Need for government and public consensus on privacy issues on information superhighway.)

Hill, Michael W. *National Information Policies & Strategies: An Overview and Bibliographic Survey.* London: Bowker, 1994.

Hoffman, Lance J., ed. *Building in Big Brother: The Cryptography Policy Debate.* New York: Springer-Verlag, 1995. (First-rate anthology of articles on all sides of the encryption debate by Steven Levy, Bruce Sterling, Dorothy Denning, Philip Zimmerman, among others.)

"Industry, Government begin Development of Security Standards for NII." *Security Technology News* 2, no. 15, July 29, 1994.

Information Resources Security & Risk Management: Policy, Standards, & Guidelines. Upland, Pa.: Diane Publishing, 1994.

Kahin, Brian, and Janet Abbate, eds. *Standards Policy for Information Infrastructure.* Cambridge, Mass.: MIT Press, 1995.

Levy, Steven."Battle of the Clipper Chip." *New York Times Magazine*, June 12, 1994. (An excellent discussion of the private sector's and general public's problems with Clipper, digital telephony, federal regulation of cryptography, PGP, etc.)

Markoff, John D. "Profit and ego in data secrecy." *New York Times*, June 28, 1994. (U.S. government versus private entrepreneurs over control of encryption standards.)

Menke, Susan et al. "Group wants security plan info." *Government Computer News*, March 20, 1995, p. 5. (Electronic Privacy Information Center [EPIC] files Freedom of Information Act suit to review Clinton administration Presidential Decision Directive 29 establishing U.S. Security Policy Board; fears amendment of 1987 Computer Security Act.)

Office of Technology Assessment. *Finding a Balance: Computer Software, Intellectual Property, and the Challenge of Technological Change.* OTA-TCT-527. Washington, D.C.: Government Printing Office, 1994.

Post, David. "Encryption—It's Not Just for Spies Anymore." *The American Lawyer*, December 1994. (Examines legal issues of PGP [pretty good privacy] and debate between government and private industry over information/computer security.)

Power, Kevin. "Iowa will be the NII test bed." *Government Computer News*, March 1995, p.1. (National information superhighway to be tested with congressional grant in Iowa; will link federal, local, and state government via Iowa Communications Network [ICN].)

Schwartz, John. "Privacy Program: An On-Line Weapon? Inventor May Face Indictment for Encryption Software Sent Abroad." *Washington Post*, April 3, 1995, p. 1. (The Phil Zimmerman case and the debate over U.S. export control law on encryption.)

Schwartzstein, Stuart J. D. "Export Controls on Encryption Technologies." *SAIS Review* 16, no. 1 (Winter-Spring 1996): 13–34.

Scott, William B. "Satellites Key to 'Infostructure.'" *Aviation Week & Space Technology*, March 14, 1994. (A new generation of communications satellites will serve both military and civilian users as part of the National Information Infrastructure.)

Sikorovsky, Elizabeth. "Guidelines expected to step up security efforts." *Federal Computer Week*, February 20, 1995, p. 6. (Industry and government convene to develop computer network security guidelines; Generally Accepted System Security Principles [GSSP].)

Sprehe, Timothy. "Federal Information: Who Owns It?" *Federal Computer Week* 9, no. 3, February 6, 1995, p. 1. (Information Industry Association of information "providers" lobbies for open dissemination of public information.)

Stahlman, Mark. "The Encryption Enigma." *Information Week*, Issue 523, April 24, 1995, p. 104. (U.S. export controls on encryption may be the result of French lobbying for continued restrictions.)

Strassman, Paul A. *The Politics of Information Management: Policy Guidelines*. New Canaan, Conn.: Information Economics Press, 1995.

Yang, Catherine. "Flamed with a Lawsuit." *Business Week*, February 6, 1995, p. 70. (First Amendment protections and the Internet).

Zurier, Steve. "Government turns to the Internet to win back public faith." *Government Computer News*, April 29, 1996.

A note on electronic sources

An extensive array of electronic information is available on subjects related to the information revolution and national security.
The sheer volume of material and the frequently transitory
nature of Internet Web sites preclude a comprehensive listing.
Here, however, are a few good places to visit:

- *Wired* magazine and its on-line version *HotWired* (http://
  hotwired.com) continues to be a principal source of good
  information on emerging technologies and information-
  age trends.

- The Electronic Privacy and Information Center (EPIC)
  (http://epic.org) archives a great deal of material on encryption, Internet civil liberties, and relevant government
  legislation.

- The U.S. Department of Defense *Defense Link* (http://
  www.dtic.dla.mil/defenselink/index.html) is an excellent locator that links browsers to sites on information
  warfare and the military.

- For the uninitiated to all things electronic, popular
  browser software like Netscape's Navigator and
  Microsoft's Internet Explorer allow users to do extremely
  easy subject searches via Internet search engines like
  Yahoo, Excite, Alta Vista, and others.

Finally, bearing in mind that the Internet houses a profusion of
sites, many of them not subject to factual verification or quality
control—*caveat emptor!*